IT'S KILLING OUR KIDS

Other works by Jerry Johnston

Books

Why Suicide?
Going All the Way
The Edge of Evil

Videos

Life Exposé
Why Suicide?
Going All the Way
The Edge of Evil
It's Killing Our Kids

IT'S KILLING OUR KIDS

Jerry Johnston

WORD PUBLISHING
Dallas · London · Vancouver · Melbourne

IT'S KILLING OUR KIDS

Copyright © 1991 by Jerry Johnston

No portion of this book may be used or reproduced in any form without the written permission of the publisher, except for brief quotations in articles or critical reviews.

Unless otherwise indicated, all scripture quotations are from the New American Standard Bible (NASB) © 1960, 1962, 1963, 1968, 1971, 1972, 1973, 1975, 1977 by The Lockman Foundation. Used by permission. Scriptures identified as KJV are from the King James Version of the Bible.

Library of Congress Cataloging-in-Publication Data

Johnston, Jerry, 1959-
   It's killing our kids: the growing epidemic of teenage alcohol
abuse and addiction / by Jerry Johnston
       p.   cm.
   Includes bibliographical references.
   ISBN 0-8499-3296-3 : $14.99
   1. Teenagers—Alcohol use. 2. Teenagers—United States—Alcohol
use. 3. Alcoholism—Religious aspects. I. Title.
HV5135.J63 1991
362-29'22'083—dc20   90-49989
                                          CIP

Printed in the United States of America

1 2 3 4 5 9 AGF 9 8 7 6 5 4 3 2 1

To my dad, John W. Johnston,
my confidant, best friend, and the epitome
of everything I want to be.

Because you would not stop believing.

Contents

Interaction!

Self-Guided Activities to Use in the War Against Alcohol Abuse

Foreword

It's Killing Our Kids points the finger of concern at the drug and alcohol problem in America, then extends a hand of encouragement, filled with workable solutions. Jerry Johnston writes from his heart as he shares painful personal experiences with drugs and alcohol. He knows what it's like to be raised in an alcoholic family. Jerry relates to kids because he, too, knows how it feels to be out of control because of personal alcohol and drug problems. He understands what it means to bring pain and grief to loved ones. He's been there—and he doesn't want your child and mine to participate in that nightmare.

Jerry knows that alcohol and other drugs are a root cause of family problems, crime, violence, declining moral values, and a host of other ills. Based on personal experience, considerable research, and daily excursions to the front lines where our young people live, he recognizes what does and does not work. His personal relationship with Jesus Christ, combined with his research and insights, have led him to some practical day-to-day solutions that have turned the lives of countless numbers of young people in a positive direction.

It's Killing Our Kids blends Jerry Johnston's spiritual commitment with his practical application of life's principles. Now mix this generously with his love for the hurting kids of America, and his willingness to work toward the solution to those problems, and you will understand my excitement for this message. Jerry reinforces this message by personally delivering his solutions through countless appearances in high schools, churches, and public seminars all over the land.

Happily married to his beautiful wife Christie and the father of three happy, healthy children, Jerry clearly understands his own stake in the youth of America. He serves as the spiritual leader, example, and mentor to his own children; but he also knows that many kids do not have the benefit of a loving home with parents who truly care for them. To many of these kids Jerry has become the father figure, the older brother, and the inspirational example that many of them so desperately need.

Jerry realizes that as we solve the drug and alcohol problem for the countless millions who are impacted by them, we are providing greater opportunities for our own children to live in a society that is literally being overrun by crime, drugs, and alcohol. That's why *It's Killing Our Kids* calls on *you* to get involved in the solution. You might answer the rhetorical question, "If not me, then who? If not now, then when?" In essence, Jerry is delivering a message to all of us because each one of us can make a difference in the lives of others. If enough of us accept the concepts of *It's Killing Our Kids,* we can and will solve the problem.

His message is clear: Each one *can* do something; each one *must* do something. If we do, America truly faces a bright future. If we don't, the consequences present such awesome repercussions that we dare not even contemplate them. Here's a book whose time has come.

Zig Ziglar

Acknowledgments

In a stage production there are so many essential people behind the curtain and lights. Their names are unknown and they never bow when the crowd roars. But without them, the show would *never* go on. The same is true with this book.

I am so blessed by the incredible people who keep me going and facilitate my unreasonable expectations. They are the true heroes of my work.

Endless thanks is always in line for my darling Christie. How could a man ever have a better, more selfless, serving mate than she is? Christie is there every night when I call late from yet another city, exhausted, after the crowd has drained everything out of me. Christie is much stronger than I. She builds me and encourages me; truly, I sense her love. In this project she coached me along, never tiring from hearing, "How does this sound?" or "Listen to this," or "What do you think?" I am as crazy about her today as the first night I was captured by her beautiful face in Holland, Michigan.

To my wonderful Danielle, Jeremy, and Jenilee, three of the best kids in the whole wide world, your patience with Daddy is to be commended. You are my life, moment by moment.

And thank God for Eileen Ackerson, my administrative assistant, who exudes professionalism and skill. Eileen pulled all the research together from a zillion places, took care of permissions, typed and retyped, and kept up with all the other endless requests I had. Thank you, Eileen. You are appreciated more than you'll ever know.

To Joey Paul, at Word, who coached me to be vulnerable and tell the truth of the Johnston family's whole ordeal, I extend my deep thanks.

Finally, to my dear irreplaceable dad and mom: Thank you. I love you. You've been the best through the ups and downs. Mom, you are in one word *courageous*. I feel certain that many readers will find life and victory because you weren't afraid to bare your soul for all to see.

Introduction

The picture shows gorgeous three-year-old Kristin with her blonde, silky, long hair, sharp glistening eyes, and a broad imaginative smile which speaks of pure satisfaction. How could she be any happier? In the photograph, Kristin's with Dad and Mom at Disneyland for the first time. Her tiny fingers finished with exquisite, petite fingernails are pressed white around a merry-go-round pole. Looking at Kristin, one imagines that experiencing Disneyland at the innocent age of three is like visiting heaven and living to tell about it.

But in just a few short weeks, Kristin will be on an ambulance stretcher, bleeding profusely with massive head injuries. Her mom, fighting for her own life, will be unable to help. Kristin will be pronounced dead two hours later in the hospital. She'll never return to Disneyland.

On the day of her death, Kristin was on her way to a birthday party. Picture her wearing her beautiful party dress, sitting in the family car beside her father, Patrick, her buttress of protection. Mom's in the back seat with Kristin's baby sister. The family happily represents the young American dream. This portrait of peace soon will be shattered, though, by a careless, oncoming drunken driver who will leave Kristin and her dad dead. For her mother, the mourning process is about to begin, and the reality of it all is like an unthinkable twilight zone.

A slogan from Mothers Against Drunk Driving is certainly appropriate here: "It's the little things that make us MADD!" It seems incomprehensible that little Kristin is only one of thousands of children already killed by drunken drivers.

This book is far more than just another treatise on alcohol abuse and its devastating impact. It does more than recount the horrors of how substance abuse can destroy lives. It also describes ways determined helpers can cope with this national problem—and make a difference in the way it affects our families, our communities, our nation. These suggestions are critically needed by parents, teens who care about themselves and their friends, and families who have been traumatized by alcohol.

This book is also a personal narrative. For the first time in my life, I am going public with the fact that I am the child of an alcoholic; I've suffered sorrow, neglect, and feelings of abject hopelessness because of substance abuse in my family. Sharing my diary of Mom's alcohol dependency within these pages makes me feel psychologically naked, and writing about it has been the most stressful experience of my life. Thank God it is all behind us now for good, and miraculously, Mom is a living tribute of complete victory over addiction. But even though it has been several years of victory, my memories of her struggles with alcohol are still as fresh and incredible as if they happened yesterday.

I wrote this book to share what my family has gone through, so you will know there is hope for the "impossible" son or daughter, mother or father, brother, sister, or friend in your own family, too. I believe in your miracle as well as my own!

And besides meaningful personal stories and practical information, this book also includes a declaration of war. In Appendix A, you'll find my friend Zig Ziglar's stirring words that describe the desperate challenge we face—and the daring steps we must take—to win this war on drugs.

I'm proud to be associated with someone who has such high credentials, and such a special rapport with the business community, as well as many other professionals. Recently I went to Mr. Ziglar's office in Dallas to seek counseling on some decisions I am making regarding my future career, and I was overwhelmed at the action steps he has formulated to try to bring sanity to our burgeoning alcohol problem. They are so succinct, and so needed, that I decided their inclusion in this book was a must. The Articles of War in Appendix A offer Mr. Ziglar's perspective of remedial steps to these problems. I would hope they could be practiced in schools and communities nationwide.

These steps are needed *now*. Alcohol is the undisputed drug of choice for North American youth. Recent studies indicate drinking on college and university campuses remains at serious levels, despite enthusiastic programs to curb it. Campus crime and the spread of venereal disease and reckless sex, among other problems, are encouraged by the sustained abuse of alcohol in this sector.

The fact is this: While there has been an overall minor reduction in the number of older people drinking, the number of teens drinking is moving in the opposite direction.

Every day, Americans consume 15.7 million gallons of beer and ale, equivalent to 28 million six-packs—enough cans to fill a stadium 30 feet deep. And every 24 hours, Americans consume 1.2 million gallons of hard liquor, enough to get 26 million people thoroughly drunk. The Centers for Disease Control (CDC) report there are more than 100,000 alcohol-related deaths a year due to, among other things, diseases like cirrhosis of the liver. Researchers with CDC calculate those deaths represent a loss of more than 2.7 million years of life (*USA Today,* March 23, 1990, page D-1).

The American Hospital Association reports that half of all hospital admissions are alcohol related (David Arterburn, *Drug-Proofing Your Kids,* page 11). The National Safety Council's *1989 Accident Facts Edition* asserts the apocalyptic fact that every twenty-seven minutes, a person dies in an alcohol-related crash. Every sixty seconds, a person is injured in an alcohol-related crash. Each year at least 24,000 people are killed in alcohol-related tragedies. The National Highway Traffic Safety Association estimates 250,000 people were killed in alcohol-related crashes in the last ten years. That is like wiping out the entire cities of Lubbock, Texas or Wichita, Kansas! About two in every five Americans will be involved in an alcohol-related crash in their lifetimes. The scenario is scary, to say the least!

The monetary cost of drunken driving is also staggering. For example, in the United States, every taxpayer shares in the cost for alcohol-related crashes to the tune of $25 a minute, for a total of $13 billion a year (*Columbus Dispatch,* July 24, 1990, "Think Before You Drink," page 1).

Now, thanks to excellent organizations like MADD who are lobbying for greater penal action against repeat drunk-driving offenders, drunk driving deaths are slowly decreasing. Just a 10 percent further reduction in drunken driving would save more than 2,000 lives and prevent 70,000 disabling injuries.

Faced with these statistics, one has to wonder why so many people drink. And in particular, why do so many kids drink?

First, obviously, there is strong peer pressure. One Atlanta teen said, "It's cool in my school to come in on Monday and talk about how drunk you got on Saturday. It's like showing how strong you are." The June 1990 *Texas Monthly* cover article on kids and drugs reported that by their senior year, more than 90 percent of America's young people have tried alcohol. Researchers with one parent-led drug-education program documented that 57.9 percent of senior-high students in Canada drank beer, 45.6 percent drank liquor, and 56.4 percent drank wine coolers during the 1987-1988 school year. The National Council on Alcoholism reports there are now more than four million teenage alcoholics in the United States.

Second, society in general cheers kids on as they drink. Often alcohol use in a teen's life is parentally sanctioned and sponsored. Movies, commercials, TV shows, and consumer ads present glamorous people drinking. Seldom is a movie produced like *Clean and Sober,* which presents the downside. Dr. Jean Kilbourne, a board member for the National Council on Alcoholism, was quoted in *SEVENTEEN Magazine* in estimating that by the time the average teen is eighteen years old, he or she has seen 100,000 TV beer commercials, which usually target a young audience. Parents often model drinking to their sons and daughters. When this is done abusively, the effects are catastrophically lived out in the teen.

The June 1990 *Texas Monthly* reported one survey of kids in treatment that estimated 50 percent of those who had been labeled as substance abusers had substance-abusing parents; the kids adopt their parents' inability to cope or communicate their problems, and turn to drugs.

The Children of Alcoholics Foundation states that children of alcoholics have a four times greater risk of developing alcoholism than children of non-alcoholics. There are 28.6 million children of alcoholics in the United States today; 6.6 million of them are under age eighteen.

Third, teens drink because many of them fail to see alcohol as a dangerous, lethal, liquid drug—identified by chemists as C_2H_6O.

As President Bush said at the White House when honoring several anti-drunk-driving groups on December 11, 1989, "We must teach our children that alcohol is a drug and irresponsible drug use is wrong."

As a drug, alcohol works as an anesthetic on the brain, impairing judgment and loosening inhibitions. This helps explain why so many teens have sex for the first time while "under the influence." Alcohol abuse blurs proper sexual choice. This brings up an alarming parallel to the issue of alcohol abuse, the fact that a majority of teenagers are ignorant of the dangers of sexual activity. Now, more than ever, information understandable to them is needed.

Chemically, alcohol has a depressing effect on the central nervous system. If enough is consumed, it will depress the functions of the system to the point that it will no longer signal the lungs to breathe or the heart to beat. Heavy drinking bombards the liver, taxing it beyond its ability to filter.

Yes, alcohol is a drug.

Fourth, some teens are hereditarily or environmentally predisposed to abuse alcohol. Recent, startling breakthroughs are helping the experts understand this addiction phenomenon. We will look into the startling new data indicating this possible danger as we seek to answer the questions: Are some kids almost "set up" to be predisposed to addiction and the abuse of alcohol? What is the genetic connection, if any? Physiologically, are some people prone to become addicts to alcohol, drugs, sex, gambling, etc.? And what psychological warning signals can be factored in?

I have asked Dr. Joe King, one of America's top adolescent psychiatrists and addiction specialists, to contribute pertinent medical and psychological data for this book which sheds a whole new light on this problem. Dr. King and I spent many hours together comparing notes and reducing the information to layman's language.

Kids also drink because they feel rebellious. Because it's available. Because they're unhappy.

The problem is enormous. But it's not hopeless. We can do something about the crisis of substance abuse, of alcohol abuse. Flip through the pages of *It's Killing Our Kids,* and you will find suggestions for things you can do about this situation—actions that can make a difference. Let's keep pushing until no kid has to be hooked and hurt.

One teenage guy, his head in a cage of surgical steel rods drilled into his skull because of a drunk-driving tragedy, asked me to sound the alarm. In front of all his friends after a high-school assembly, he pointed to the cage and said, "We didn't listen. Tell them, Jerry."

This book fulfills the promise I made to him that day.

Jerry Johnston
Kansas City

PART ONE

Challenges

As a young man, the poet Carl Sandburg once took his college roommate home to meet his hard-of-hearing aunt.

"Auntie," Carl said, "this is my roommate Al Specknoodle."

She shook her head and cupped her ear.

"Auntie," yelled Carl, "I want you to meet Al Specknoodle!"

She shook her head and frowned.

Exasperated, Carl shouted the name again and pointed to his friend: "Specknoodle! Al Specknoodle!"

"Carl," his aunt finally cried, "it's no use. No matter how many times you say it, it still sounds like . . . Al Specknoodle!"

How often and how loudly do we have to hear something before we'll really listen?

1

Russian Roulette on Wheels

I remember the sirens that night. I remember glancing out the front window of Mom's room to see the neighbors blustering out onto their porches to watch the police cars pull up at our house.

It was just a couple of years ago, but as I drive north out of Los Angeles under ominous afternoon clouds, I need to refresh my memory. The radio is appropriately playing the old UB40 song, "Red, Red Wine" as I pop a cassette into the tape player. It's the cassette Mom recorded about her recollections of that night.

"Jerry, let me relive that night with you." Her voice is mature, controlled. "Naturally, I'd been drinking all day. I don't believe I'd talked to any of you five boys all day, and John, your father, was out of town. So I drank and was watching television in my room when you knocked at the front door.

"The five of you came up to my room and I believe it was you, Jerry, who said, 'Mother, we're going to take you to the hospital. We know you have an alcohol problem and we've made arrangements for you to go in and stay for twenty-eight days in a rehabilitation center.'"

Now, a couple of years—but what seems a lifetime—later, I pull off Interstate 5 to listen to the rush of memories, to review one of the many chapters of my family's part in what the experts call "substance abuse."

3

This chapter is about our culture's drug of choice: alcohol. I've been dredging through hundreds of people's stories about kids on drugs, and alcoholics, and addiction-prone tendencies. After talking face-to-face in high-school assemblies with more than three million kids, hearing their tough, disturbing, convoluted stories, you'd think I'd be pretty well desensitized to the drama of my own story. But as always, it hits me full-force as my mom says on the tape:

"I was mad. I usually didn't get mad when I drank; but that time I really got furious. I thought, *nobody's going to take me anywhere—especially my own sons.* So I dialed the emergency number 9-1-1. I told the police that somebody was trying to physically take me out of my home and would they please come to the house. I remember standing there looking at you and your brothers, Jerry, having trouble remembering that I'd actually given birth to you five boys. The sirens were going. Neighbors came out on their front porches to see what had happened.

"The police rushed into the house and interrogated each of you. And one of you—I can't remember which one—kept insisting that everything was all right, that you were just trying to help me and take me to the hospital.

"The police finally left. Then one of you said, 'Come on, Mother, get in the van. We'll just go to the hospital for a while.' So somehow I gave in to go for just a while.

"At the hospital, Jerry, they put me in a little room. Then a nurse came in to tell me I would be locked up for twenty-eight days, that my sons had just signed me in. And I remember pleading with each one of you, 'Don't make me stay here!' I'd never been incarcerated, or anyplace that I couldn't leave by my own free will. I told you I would do anything if you'd take me home. And none of you would."

At that point, my own voice comes on the tape: "You were really upset with me."

Mom answers, "I really hated all my family. And it was you, Jerry, who was the instigator."

I listen to more of the tape, to Mom's traumatic rehab experiences. Then I wince as she confesses her relapse back to the bottle after I had taken her with me to Anchorage on one of my trips as a youth lecturer. My topics on that trip? Suicide. Drugs. And, as if it were a problem in somebody else's life, I gave my well-honed presentation on alcohol.

Sleeping Beauty

That's the way Tiffany Delaney's family always felt—that alcohol was somebody else's problem. But that was before the terror of January 27, 1989.

They were right, in a way. Booze was a problem to Anders Grunberg, the twenty-eight-year-old Encino, California, geologist who is now considered a fugitive from the law, hiding out presumably in Europe. And his problem became the Delaney family problem when Grunberg's yellow Nissan pickup blasted into Tiffany's Volkswagen Rabbit.

Thinking about Tiffany, I turn off the tape player, get back on the freeway, and drive out of the Los Angeles smog past Northridge. Rough ridges of the San Gabriel Mountains loom to the southeast as I exit to Quartz Hill, a rather stark development of houses among the Joshua trees of this area just west of the Mojave Desert. I pull into a cul-de-sac and amble up to the open garage door of a large house. A man resembling a movie star strides out, wiping grease from his hands. "Larry Delaney," he says, introducing himself and apologizing for his dirty hands. "Sorry, I've been trying to readjust some plumbing on the water heater. We were using so much hot water with the diameter pipe they'd installed. . . . Well, listen, come on in."

"Anybody ever tell you you look like a young Clint Eastwood?" I ask; but Larry is through the front door, already calling to his wife, "Pam! Hot water in the sink yet?" I wander into the family room with its high white walls and view of the landscaping construction messing up the backyard. Larry comes in and insists that the first thing I need to see is the video segment about his daughter Tiffany broadcast by the investigative TV magazine "Hard Copy."

The Delaneys' wide-screen television bursts to life with commercials featuring sweet-faced little blonde kids. One quick snippet shows a fresh little girl dueling repartees with Bob Hope. Larry explains, "Tiff and her brother and sisters all have been in some print and several television commercials—Gerber Baby Foods, Mattel, Coca-Cola, Kool-Aid. That Bob Hope bit was from his wacky 'Bob Hope for President' special back in 1980."

Next are several formal poses of Tiff as the gorgeous teenage model, and as the vivacious cheerleader friends teased with the nickname "Barbie." Then the video clip takes an ugly turn: twisted wreckage, the noncommittal look of accused drunk driver Anders Leif Grunberg in his mug shot; a long, sad view of Tiffany, now seventeen, her blonde hair spread across the pillow in the hospital—the tubes and equipment of her life-support system sprouting from the side of her hospital bed.

"Anders had been skiing," Larry says, settling on the couch. "He was coming back from the mountains, and had probably had a few beers on the way." He hands me copies of the police report.

The accident had occurred about 6:30 on that dark January evening. Anders was barreling along Topanga Canyon Boulevard at about fifty miles per hour when he allegedly crossed the double-yellow center line to smash into Tiffany's white VW convertible. Also in the VW was Tiff's twelve-year-old sister Sabrina. Grunberg's pickup lost its camper shell, which flipped down the street to shatter under the front of a Chevy Blazer traveling two cars behind the VW. Grunberg's truck rolled and slid to a stop on its top in the middle of the boulevard. Tiffany's Volkswagen careened over the curb.

The police report tersely describes the injuries: "P-1 [Grunberg]: Superficial contusion to the forehead & complained of pain to the left hip. WIT#1 [Sabrina]: Fractured legs (both) & lacerations to the head and face. Unknown other injuries. WIT-1 airlifted by air ambulance to Northridge Hosp. P2 [Tiffany]: Multi-fractures to both legs, head & face. Lacerations and contusions; concussion, unknown internal & closed head injuries. Termed 'Critical condition' by hosp. staff. Airlifted to Northridge Hosp."

The statements recorded by those involved in the "accident" were just as stark: "P-1 [Grunberg]: 'I was going down Topanga. The white car made a left turn from a side street or driveway. . . . I think they cut off the truck [Blazer] while the white car was in my blind spot. I slammed on the brakes but hit the turning VW. The truck just kept going and didn't stop.'

"P-2 [Tiffany]: Unconscious. Not interviewed.

"WIT#1 [Sabrina]: Not interviewed due to serious nature of injuries.

"P-3 [driver of the Blazer following second behind Tiffany's VW]: 'I was going north on Topanga in the far right lane. I saw a yellow vehicle coming toward the VW a couple cars ahead of me.'

"WIT#2 [driver of the car immediately following Tiff's]: 'I was northbound on Topanga behind the Rabbit. Suddenly there was a huge crash in front of me. I locked up my brakes and skidded between the pickup on my left and the VW on my right. Something [camper shell] flew over my car and damaged the Blazer behind me. I know the Volkswagen was going straight in the number one northbound lane when it happened.'"

The police report's "Observations" section includes a couple more disturbing details: "Upon interviewing [Grunberg], we noted multi-objective symptoms of intox. In our opinion deft [defendant] was too intox. to safely operate a motor veh. & was therefore DUI at the time of the traffic accident. . . . No California op. license in his possession. DMV records show the deft's license suspended except during course of employment. On DUI probation 3 years beginning 8/88—terms state 'no driving while alcohol in blood.'"

Under "Remarks," the report describes a picture Larry and Pam Delaney never wanted to imagine of their beautiful, fun-loving daughter: "P-2 [Tiffany] was ejected from vehicle on impact & came to rest at the left door of the vehicle. The left rear tire of vehicle was on P-2's hair—holding P-2 to the ground 'til freed by parameds."

Grunberg was taken into custody, but was released the next day when his parents paid a $2,500 bond. He never showed up for his arraignment. Now in the darkening afternoon in the Delaney home, Larry says, "He called the police station a couple times in the days after the crash to ask about his pickup, his skis, and some stuff he left in the truck. He never once asked about anyone else hurt in the crash."

Larry hands me the clippings of the local newspapers' accounts of the incident. "We don't think of it as an 'accident,'" Larry smiles wearily. "It's like someone playing Russian roulette. He knows he's putting a bullet in the chamber—he knows he's ingesting alcohol, and he knows at that time that he will be stepping into a three-thousand-pound battering ram of steel that can travel nearly a hundred miles an hour. The only difference between driving drunk and Russian roulette is that instead of pointing the gun at himself, the player is pointing the barrel at you, or at your kids, and pulling the trigger to see what happens.

"And what happened for us," Larry says, "is that Tiff was left unconscious, not expected to live. We called her Sleeping Beauty when she was in the coma. Then came the five months of comatose treatment at the hospital. Our $600,000 of insurance ran out just a few months after she was admitted."

I notice in Larry's clippings a few scraps of medical bills, and feel the dread of reality—a drunk-driving tragedy isn't just a physical, emotional trauma. Hospital costs for a single day of Tiffany's care list $122 for an injection, $760 for her intensive-care room and board, $100 for another injection, $43 here, and $146 there, along with dozens of other daily charges.

"How can you survive financially with all this?"

Larry smiles. "I'm a twenty-one-year vet with the L.A. Fire Department—Station 8 on the B shift. Firefighters helped us a lot after the insurance topped out. Others have helped, too. We're going to make those donations last as long as possible; we're pacing ourselves for the long haul since Tiff will always need care. It's going to take years and years."

"What's this?" I ask, noticing a sheet titled "Tiffany Brooke Delaney."

"Pam wrote that poem when Tiff was a few months into the coma," says Larry. "Maybe it gives a hint of what a mother goes through when her daughter's entire life is violated."

I carefully read the poem:

A brief life curtailed, dreams of no use
Tears that overwhelm for a shattered youth
Her eyes once sparkled—now they're dimmed with pain
A voice that was eager lives in silent domain
Intelligence and beauty—they once were her own
The light now is shrouded like a spent candle blown
A childhood memory that long ceased to be
A game that was played by the children and me
Whenever afraid or alone and unsure
They would take Mom or Dad's hand, holding firm and secure
Three little squeezes, then the adult's turn came
Returning three squeezes—that was the game
As I sit and I watch her I still play the game
I hold on to her hand and whisper her name
I don't know if I can reach her—I pray I get through
Please, Tiffany, don't you remember
Three squeezes mean I love you?

A Happy Ending?

As I gradually absorb the integrity and bonding of this family, the Delaneys' story climbs out of the morass of statistics that we all vaguely know about our culture's bizarre mix of drinks and horse-power. I vow to keep trying to put faces on the numbers—such as the 23,351 people killed in the United States in 1988's alcohol-related car crashes. Every year about a half a million Americans suffer injuries in alcohol-related traffic accidents—an average of one person every minute. Think of it: How many minutes have you been reading with me? That many Tiffanys have been hurt in drunk-driving incidents in that time.

I find myself sinking back into the Delaneys' couch, overwhelmed by the enormity of the carnage, wishfully thinking that most of those injuries aren't as shattering as Tiffany's.

My curiosity gets the best of me. "May I see Tiff?" I ask.

"Sure," Larry says. "After the five months she was in the coma and the past year of hospitalization, I built on this special room for her. We want her home. Let me see if she's ready for a visitor."

Larry steps out while I scan a clipping about Tiffany's remarkable struggle back from the horrific beating her head and body took in the crash. "Crash Victim Defies Prognosis" says one front-page headline in the December 10, 1989 *San Fernando Daily News.* "After 10 months in a hospital bed—half of that time spent in a coma—19-year-old Tiffany Delaney motioned her mother to her bedside. 'I love you, Mom,' she said. They were her first intelligible words since January 27." The article by Tom Mallory goes on to say that although she awoke from the coma in the summer of 1989, doctors caution that Tiff will never fully recover.

Larry pokes his head around a doorway and motions me into Tiffany's wheelchair-accessible room. A "Bonanza" rerun is blaring on the TV hung high on a wall. Tiff's sister Sabrina is snuggled against Tiffany, who rests listlessly in green hospital-style pajamas, watching the show.

Larry says, "Sabrina herself went through quite a deal. Eight weeks in the hospital with a ruptured spleen, arms and legs broken in several places."

Sabrina smiles and shakes my hand.

I walk to the side of the raised hospital bed, and say, "Hello, Tiffany. I'm wanting to write about you in a book. What do you think?"

Tiffany glances sideways, one eye not as wide as the other, and smiles a little lopsidedly. "I work hard," she says softly. "I'm number one."

I later learn that she can walk now with difficulty. Although she sometimes falls back into using the sign language she invented while still unable to speak, she can communicate in brief sentences now, and she regularly pops out with a healthy sense of humor. When asked about her physical therapy sessions three days a week at nearby High Desert Hospital, Tiffany quips, "I get a kick out of it," with a sharp kick of her right leg. Her left leg is slow in responding to therapy sessions.

She's beginning to remember details of the crash, itself: "The truck came into my car. It was a shock. I was cold. I remember I was freezing. I was very cold."

Back outside in the driveway, I ask about Grunberg, the drunk driver. "We've got enough to worry about without being obsessed with his capture," Larry says. "There's one cop who's sticking to the case; but when the guy is probably hiding out in Europe, what can you do?"

"I suppose so," I say. "But this stuff always just makes me mad. Can we help somehow with Tiff's trust fund?" Larry shrugs and jots down an address for contributions: Tiffany Delaney Fund, Fireman's Credit Union, 2900 West Temple Street, Los Angeles, CA 90026.

"Thanks," I say.

"Thank you," he answers. He walks me to my car and says, "When she was in the hospital, we'd squeeze her hand and she'd squeeze back. That was it. She was never expected to recover at all. She's beating the odds. Now she's always telling us how much she loves us. She's such a special spirit, so loving and childlike. We're really blessed to have her with us."

I climb heavily into my car, wave to Larry as he heads back to his water-heater repairs in the garage, and drive in the deepening sunset to the freeway. Taillights zing past as I accelerate down the freeway on-ramp. The cars suddenly look lethal, huge and powerful. As darkness lowers across the desert, I find myself wondering how many drivers are drunk. How many are playing Russian roulette with me, with my wife, my kids?

Every 27 Minutes

The article reprinted below isn't new. In fact, since it was first published, the deadly countdown it describes from one alcohol-related

ABOVE: **Drunk-driver assailant Larry Mahoney is serving only a sixteen-year sentence. He struck a church bus carrying sixty-seven people in Kentucky. Twenty-seven passengers, most of them young people, were immediately incinerated. (AP/Wide World Photo)**

While making a poster about drinking and driving, people at Johnson County (Kansas) Community College play dead. They are representing the hundreds of people killed each month in alcohol- and drug-related crashes. (Photo by David Brandt, Sun Publications.)

LEFT: Tiffany Delaney, standing, and her younger sister Kelsey modeled in several television commercials before Tiffany was severely injured in a car crash in California. Anders Grunberg, the driver of the other car, was charged with driving under the influence of alcohol.

BELOW: Tiffany Delaney was not expected to live after the crash with a drunk driver. She was comatose for five months, and hospitalized a year as she valiantly fought her way back to life through therapy and faith.

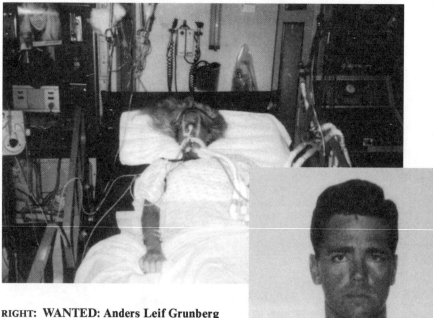

RIGHT: WANTED: Anders Leif Grunberg jumped bail after being charged with driving under the influence of alcohol in California. Teenager Tiffany Delaney was almost killed in the crash when Grunberg's pickup allegedly crossed the double-yellow center line and smashed into Tiffany's Volkswagen convertible.

LEFT: Jerry Johnston: "I am convinced we have turned the corner and can win the war against substance abuse—if we work together."

RIGHT: Jerry offers a listening ear and a caring heart to teenagers searching for just one glimmer of hope.

LEFT: John W. Johnston, Jerry's dad, believes there is hope for every alcoholic.

LEFT: Kevin Tunell was convicted of driving while intoxicated after crashing into a car driven by Susan Herzog. Susan, eighteen, was killed in the wreck. Tunell, who was uninjured, was ordered by the court to send one dollar every Friday to Susan's parents, Lou and Patty Herzog, above, as a memorial to their daughter. (Photo of Tunell by Stanley Tretick/*People Weekly* © 1990 The Time Inc. Magazine Co. All rights reserved. Photo of Lou and Patty Herzog by Robert Sherbow/*People Weekly* © 1990 The Time Inc. Magazine Co. All rights reserved.)

RIGHT: More young people are killed each year by drunk-driving tragedies than by any other cause.

death to the next has decreased from twenty-seven minutes to twenty-three. But the grim reduction in time only sharpens the effectiveness of this powerful writing. I think it will prepare you even more deeply for our further investigation of the personal side of the ravages of alcohol abuse. Consider reading the following aloud to a teenager—it might go down a little smoother than a sermon would:

My husband and I went to a funeral a few weeks ago. The man we honored had not been ill. He was killed on a Sunday night while driving home. An oncoming car jumped the highway median and hit two other cars before smashing head-on into his.

According to the newspaper, the offending driver, who was returning from a wedding, told police she had drunk two bottles of beer and two glasses of champagne.

A wedding.

Followed by a funeral.

I wish she could have been there to see all the lives her act has changed forever: the widow, the four children, the extended family, the hundreds of friends who sat listening to words that barely touched the depths of their grief.

Strange to think that, according to the National Highway Traffic Safety Administration, this happens in America every 27 minutes.

Somebody drinks.

Somebody drives.

Somebody dies.

The day before the funeral, I had run into a longtime acquaintance while shopping. I was hobbling around with a broken leg, and he commented on my crutches. I asked if he had ever broken his leg.

"Oh, I have a long rod in one thigh," he said, "from an automobile accident I was in two weeks after I came back from Vietnam."

"That's ironic. To leave a war zone and get injured," I teased him. "You're lucky it wasn't worse."

"Well, my wife was killed and so was the wife of the other driver," he said uncomfortably. Then he added, "We were hit by a drunk."

I've known this man for years, yet here was a chapter of his life he'd never mentioned. He said he'd remained in the hospital seven weeks, aware all that time that his wife was dead. It was hard to know what to say, for there are questions you can't ask in a casual conversation, like "How could you bear it?" or "What did you do about wanting revenge?"

I wish I knew the answers so I could offer them to the woman who, overwhelmed by grief, could barely walk as she followed her husband's coffin from the synagogue.

At the high school where she teaches, my friend Lynn saw a movie in which the young male narrator recounted how he'd killed someone while driving drunk. "He said he didn't know how he'd stand it if he'd killed someone he loved, " Lynn told me. "That really bothered me. Isn't everyone someone that somebody loves?"

Every 27 minutes, who dies?

A mother who will never comfort the child who needs her. A man whose contributions to his community would have made a difference. A wife whose husband cannot picture the future without her.

Every 27 minutes, who dies?

A son who involuntarily abandons his parents in their old age. A father who can never acknowledge his children's accomplishments. A friend whose encouragement is gone forever.

Every 27 minutes, who dies?

A child who will never fulfill his promise. A bride-to-be who will never say her vows.

Every 27 minutes.

A void opens.

Someone looks across the table at a vacant chair, climbs into an empty bed, feels the pain of no voice, no touch, no love.

Every 27 minutes.

A heart breaks.

Someone's pain defies the soothing power of tranquilizers. Sleep offers no escape from the nightmare of awakening to the irreversibility of loss.

Every 27 minutes.

A dream ends.

Someone's future goes blank. The phone will not ring, the car will not pull into the driveway.

Every 27 minutes.

Somebody wants to run. Somebody wants to hide.

Somebody is left with hate. Somebody wants to die.

And we permit this to go on.

Every 27 minutes.

(By Linda Weltner. Reprinted with permission from the February 1987 *Reader's Digest.*)

The Booze Blues

I keep thinking about Grunberg as a fugitive, wondering about his conscience. And I keep thinking about how my next story to research is going to be a lot tougher emotionally. I need to remember that the man I'll be studying is just as human as I am, even though I'm not the one who played alcohol roulette with the lives of twenty-seven people—and lost.

2

Dead Drunk

(The following account is reconstructed from articles published in 1988 and 1989 by the *Louisville Courier-Journal,* which has granted its permission.)

May 14, 1988, is a day Larry Mahoney cannot fully remember, but it is a day he most certainly can never, ever forget. Larry, described in press reports as a soft-spoken, twice-divorced chemical worker of thirty-four, was having problems reconciling with his first wife because of financial problems. That day in northern Kentucky, he drank seven or eight beers, then drove to a friend's house that evening. There he was offered a mixed drink, although he says he prefers beer.

"I took a big swallow," Mahoney said, "and it choked me, took my breath. I heard some people giggling, laughing."

He had a couple more mixed drinks.

"You do it sometimes because somebody says you're not man enough to take a drink," he said, meaning hard liquor. "You just do it to show you can take a drink. But I hate the stuff."

As Mahoney left in his Toyota pickup truck, the liquor, plus the beer, numbed his memory of what happened next.

Clint Bradley, a motorist driving south on Interstate 71 that night, saw Mahoney's pickup. "It was coming out of the northbound lanes," Bradley related, "and made a U-turn across the grass and started going south. He pulled around behind me with his bright lights on, and just about blinded me."

The pickup passed Bradley and was driving erratically, so he took an exit "to just let that pickup truck get down the road." When Bradley got back onto southbound I-71, he soon saw the pickup "pull out of the median and start driving north on the southbound lanes. It really shocked me. . . . I flashed my lights and blew my horn."

That evening, a group of kids from Radcliff, Kentucky, were returning from a church outing at an amusement park north of Cincinnati. Many of these ten- to nineteen-year-olds were active in Radcliff First Assembly of God's youth group called LIFE, for Life Is For Everyone. But it was getting to be about 10:55 P.M. as the bus neared the town of Carrolton. The liveliness was draining from the kids after a full day of adventures on the drenching Amazon Falls water ride, the Beast roller coaster, and the thrills and scares of other rides.

John Pearman, the thirty-seven-year-old associate pastor, was driving the fully loaded church bus with its sixty-seven tired but happy occupants. Suddenly he slammed on the brakes, crying, "Oh, no!"

"I could hear the skidding," said Janie Padgett, one of the four chaperones. "I'll never forget the skidding, the skidding."

The bus swerved; but Mahoney's pickup was coming right at them. Bus passenger Tom Hertz, fifteen, thought, *No, we won't get in a wreck; that never happens to me.*

As the pickup hurled into the right front corner of the bus, a gash ripped into the bus's fuel tank, just behind the front door, making it unusable.

A narrow trail of fire was on the road. Flames shot out from the right side of the bus.

Now flames were inside, rushing from the stairwell to the ceiling. Intense light silhouetted the children.

Driver Pearman was shaken but not seriously injured. He turned to the back and hollered, "Open the door and get 'em out!"

Conrad Garcia kicked open the emergency door and jumped.

As other children tried at once to squeeze through the opening partly blocked by the back seats, it became clogged.

In the heart of the fire, youth leader Chuck Kytta raised his hands. "Lord, I'm coming home!" he cried.

In a flash, the flames outside the bus rose halfway up the windows. Inside, the passengers quickly moved back. Padgett thought, *Oh, God! We're in trouble! . . . We're all doomed.*

As the heat hit her, this small woman squeezed through a nine-by-twenty-four-inch window opening. Somehow she was out—singed, but lying safely on the pavement.

Most of the windows were shut, transforming the bus into an oven filled with thick, black smoke. Oxygen was getting scarce.

Jamie Hardesty, a farm boy, found the aisle to the rear blocked, so he hurtled over seats to the exit. There, a pile of children was blocking freedom. He dived over the bodies out onto the highway pavement.

Kim Farmer got to the last row of seats. "I was pushing on people in front of me. Then the smoke, it got real black and I passed out. And I just quit. It was like just drifting off."

In the crush of passengers pushing their way through the aisle was Juan Holt. After an eternity, he strained within reach of the exit. Then he was falling, with an avalanche of falling children from behind burying him. "Get off me! Get off me!" he screamed as he lost consciousness. He was pulled off the bus.

Others couldn't move; the aisle was completely blocked. Terrorized children pushed, pleaded, shoved, screamed. Then came more smoke, darkness, disorientation—and blackout.

Christy Pearman, fourteen, turned to see her father, still up front. He had a fire extinguisher. "C'mon, Dad!" she yelled. "Get off the bus!" She tried to push toward the front, against the desperate flow. She must help him! Then someone grabbed her leg, and she went down, crashing to her knees.

Tom Hertz kicked and kicked his window. It wouldn't shatter. He grabbed hands with seatmates Kristen Williams and Mike Jefferson, and they leaped over seat backs.

They saw boyfriend and girlfriend Chad Witt and April Mills in a desperate hug. "They wouldn't move," Tom said. "Everyone was yelling at them, 'Come on; get out!'" But they didn't.

Children kept falling in the aisle on top of each other. "One person would trip," Tom said, "and everyone behind him would start falling down . . . falling and tripping and trying to get out." Some were panicking; others passed out. One said later it felt like the smoke was "eating your lungs apart."

Motorists stopped and ran to the burning bus, now filled with flames clawing at its ceiling. Children inside cried, "Help me!" "Mom!" Many of them were in flames.

A child stuck a hand out a window, and a passing motorist tried to help, but said later, "When I was ready to reach up there, then the explosion came." There was a huge blast. Afterward, he said, "There was just muffled sounds in there for a few seconds, and then it was all over."

Those who perished: twenty-four children and three adults. Dental records were required to identify every victim.

Numerous fire engines, police cars, and ambulances lined the interstate in both directions. The most seriously injured were airlifted by helicopter. The rest of the injured were taken by ambulance to three different hospitals. The bus was now a charred hulk, at last without windows and doors.

Those who survived: thirty-nine children, one adult chaperone—and Larry Mahoney.

That night still deeply affects the survivors. Many will always have scars, both emotional and physical.

When Tom Hertz returned to school, he couldn't bear passing the lockers of his sixteen missing schoolmates. "So I came home," he said. He couldn't go back, at least not for a while.

Now fatherless Christy Pearman is terrified of fire. At night in the hospital she had to have her burned arms tied in splints to the bed to help healing. Being tied down was horrifying for her; she feared the hospital might catch on fire.

For many children, the horrific night strengthened their faith in God for saving them and some of their friends.

As for Mahoney? His blood alcohol level at the time of the crash was over twice the state's officially drunk level. It was learned he had been fined previously for drunk driving.

He was tried for twenty-seven murders under Kentucky's law, which states that "voluntary intoxication" in such cases constitutes wanton disregard for human life—which amounts to murder. Intent does not need to be proved.

Lee Williams testified at the trial, but was restricted by law to giving only a few details. He had lost his wife and two daughters in the crash. He turned from the jury and stared at the defendant. "All three of my family members—my whole family was killed on that bus."

During the testimony, Mahoney never looked up.

When Mahoney later testified, he said, "I've been waiting a long time to do this. I just want to say something to everyone, especially the families of the people involved in the accident. I know you've been waiting for me to say something, to tell you I'm sorry, and that's what I do want to do. But I was told not to say anything.

"But I want you to know I really am sorry. I mean this. I don't know if there is anything else I can say or something else I can do any differently—maybe that I would probably feel the same way about me that you do. . . . I'm sorry."

Mahoney's mother cried, and so did the victims' relatives.

There had been tears from many people who had to testify at this murder trial. One of those was Katrina Muller, fifteen, who was fortunate enough to escape. The defense attorney asked her why she had sent Mahoney a tape offering forgiveness.

Katrina broke into tears. The families in the courtroom also cried.

The girl said, sobbing, "In my church, I was raised that you couldn't go to heaven if you hate someone. I forgive him for what he did. But I still feel he needs to be punished for it."

The sequel to the story? Most of the parents felt sure the trial and outcome of this case would finally send the solid warning to every drinker in our society: Don't even *think* about drinking and driving.

Other relatives of the dead wanted personal apologies, not the one-size-fits-all apology Mahoney gave in court. Some wanted the deaths of their loved ones acknowledged with a charge and conviction of murder.

Larry Mahoney was convicted after a seven-week trial in Carrollton. The jury of the Carroll Circuit Court found Mahoney guilty of manslaughter, wanton endangerment, and assault. His sentence for being responsible for twenty-seven deaths? Sixteen years in prison— eligible for parole in eight. The sentencing came after Mahoney's defense lawyers asked that he simply be placed on probation.

The "deadliest drunk driver in the history of United States" said in a February 26, 1990 *People* magazine article that he wishes he'd been locked up the first time he'd been caught driving drunk in 1984. He said, "If I'd have stayed 30 days in jail for that first time, I'd have never been back out on that road no more." His sentence at that time? A small fine.

First Assembly's pastor—who originally had been designated to drive the bus on that fateful May night—was cordial, but not enthusiastic about my request to come to Radcliff and interview the families.

"Let me check with some of the parents and see, Jerry," was his reserved reply.

But in a later call, the pastor said, in effect, "Please don't come. We are still in a healing process. Some of the families have moved away." Worse yet, he said, some of the families have fragmented as a result of coping with this tragedy.

So I called off the trip, respecting their grief. Down deep inside, though, I know that lingering in Radcliff's mourning survivors are words that might just be the motivation which could keep someone else from causing another bloody I-71 disaster.

As for Larry Mahoney, he is what seems to be mute. In spite of attempts by *Playboy* magazine, the "Oprah Winfrey Show," myself, and others to penetrate his cocoon, attempts to get him to agree to an interview are to no avail. His message to others could be a tragic but inspiring reminder of the deadly perils and life-changing disasters drunk driving can cause. Unfortunately, he has chosen to follow his attorney's advice to remain silent, and has lost this opportunity.

Drunk and Deadly

Drunk driving is one of the leading causes of death in Canada as well as in the United States. "The problem persists," says the Canadian government's magazine *Smashed,* "because driving and drinking are important parts of many Canadians' lifestyle." More than fifteen million licensed drivers in Canada drive more than 180 billion kilometers each year. Meanwhile, the average adult consumes twelve drinks of alcohol weekly. The deadly combination has prompted a catch-phrase in the Canadian drunk-driving law books: "Alcohol-impaired driving is not only unacceptable, but also criminal."

The problem is similar in the United States. The statistics, shown in Table 2-1 on page 20, are impersonal but impressive.

But the statistics need to be personalized if we are ever to be moved to stop the carnage on our nation's highways. According to the National Center for Statistics and Analysis, in one twenty-four-hour period on May 17, 1986, 116 people were killed in alcohol-related crashes.

Who was killed? A gripping video lets us see some of the faces of these statistics. Pyramid Film and Video offers one of the most

Table 2-1

Alcohol-Related Traffic Accidents and Fatalities

| | Drivers Age Twenty and Over | |
Year	Total Fatalities	Alcohol-Related Fatalities
1988	36,984	19,265
1987	36,305	19,450
1986	36,084	19,795
1985	34,363	18,590
1984	34,637	19,273

| | Drivers Age Fifteen to Nineteen | |
Year	Total Fatalities	Alcohol-Related Fatalities
1988	3,599	1,422
1987	3,700	1,419
1986	3,577	1,581
1985	3,279	1,427
1984	3,418	1,621

| | Drivers Age Fifteen to Nineteen | |
Year	Involved in Fatal Alcohol-Related Accidents	Survivors of Alcohol-Related Accidents
1988	2,447	1,025
1987	2,461	1,042
1986	2,717	1,136
1985	2,408	981
1984	2,769	1,148

(Information obtained from the Fatal Accident Reporting System maintained by the National Highway Traffic Safety Administration.)

effective resources I've seen on drinking and driving. *Drunk and Deadly,* a video and study guide for groups, chronicles the details of the 116 fatalities on that day. In many cases, the victims are named, and survivors of the crashes are interviewed. Viewers hear the stories of the real people involved, the heartaches left behind, the idiocy of it all as the video reviews the drunk-driving incidents of that typical day. Believe me, it'll keep you—and your teenagers—sober about drinking and driving. These 116 deaths in twenty-four hours are more than statistics; they are names, lives, fathers, wives, children, cousins, neighbors, and friends. Yet they comprise only a fraction of the twenty-three thousand very normal people who die every year in the United States alone in alcohol-related accidents.

Read through the listing of the dead from May 17, 1986, in Table 2-2. Think about how old each person was. Look at the time and place each one died. Think of this stark, simple memorial list as if it's the wall that stands in Washington, D.C. as a memorial to the Vietnam dead.

If we could ever visualize the faces, the lives, the families, and lost futures of the quarter of a million Americans killed in booze-related auto wrecks in the past decade, I think every one of us would simply and finally say, "I will never drink and drive."

To order *Drunk and Deadly* for your school or civic group, your family, or yourself, contact Pyramid Film and Video, Box 1048, Santa Monica, CA 90406; phone 213-828-7577.

The film is not grotesque or gory. It's simply dumbfounding and bewildering as it shows how we allow this to happen day after day. It happens even though we know the simple effectiveness of choosing a designated driver who won't drink and then will drive everyone else home.

You don't have to drink and then drive if you plan ahead. So take another run at what is to many people a difficult, challenging vow: "I will never drink and drive."

If it's still tough to convince yourself that you could actually mean those words, despite the grim statistics that predict two out of every five people will sometime be involved in an alcohol-related

Table 2-2

Total Fatalities in Crashes When Alcohol was Present for Driver, Pedestrian, or Pedalcyclist on May 17, 1986

No.	State	Age	Sex	Person Type	Time of Death
1	Alabama	43	F	Passenger	330
2	Alabama	50	M	Pedestrian	Unk.
3	Alabama	28	M	Driver	2310
4	Alabama	24	M	Driver	1540
5	Alabama	27	M	Driver	Unk.

Table 2-2 *(Continued)*

No.	State	Age	Sex	Person Type	Time of Death
6	Alaska	41	M	Driver	Unk.
7	Arizona	16	M	Pedestrian	1650
8	Arizona	4	F	Passenger	2005
9	Arkansas	65	F	Driver	1850
10	California	20	M	Passenger	52
11	California	30	M	Pedestrian	415
12	California	46	M	Driver	1800
13	California	21	M	Driver	1853
14	California	??	M	Pedestrian	2201
15	California	33	M	Driver	2306
16	California	29	M	Driver	2316
17	California	35	F	Driver	1916
18	Connecticut	24	F	Driver	105
19	Connecticut	37	M	Driver	2030
20	Delaware	26	M	Driver	1130
21	Florida	37	F	Passenger	216
22	Florida	??	F	Pedestrian	1305
23	Florida	15	M	Passenger	1851
24	Florida	43	M	Driver	139
25	Florida	??	F	Pedestrian	2155
26	Florida	43	M	Pedestrian	255
27	Florida	65	F	Pedestrian	2023
28	Georgia	27	M	Driver	2137
29	Georgia	29	M	Driver	1645
30	Georgia	20	M	Driver	230
31	Georgia	36	M	Pedestrian	2337
32	Georgia	16	M	Driver	1350
33	Hawaii	17	F	Driver	100
34	Hawaii	25	M	Driver	225
35	Idaho	21	M	Driver	1504
36	Illinois	25	M	Driver	720
37	Illinois	31	M	Driver	335
38	Illinois	22	M	Driver	544
39	Illinois	25	M	Driver	537
40	Illinois	43	M	Pedestrian	500
41	Illinois	17	M	Pedestrian	1210
42	Kansas	21	F	Driver	2038
43	Kansas	37	M	Driver	2040

Table 2-2   *(Continued)*

No.	State	Age	Sex	Person Type	Time of Death
44	Kansas	24	M	Passenger	2040
45	Kansas	5	M	Passenger	2040
46	Kansas	18	M	Pedestrian	22
47	Kentucky	30	F	Passenger	103
48	Kentucky	12	M	Passenger	103
49	Kentucky	28	M	Driver	355
50	Kentucky	20	M	Driver	56
51	Kentucky	24	M	Driver	1928
52	Louisiana	20	M	Passenger	701
53	Louisiana	29	M	Driver	10
54	Louisiana	18	M	Passenger	310
55	Massachusetts	30	M	Driver	344
56	Massachusetts	25	M	Pedestrian	250
57	Massachusetts	28	M	Passenger	215
58	Michigan	24	M	Driver	1512
59	Minnesota	18	M	Passenger	210
60	Minnesota	13	M	Driver	113
61	Minnesota	41	M	Pedestrian	2220
62	Minnesota	3	M	Pedestrian	1823
63	Missouri	20	M	Driver	550
64	Missouri	20	M	Driver	1929
65	Montana	16	M	Driver	530
66	Nebraska	21	M	Driver	255
67	Nevada	30	M	Driver	1447
68	New Jersey	22	M	Driver	240
69	New Jersey	23	M	Passenger	240
70	New Jersey	34	F	Driver	250
71	New Jersey	39	M	Passenger	457
72	New Jersey	28	M	Driver	801
73	New Mexico	17	M	Driver	220
74	New York	18	M	Pedestrian	810
75	New York	20	M	Passenger	400
76	New York	72	M	Pedestrian	253
77	North Carolina	44	M	Passenger	2100
78	North Carolina	24	M	Passenger	1540
79	Ohio	18	M	Driver	557
80	Ohio	26	M	Driver	1221
81	Ohio	33	M	Driver	2005

Table 2-2 *(Continued)*

No.	State	Age	Sex	Person Type	Time of Death
82	Ohio	24	M	Passenger	655
83	Oklahoma	29	F	Driver	1320
84	Oklahoma	42	F	Driver	Unk.
85	Oregon	26	M	Driver	2228
86	Oregon	40	M	Driver	1910
87	Oregon	18	M	Driver	315
88	Oregon	19	M	Passenger	225
89	Pennsylvania	24	M	Driver	1910
90	Pennsylvania	17	F	Passenger	1910
91	Pennsylvania	45	M	Driver	315
92	Pennsylvania	24	M	Pedestrian	1530
93	South Carolina	24	M	Passenger	Unk.
94	South Carolina	24	M	Driver	2230
95	South Carolina	41	M	Pedestrian	2300
96	Tennessee	26	M	Driver	Unk.
97	Tennessee	22	M	Driver	Unk.
98	Tennessee	53	F	Passenger	Unk.
99	Tennessee	25	M	Driver	2135
100	Texas	18	M	Occupant of parked car	2310
101	Texas	25	M	Driver	1350
102	Texas	17	M	Passenger	1350
103	Texas	52	F	Passenger	1237
104	Texas	25	M	Passenger	351
105	Texas	27	M	Driver	1732
106	Texas	34	M	Passenger	1732
107	Texas	17	M	Passenger	410
108	Utah	25	M	Pedestrian	5
109	Utah	19	F	Passenger	2232
110	Virginia	20	M	Driver	200
111	Washington	19	M	Pedestrian	1820
112	Washington	20	M	Driver	153
113	West Virginia	29	M	Driver	822
114	Wisconsin	37	F	Pedestrian	2217
115	Wyoming	26	M	Driver	2100
116	Wyoming	25	M	Passenger	2155

?? = Age unknown
Unk. = Time unknown
Source: National Center for Statistics and Analysis

accident, then visit with Kevin Tunell, who killed eighteen-year-old Susan Herzog.

The Price Is High

"Nothing will ever happen to me." How many teenagers—or adults, for that matter—say that? Kevin Tunell of Fairfax, Virginia said it on New Year's Eve, 1981, before leaving a friend's party.

Kevin was seventeen that night—and drunk. He lost control of his Chrysler station wagon and slammed into Susan Herzog's blue 1973 Volkswagen beetle. Susan was killed instantly. Kevin didn't suffer any injuries—until later.

Pleading guilty to manslaughter and drunk driving, Kevin was sentenced to three years of probation and a year of community service. For his community service Kevin began speaking to schools and youth groups on "The Perils of Drinking and Driving." Susan's parents, meanwhile, were to be given recompense for their tragic loss in another way.

The death of the Herzogs' third and youngest daughter would be memorialized as Kevin was ordered to send a check for one dollar every Friday until the year 2000. Those eighteen years of weekly checks would symbolize Susan's age at the time of her death.

Kevin performed his community service role diligently. But he faltered on sending the weekly checks regularly. As a result, in the spring of 1990, the Herzogs took him to court. "Susan's death is there every waking moment," fifty-seven-year-old Lou Herzog told *People* magazine (March 1990, page 18). "But every time we don't get a check, there's only one thing that comes to our mind: he doesn't remember."

Incredibly, in 1987 the Herzogs' second daughter, Deborah, was struck by a drunk driver as Deborah was driving through Florida. As a result of the two broken legs she suffered, Deborah now walks with a permanent limp. A photo caption in the *People* article sums up the situation: "'We realize everyone has tragedy in their lives,' Susan's mother Patty Herzog says. 'This is our tragedy.'"

Kevin Tunell is quoted in the article as saying, "You get to a point where you kind of snap and you say, 'It hurts too much.'"

I wonder how he feels. I wonder if he ever drinks and drives.

During a trip to California, I notice the headline over Ann Landers's column is "Driver Pays for a Life at $1 a Week." A letter writer, signed "Undecided in Missouri," apparently thought the Herzogs were a bit cruel in their insistence that Kevin remember he killed Susan every week by sending the checks that will total $936 by the year 2000.

Ann's answer?

> Dear Missouri: Kevin Tunell killed Susan Herzog and she is just as dead as if he had shot her with a gun. Of course it's a nuisance to have to mail a check for $1 every Friday for 18 years. But Susan's parents want Kevin to be reminded of what he did every Friday until the year 2000. You can be sure the Herzogs would be thrilled to send a check for 100 times that amount every Friday to Kevin Tunell if they could have their daughter back. Does that answer your question?
>
> (Ann Landers/Creators Syndicate, *Los Angeles Times,* July 8, 1990. Used by permission.)

I decided to call Kevin.

"It's just time to move on. I can't think of it as a vendetta. My focus is simply to get on with life," Kevin said. "There's been so much written about my whole incident these past six months that it's impossible to keep up with it; so I just don't read it."

"Is there anything you'd like to add to the account? Any particular thing you'd like to say?" I ask.

"Yeah," Kevin says quickly. "If there's anything I'd like, it would be to leave me and my story out of the book. It's time to get on with other things."

Like Larry Mahoney, Kevin is declining an opportunity to touch others with the vivid message he could share. I can't help but wonder if Kevin's story, if he would share it, could save a life sometime in the future by keeping someone somewhere from driving drunk.

The Booze Challenge

Not all the drunk drivers who get soused and then get into their 3,000-pound, 110-mile-per-hour machines and kill get caught by the law. Sometimes they're the ones who die.

In a more poignant way than I could ever tell you the story, Carolyn Burnam shares her thoughts on the death of her son Darrin:

Standing there feeling so all alone, I stared in disbelief at the casket of my seventeen-year-old son, Darrin, who died in a car accident because he and a friend made the fatal mistake of drinking and driving.

He was my second son—there were almost six years between him and my first son, Danny. I had to go to work after Danny was born, so when Darrin was born I decided to stay home and take care of him, myself. Darrin was with me constantly; I hardly ever left him with anyone else. He was my whole life.

He grew into a very nice-looking boy; he was tall and slender with dark, curly hair. He loved practical jokes and making people laugh. He loved life. I don't think I ever saw him bored. Like all teenagers, Darrin liked movies, rock concerts, girls, and talking on the telephone.

I don't know why he started drinking, unless he thought he had to so he would be accepted by his friends. Unfortunately, I didn't think anything was wrong with his having a beer or two with his father, older brother, or friends. That was my first mistake. Pretty soon it got uncontrollable, and I got help for him. He seemed to be doing great, but I guess the peer pressure got the best of Darrin.

On spring break in 1983, Darrin and a friend bought two bottles of bourbon; the liquor store clerk didn't bother to ask for any identification—a big mistake because it helped get my son killed. She even gave them two ice-filled glasses. My son and his friend were on their way to meet all of us at our beach house in Corpus Christi. They never made it.

The other boy told me that because they had been drinking, they got on the wrong highway—a dark and lonely road—and he thinks my son fell asleep and lost control of the car. Then he grabbed the wheel but overcorrected, causing it to flip over several times, throwing my son out onto the pavement.

The boy got out of the car, searched in the darkness for my son, then flagged down a car for help. Crying, the boy told me he sat with my son's head in his lap, holding it up so he could breathe. He said there was blood running from my son's ear, nose, and mouth. Darrin never said a word.

Now the only way I can talk to him is through a marble mausoleum wall with his name on it. The only birthday and Christmas presents he can get are flowers.

(Reprinted by permission of *Friendly Exchange,* the magazine of Farmers Insurance Group of Companies, © 1990. Page 11.)

Carolyn's heartbreak reminds me of the famous piece Abigail Van Buren has reprinted several times in her syndicated newspaper column "Dear Abby." It always renews my own commitment to seeing that whether the problem is booze or just recklessness, not another kid needs to die on the highway:

Please God, I'm Only 17

The day I died was an ordinary school day. How I wish I had taken the bus! But I was too cool for the bus. I remember how I wheedled the car out of Mom. "Special favor," I pleaded. "All the kids drive." When the 2:50 bell rang, I threw all my books in the locker. I was free until 8:40 tomorrow morning! I ran to the parking lot, excited at the thought of driving a car and being my own boss. Free!

It doesn't matter how the accident happened. I was goofing off—going too fast. Taking crazy chances. But I was enjoying my freedom and having fun. The last thing I remember was passing an old lady who seemed to be going awfully slow. I heard a deafening crash and felt a terrible jolt. Glass and steel flew everywhere. My whole body seemed to be turning inside out. I heard myself scream.

Suddenly I awakened; it was very quiet. A police officer was standing over me. Then I saw a doctor. My body was mangled. I was saturated with blood. Pieces of jagged glass were sticking out all over. Strange that I couldn't feel anything. Hey, don't pull that sheet over my head! I can't be dead. I'm only 17. I have a date tonight. I'm supposed to grow up and have a wonderful life. I haven't lived yet. I can't be dead. Later I was placed in a drawer. My folks had to identify me. Why did they have to see me like this? Why did I have to look at Mom's eyes when she faced the most terrible ordeal of her life? Dad suddenly looked like an old man. He told the man in charge, "Yes, he is my son."

The funeral was a weird experience. I saw all my relatives and friends walk toward the casket. They passed by, one by one, and looked at me with the saddest eyes I've ever seen. Some of my buddies were crying. A few of the girls touched my hand and sobbed as they walked away.

Please—somebody—wake me up! Get me out of here! I can't bear to see my mom and dad so broken up. My grandparents are so racked with grief they can hardly walk. My brother and sisters are like zombies. They move like robots. In a daze, everybody. No one can believe this. And I can't believe it, either.

Please don't bury me! I'm not dead! I have a lot of living to do! I want to laugh and run again. I want to sing and dance. Please don't

put me in the ground . . . give me just one more chance, God. All I
want is one more chance!
  Please, God, I'm only 17!
      (TAKEN FROM THE DEAR ABBY COLUMN, ABIGAIL VAN BUREN.
                Copyright 1990, Universal Press Syndicate.
                        Reprinted with permission.)

Take the Pledge

In spite of the wonderful alcohol commercials, the happy faces, and
the exuberance of the ads . . .

Regardless of the sophistication, the ease, the maturity oozing
through the cocktail party . . .

Despite the romantic sheen, the soft edges, and pleasure of the
wine or liquor with dinner . . .

Without worrying about the frowns or jabs of beer-drinking
friends cheering around the televised game or singing around the
pizza feast . . .

Promise me, for the sake of tens of thousands of lives—and for
your own sake—that you won't drink and drive. Say it aloud; write it
down somewhere: "I will not drink and drive."

Maybe you're almost considering an even simpler commitment—a commitment about not drinking in the first place. Let's look
at the phenomenon of drinking, itself. Could alcohol be a problem
for you?

3

I'm Not a Child;
I Can Handle It

The problems of drinking and driving, of course, lead us back to the basic problems of drinking, period. This is the case in Canada, where the decision to fight that country's horrendous statistics of alcohol-impaired driving will surely lead researchers to study how many Canadians have drinking problems and why. As we narrow our focus to teenage drinkers, sit with me in a television studio in Toronto, where I'm interviewing an energetic man with a mission.

JERRY: Canadian young people, as in America, are falling victim to alcohol abuse, and the number-one killer of Canadian teens is exactly what it is in the United States—alcohol-related car crashes. With us today is John Bates. John, you are president of PRIDE, which is the Ontario chapter of MADD, Mothers Against Drunk Driving.

JOHN: That's right, Jerry.

JERRY: Now tell us, why did you get involved here in Canada with the alcohol-abuse problem? And tell us what is going on?

JOHN: Well, it goes back many years ago, when a young lad called Casey Frame was killed by a drunk driver going the wrong way on Highway 401. Casey was twenty years old, the son of a brilliant and lovely woman, June Caldwin. He was going back to take his final engineering exam at . . . Queens, which means he was going eastbound. A drunk coming westbound killed him.

Casey was a friend of my daughter in high school, and we became very upset about this. I guess it takes something like this to sort of jog people into action, and we formed the organization with just a few people around the kitchen table nine years ago. Now we are three thousand strong across this province, and we act as the Ontario chapter of MADD, Mothers Against Drunk Driving.

JERRY: Give me the alcohol-abuse scenario of Canada. What's happening? How many people are dying in alcohol-related tragedies? What's the government's position on this?

JOHN: In 1989, 18,000 people in this country died from alcohol abuse. Then we have this huge thing on drug abuse which is certainly bad enough. We lost 280 people to drug abuse in this country. That includes homicides, murders, overdoses, and so forth.

JERRY: So 280 died from drug abuse.

JOHN: That's right—illicit drugs.

JERRY: And 18,000 died from alcohol abuse. What does the government say?

JOHN: Virtually nothing. What they are doing is coming out with, "Gee whiz, we are really going to fight this drug-abuse thing." In Ontario

AUTH, copyright 1990 *Philadelphia Inquirer.* Reprinted with permission of Universal Press Syndicate. All rights reserved.

alone, they have a $54 million directive set up. But that drug directive deliberately, by design, and despite protestations from groups like ours, has deliberately ignored alcohol. They will not consider that alcohol is a drug.

And it is an addictive drug. It is a poison that causes all kinds of diseases. Among the total population there is something like $4 million to $5 million in excess health care costs because of alcohol abuse. That's what it's costing us in money, let alone 18,000 deaths. It's incredibly shortsighted to not recognize the seriousness of alcohol.

JERRY: Why is it, John? What are the legislators trying to protect? Is it their own alcohol consumption?

JOHN: That actually may be partly it. It's also revenue, you know. In Ontario, for example, we know that the government takes in something like a billion dollars in alcohol revenue. There is a tremendously powerful alcohol lobby out there. But people don't like to talk about that kind of thing.

JERRY: Is this taxation money that alcohol brings in?

JOHN: Yes. So it's tough to get legislators to suddenly admit this is wrong. They simply won't do it. Now, for example, we know we can start saving teenage lives tomorrow morning by simply raising the drinking ages as they've had the courage to do in the States. Since the States passed the National Minimum Drinking Age Act in 1984, they've had some 17 to 20 percent reduction in the killing of young kids. We think it is unconscionable that the government here will not even form a task force to look at it.

JERRY: Is it still eighteen years of age?

JOHN: It is nineteen in Ontario and eighteen in most of the other provinces. It's as if the government is behaving like the bishops who refused to look through Galileo's telescope because they were afraid he might be right.

It's a public-awareness problem as well. Impaired driving and this horrendous carnage being done to our young people is something people in general don't want to talk about it. We have trouble being listened to when we say Canada should lower the BAC from .08—which is lower than what they have in the States, by the way.

JERRY: The BAC is the blood alcohol content. Most of our law-enforcement agencies in the States define intoxication at .10 percent BAC.

JOHN: If you say the BAC is .08 that is eighty milligrams of alcohol per one thousand milliliters of blood. Now we maintain that people who drink and drive have got a problem, a drinking problem. If they didn't, they wouldn't chance the penalties they may have. We have 600,000 alcohol abusers in Ontario alone on our roads!

JERRY: Six hundred thousand alcohol abusers in Ontario?

JOHN: There are six million drivers roughly in Ontario alone. We know that 10 percent, according to the Addiction Research Foundation, are problem drinkers. That means 600,000 people who are having alcohol problems are behind the steering wheels of cars. What we are saying is, we have to treat this thing as an alcohol-abuse problem.

All our bumper stickers and public-awareness campaigns say, "Don't drink and drive!" But that's not what the law says. The law says, go ahead and drink until you are drunk; but don't drive after you are drunk! Until we can get a BAC limit of .08, there is a mixed message in that the law says go ahead and drink and drive—while everybody else says don't drink and drive. We say it should be a consistent message.

Besides, the BAC reading is often unaffected by the presence of other drugs like cocaine or tranquilizers in the drinking driver. This mixing of substances greatly increases the effects of the alcohol. But it will be undetected. The only way we can really get at that is to say, "Don't drink and drive at all," because there is always this cross-addiction problem.

We don't need these people on the roads. We need to say that only those people who can drive safely can drive at all. I mean, look at the consequences: 40 percent of all the people killed on the roads in this country are under the age of twenty-five. That's a terrible waste.

JERRY: How many teenagers would you estimate in Canada are dying due to alcohol-related tragedies?

JOHN: We can put it this way. About 5 percent of the licenses are held by young people under the age of twenty-one. They cause 17 percent of all impaired crashes, and are responsible for 18 percent of all the deaths! Terrible waste! And what are we as a society going to do about it? What? It simply drives us to distraction that we cannot get the government to move on this thing. They will give us funding to go around saying it is a terrible thing, to run advertising campaigns saying it is a terrible thing—but that's where it seems to stop.

JERRY: But the brewers are also running ad campaigns that are competing for the attention of young people. In the United States, by the time teens are eighteen, they have witnessed 100,000 beer commercials. How can we compete against these powerful multi-billion-dollar companies?

JOHN: Jerry, that's exactly the problem! That's exactly it! The beer companies in this province in this country have $200 million worth of advertising aimed directly at kids. If they're not actually targeting youth, we ask why are beer companies the largest owners and sponsors of rock concerts? We have beer companies who offer incentives to young people to go to events like stock-car races—which are sponsored by the beer companies. Often children under twelve are admitted free to a beer-sponsored event. This is utter madness! Utter madness! Here are automobile races being sponsored by beer companies; isn't this association absurd? If they really want to reach an older-age group, Why can't they sponsor something else like shuffleboard tournaments or something or flower shows or something that has nothing to do with thousands of young deaths every year?

They have one commercial that shows what seems like insane people on motorcycles tearing down trees and falling over in the water, and acting like fools. Then they go and get their beer at the end of the commercial. Craziness!

JERRY: Can you give me an idea of the problem of alcohol abuse from province to province?

JOHN: It doesn't vary much. Something like 10 percent of the entire adult population has an alcohol problem in this country.

JERRY: Now there are about 27 million Canadians.

JOHN: And 10 percent of those are alcohol abusers.

JERRY: So we are talking about 2.7 million people!

JOHN: That's right! That's right!

JERRY: In Washington, we were informed that the War on Drugs legislation had been purposely worded to specifically omit alcohol in its declarations.

JOHN: That's right! That's right!

JERRY: It's rumored they did it because they didn't want it. And the lobbyist groups of the breweries are so strong many felt including alcohol as a drug would create a war. But, John, isn't the bottom line of this thing money? I mean, aren't we talking about money here?

JOHN: Absolutely!

JERRY: Money means more to people than the human lives that are being wasted?

JOHN: Jerry, that is the obscenity of this whole thing. That lobby is so powerful. First of all, it's the manufacturers, and the advertisers themselves—then the media that accept the advertising. And, of course, next come the government officials who are influenced by the media advertisers. For example, this province has the most relaxed alcohol advertising rules in the world. Advertising can say just about anything it wants, anytime and in any media. There is $200 million worth of advertising going to the media, which renders a most congenial atmosphere for encouraging alcohol advertising. What that also does, of course, is stifle any debate against such advertising ever appearing in the media. You cannot get a debate on alcohol abuse going in any major medium at all. It has to be either underground media or promoted by private or nonprofit organizations.

JERRY: We've got two minutes left on the program. Give me the agenda that you feel the Ontario government needs to immediately curb this problem, with any applications to Canadian youth. What message do we need to get to them?

JOHN: First, we have to say we want the drinking age raised to twenty-one. All we are saying to the government is this: Form a task force and look at the problem. People from the National Highway Traffic Safety Administration in Washington, for example, need to testify before such a task force to help find out whether we are right or wrong in our contention that an older drinking age would help relieve the carnage on our highways.

Secondly, we want the Ontario government and the Canadian government to come out with a strong policy about alcohol abuse. Simply tell the people: Are you against alcohol abuse or are you in favor of alcohol abuse? Simple as that! Of course, once they say they are against alcohol abuse, then we can say, okay, how come you are not raising the drinking age? How come you allow these advertising campaigns and so forth?

JERRY: So it's not a prohibition move. You in PRIDE are just saying, come out against the abuse of alcohol.

JOHN: That's all we are saying, for goodness' sake! Now 50 percent of all violent crime is alcohol-related. Frankly, it's perfectly safe to fight the drug war—a terrible thing, I admit. But when alcohol is not considered as one of the drugs in that war, the abuse of other drugs is a very tiny problem compared to the problem of alcohol.

JERRY: Eighteen thousand Canadian deaths last year due to alcohol abuse. Something has got to be done!

I'm Not a Child; I Can Handle It

These days, kids in Canada and the United States are drinking long before they can even get a license to drive. The following vignette could be one girl's description of how North American teenagers think:

> Jennifer passed me a note in Home Ec. class—*They're gone again.*
> What great parents . . . gone all the time. They travel on business, go to weekend retreats to "save their marriage," or practice "The Basics of Enlightenment" and stuff. Basically, who cares? What it means is, the house is ours. We're in charge, in control for a change. I mean, we've got rules at home, rules at school, rules at church, and laws to obey. It's like I'm almost old enough to vote, and I can't even breathe without somebody wanting to know when I'm going to breathe, how long, with whom, and what time I'll be done.
> I can just picture sitting down to an hour of TV before dinner and having a couple glasses of wine with my folks. Right. Dad would, as

he loves to say, "Knock me into the middle of next week," for even suggesting it!

Jenny's folks are totally cool. They serve her wine before dinner. They want her to be comfortable with alcohol and learn to handle it so it's not a big, glamorous "no-no" for her.

The first time I went to Jenny's when her parents were gone, I felt like a complete dweeb. Jenny held her glass so naturally, with her hand kind of half-cupped around the bottom. I gripped the stem like it was a garden hose. At first I had to hold the stuff in my mouth and force myself to swallow. It tasted bad. After a couple of glasses, I didn't mind it. In fact, I didn't mind anything.

Jenny's eyes got brighter and she danced pretty loose to the television, but she really kept it together. I totally embarrassed myself by getting the giggles. I probably laughed for an hour. Felt good. I remember trying to tell Jenny, "They lied. They all lied, the youth pastor, the drug-abuse class at school, Mom and Dad. There's nothing wrong with this. What's the world got against laughing?"

We move on to gin and tonics with just a squeeze of lime. Jenny is so bizarre. She's a total character. She chews Bubble Dazzle, the glow-in-the-dark gum, while she mixes the drinks. We down a few, then go play at the playground like a couple of five-year-olds. What a gas! Gin tastes like a combination of vinegar and juniper bushes—you know, those ugly bushes they always plant around dentists' offices.

We tell each other deep and secret things—things you would never talk about if you weren't feeling good.

The next day Jenny helped me clean the spots on the rug and the couch and she never even put me down. She's not judgmental like a lot of my so-called friends. Becky and Trudy, my old infantile youth-group friends tried to tell me, "Jenny's a drunk. She just wants somebody to drink with." Is that judgmental or what!

Jenny brings alcohol in her thermos every day and I just say no, not at school, and she accepts it. My old friends are jealous 'cause Jen's so popular. Monday mornings I stand around with all the really cool people and we compare how much we drank and how sick we got over the weekend. It's hilarious, and best of all, it's like, I've arrived. I used to stand around with my old friends and we'd try to act like we were having a great time, but we were really watching the cool kids, wishing we were with them and now—I am.

Some of the kids' parents are so righteous, they say, "We drink at home, so if our kids are going to drink, let them do it at home." They just take everybody's car keys when we show up to party hearty. Only two kids have died from driving drunk and this is a big school. I tried to talk to my parents, but they are totally old world. My dad says, "Well, we have sex at home, too, so we're supposed to let you have sex at home?"

I know everything there is to know about alcohol. I've heard it all. So what? Like me and Jenny and our friends partying on the weekend is the same as the old winos down on State Street walking around with their grocery carts full of trash begging for money for cheap wine. Right. Come on.

If I ever feel like my drinking's getting out of control, I'll just stop. I'm not a child. I can handle it.

I answer Jen's note:

Jen—Perfect. I'll tell my folks we're going skiing! See ya—Stace.

That little vignette could have been written by any fifteen-year-old teenager in North America. It was actually written by adult Diane Kesey, an author from Eugene, Oregon, in response to my question of "What do you think it feels like as a teenager to begin the slide into alcohol problems?" The teenagers I read the piece to agree it sounds pretty accurate. How do they know? As one kid told me, "They're drinking like fish out there!"

Kids and Booze

The picture isn't all horrible, you know. Not every teenager in North America thinks it's incredibly sophisticated to drink. One seventeen-year-old told me he finally went with a bunch of buddies to just drink until they dropped a few weekends ago. In his small South Dakota town, "the boys" got an older friend to buy three cases of a cheap brand of beer.

"First," he said, "we drove around trying to find someplace to have a party and ended up just kind of standing around behind a closed gas station drinking cans as fast as we could to get drunk fast. It really tasted just kind of watery and like bad well water. There were five of us, and after we'd finished off about four cans apiece, we drove out to the cemetery and each of us drank about four or five more. I didn't, though. I could only stomach about three more cans, and then we all started throwing up behind the tombstones. I remember laughing my head off at it all, because I kept thinking of all the neat beer commercials. And there we were, a bunch of stupid kids trying to tell ourselves this was great. I don't know how I got home, but I was sick to my stomach for about three days. Pretty stupid, huh?"

I tried to look nonjudgmental as I nodded, "Yup."

Many teenagers see how the ravages of alcohol and other drug use have worn on their 1960s-and '70s-era parents. And many of them are going straight—no booze, no drugs. They want to keep their brains intact and be healthy for the hundred years they plan on living.

Even former users are giving up the illusion that it's sophisticated or brave or spiritual or independent to slur their speech, vomit in public, make a fool of themselves, fall into sexual encounters with people they wouldn't even fantasize about if they were sober, have dead-smelling breath and bloodshot eyes, get into ridiculous arguments, spend all kinds of quick money without meaning to, risk alcohol-related diseases, drive and get arrested and hassled when their licenses are revoked or do jail time with the tough new laws, shame their families, and impair their sexual responses—all for booze!

Alcohol use by younger teenagers has been dropping in recent years. Still constantly high in the college-aged older teen group, the level of alcohol consumption among twelve- to seventeen-year-olds declined from 31 percent in 1985 to 25 percent in 1988, according to the National Institute of Drug Abuse and Alcoholism (*USA Today,* August 1, 1989, pages A1-A2). Alcohol use as reflected in each year's NIDA survey is expected to continue to drop just as overall drug use in the United States has been declining for the most part since 1979.

And yet, there are millions of kids—some four million of them, actually—who are addicted to alcohol, who are still guzzling booze like there's no tomorrow. Kids who are just like Jack was.

"Like Hands on My Shoulders"

Arriving for a speaking appearance in Detroit, I was met at the airport by a tall, slim, young man named Jack, who was to drive me to the auditorium. He talked freely as we drove through the rain-slick streets, and eventually the conversation turned to one of my persistent themes—kids and alcohol. It was a subject Jack had known intimately in his own teenage years.

"A bunch of us guys were drinking regularly then. We'd plan all week our exploits for Friday and Saturday nights. We wore boots so we could hide little flasks of Everclear at football games. Then we'd get together after school sometimes. Then for a while we actually got together about six in the morning before school to drink—kind of as a game to see how much of a buzz we could catch without anybody knowing during classes. That's why a lot of problem drinkers drink vodka, you know—no real boozy smell on your breath."

"No," I said. "I didn't know that."

We drove south across town on the wet, deserted freeway.

"Is it something you can talk about?" I asked.

"Yeah. In fact, I talk about it in high-school meetings and school assemblies sometimes now, since it's bound to help some kid somewhere who's getting into the game."

Jack talked quietly as he drove. "I first tasted beer in eighth grade—hated it, but you've got to be cool in eighth grade, right? Then in tenth grade these two jocks and some more real popular guys asked me to go with them out to a lake late one night. I said, 'Sure, man, let's get smashed.' That's the first time I remember drinking to get drunk. It was no big deal, you know?"

"That's the problem, right, Jack?" I answered. "It's never any big deal at first. And there's no way to convince kids that alcohol could get a grip on them because it's not going to happen to them, right? It's always going to be just no big deal to drink a little when you're with friends, to be cool and get drunk only once in a while when you feel like just getting smashed."

Jack's reminiscences weren't coming so easily now. He cleared his throat several times as he continued: "In our senior year, my girl-friend committed suicide. And I found out something—something shocking about my mother. And . . . that's when I realized I had started drinking just by myself. Then I tried college, and basically couldn't hack it. I worked the graveyard shift in this convenience store, and about three in the morning, the customers would quit coming in, so I'd sit back in the storeroom on a case of Cokes and down beers. I told myself I was doing it so I could sleep when I got home in the morning; but I was doing it because I was depressed. I know that now.

"Then I'd have a few more when I got home so I could sleep. Then when I'd wake up in the afternoon, I'd drink some more; after I drank a few beers I'd get sleepy, but if I'd keep on drinking I'd get hyper, you know. So I was drinking to get energetic for the night shift again. My roommate would argue with me like crazy that I had a drinking problem, but I wouldn't see it. We had some real fights over it."

I said, "Still bother you?"

"About three years, ago, Jerry, I was at one of your rallies and I gave my life to Christ. I can't say the drinking stopped altogether right then, but it's stopped now. Still, sometimes I'll see a billboard advertising beer or I'll go into a convenience store and walk by the beer section, and it's like hands on my shoulders, like something grabs me and whispers, 'Come on man, come on.'"

"It started as a game with hiding Everclear, huh?" I said.

"The thing that clinched it, though, I think," Jack said, "was my girlfriend's death. I just couldn't quite handle it without escaping into a buzz. Then my Mom. I found out she—"

"You don't need to tell me," I said, looking out at the dark rain over the yellow Detroit streetlights.

"That she was a lesbian," he said.

I said nothing; but I wondered how many youth across the continent were driving around with thoughts they couldn't quite handle, determined to get lost in a cheap, well-advertised, semi-respectable alcoholic buzz.

Teenagers Who Drink

Generally, teenage drinkers divide themselves into three categories. And remember, where the legal age limit to drink is twenty-one—in all the states of the United States, for example—these teenage drinkers are all breaking the law.

• *Light Drinkers.* Frankly, these people have a take-it-or-leave-it attitude about alcohol. For example, if they arrive at a party and find no alcohol, they never even consider leaving in disgust or getting irritated at the hosts. If they don't drink when booze is served, they may feel childish or slightly socially unsophisticated, but they have no sense of feeling incomplete.

• *Problem Drinkers.* Although these teenagers, themselves, might not notice, it's apparent to others that they have trouble controlling the amount and the frequency of alcohol consumed. This is the critical stage of determining whether the drinker is in control of the drug or the drug is in control.

• *Alcohol-Dependent Drinkers.* Booze is a must for this person, a core part of life. As one teenage alcoholic told me, "It's not just what I do; it's how I think." There is no rock-solid definition of alcoholism, but most experts seem to line up behind the National Council on Alcoholism's description that alcoholics are those who cannot consistently choose, despite their best intentions, when they will drink and how much they will drink. Alcoholics are people who have lost control of their drinking—to the point that it interferes with at least one area of their lives, such as family, relationships, work, school or health ("Alcoholism," *Kansas City Star,* March 2, 1989, page 4-D).

Could alcohol be a part of the life of a teenager close to you? Materials from the U.S. Department of Health and Human Services describe some of the early warning signs:

• Abrupt changes in mood or attitude

• Sudden decline in attendance or performance at work or school

• Sudden resistance to discipline at home or school

• Impaired relationship with family or friends

• Ignoring curfews

• Unusual temper flare-ups

• Increased borrowing of money, possibly stealing from home, school, or employer

• Increased secrecy about possessions, actions, and use of money

• Associating with a new group of friends who use booze and other drugs

Could alcohol be a big part of *your* life?

The Jigsaw Puzzle of Your Life

Even before you're of legal drinking age, you can evaluate your susceptibility to getting in over your head with booze. And if you're an adult who now drinks, you can evaluate if your drinking is or could become a problem. Here are some indicators that alcohol just might come to mean more than it should in your life. More than three "yes" answers indicate you should get serious about your involvement with booze.

Alcohol and You: A Self-Test. Part I

Is there a history of alcohol abuse in your family tree? (See instructions for developing a genogram to chart possible dysfunctions in your family in chapter 6.)

List areas of stress and pressure in your life now. Think through the list and consider whether, if any of these pressures worsen, you might feel overwhelmed and unable to cope?

Give yourself a physical and psychological checkup. Do you constantly feel:

- physically tired or ill?
- emotionally worn out?
- lonely?
- hurt by significant losses as in a divorce, a death, loss of friendship, or other experience? (When a teenager endures this kind of loss, it may not seem significant to others. But the teenager's self-esteem has been beaten up. Maybe it was a lost election for a school office or cheerleading position; maybe it was an F in a course the teen usually excels in. This kind of loss can occur in several ways, but it always involves public embarrassment, and a feeling that the teenager has "lost face.")
- spiritually cynical?
- misunderstood by parents and/or peers?
- compelled to "take the edge off" your day with alcohol?

More than three affirmative answers could indicate that you're a prime candidate for letting alcohol come to mean more to you than it should. Even if you're not drinking now, you're possibly *susceptible* to problem drinking, and it's a good time to get some early help from your pastor, counselor, local mental health association, or support-group organization. (See the Resources listing in Appendix B of this book.)

Booze. It's amazing that after thousands of years of using and abusing alcohol, we still don't know much about it. Nor can we agree on what we do know. For example, the American Medical Association and the National Institute on Alcohol Abuse and Alcoholism consider alcoholism a disease. But the U.S. Supreme Court does not. In 1988, the court reviewed the case of a veteran claiming benefits from the Veterans Administration for his illness of alcoholism. The verdict made it clear that the court didn't want to declare alcoholism a disease, calling it instead, "willful misconduct" ("Alcoholism," *Kansas City Star,* March 2, 1989, pages 1D, 4D).

If the experts aren't clear on alcohol and its effects, it's a good possibility you don't know about some of the effects of alcohol in your own life. If you're a drinker, think through another self-test to consider any red flags in your drinking habits.

Alcohol and You: A Self-Test. Part II

Do you sometimes drink a lot after a letdown or a fight?

Do you drink more than usual when under pressure?

Have you noticed that you're able to "handle" more alcohol than you could when you were first drinking?

Do you ever wake up on the "morning after" and discover that you can't remember part of the evening before?

When drinking with other people, do you try to have a few extra drinks when they won't know it?

Do you often find that you want to keep drinking after your friends say they've had enough?

Do you often regret things you did or said while drinking?

Have you often failed to keep promises you've made to yourself about controlling or cutting down on your drinking?

Do you try to avoid close friends while you're drinking?

Do more people seem to be treating you unfairly?

When drinking, do you often wonder whether life is worth living?

After periods of drinking, do you sometimes see or hear things that aren't there?

Do you get frightened after you've been drinking heavily?

According to the National Council on Alcoholism and Drug Dependence, any "yes" answer indicates a probable symptom of problem drinking or alcoholism. More than one "yes" answer indicates its presence. If you think you're developing a problem with alcohol (or someone you know is), look for help immediately. (See the Resources section in Appendix B.)

Help a teenager through the following simplified self-test:

Alcohol and You: A Self-Test. Part III for Teenagers

1. Do you drink because you have problems? To face up to stressful situations?

2. Do you drink when you get mad at other people, your friends or parents?

3. Do you often prefer to drink alone, rather than with others?

4. Are your grades starting to slip? Are you goofing off on the job?

5. Do you ever try to stop drinking or drink less—and fail?

6. Have you begun to drink in the morning before school or work?

7. Do you gulp your drinks as if to satisfy a great thirst?

8. Do you have blackouts—times when you don't remember what has happened?

9. Do you avoid leveling with others about your drinking?

10. Do you ever get into trouble when you are drinking?

11. Do you often get drunk when you drink, even when you do not mean to?

12. Do you think it is cool to be able to hold your liquor?

If you answer "yes" to more than one of these questions, it indicates you need to talk with a counselor who has expertise in this area.

Maybe you were able to answer every question "no." Booze might not have been a part of your life at all. But perhaps, like millions of others, alcohol problems have been a part of the life of someone near you. Maybe you never drink, and yet someone else's use of alcohol has deeply affected the shaping of your own attitudes, outlook, and personality. Let's look at a phenomenon of the substance-abuse world that has affected me personally: the codependency of a child of an alcoholic.

4

Codependency: Guarding the Secret

"I *think* I can talk about it."

Large, dark eyes squint determinedly as twenty-two-year-old Lori Marchant—not her real name—catches her breath after basketball. "My brother and I are probably about as close as you can get to being cases of classic codependents."

To protect Lori's identity, let's say I'm in Denver, even though I'm not. Let's say I'm on the campus of a prominent school. I've wandered between campus buildings to find the old gym where afternoon basketball practice is keeping students' minds off upcoming midterm exams.

The old gym is cool and dark except for the lighted court with its squealing players and squeaking shoes. The place has that familiar smell of lacquer from the wooden floor, mixed with dust and sweat; after all my years of doing my song and dance in thousands of gymnasiums across the country, I feel pretty much at home as I sit behind the scorer's table at the edge of the court.

As a wild coed game plays full-court, Lori leaves the action, plops into a folding metal chair, and towels off her face. She unbuckles a blue leg brace. "Old knee injury," she explains.

Lori says she thinks she can talk about being a codependent. But watching her, I wonder if she really can. I just finished reading a startling book about kids who grow up in alcoholic families. In *It Will Never Happen to Me!* Dr. Claudia Black identifies and explains three primary rules of codependence: Don't talk, don't trust, don't feel.

"What do you think, Lori, about the way codependency seems to be a fad?" I ask. "It seems as if everybody who has any kind of personal problem now is blaming it on his or her upbringing. It's sort of like saying, 'I'm not responsible for myself—I'm codependent.' What do you think? Am I being too cynical?"

"Yup," she says decisively.

Earlier, I shared with Lori my own family's history of substance abuse. Now she says, "Maybe you're overlooking something in your own life, Jerry." She tosses the sweat-drenched towel aside and pulls a battered bookbag onto the scorekeeper's table. "Simple yes or no answers, please."

Then she quizzes me. Am I a full-blown codependent because of my background? Here's the quiz Lori rattles off. If you've lived with someone whose compulsive behavior has affected you, go ahead—test yourself!

Codependency Self-Evaluation. Part I

_____ Do I often feel alienated from people, especially authority figures?

_____ Do I have low self-esteem?

_____ Do I judge myself severely?

_____ Is it really difficult to evaluate my own faults?

_____ Is it easier to be concerned with meeting others' needs than with my own responsibilities?

_____ Am I overly concerned about gaining approval, even if it means losing my own identity?

_____ Do I feel guilty when I stand up for myself instead of giving in to others?

_____ Do I fear criticism?

_____ Am I overly afraid of expressions of anger, of angry people?

_____   Do I often feel I'm a victim in personal relationships and on the job?

_____   Do I confuse love with pity and tend to love people I can pity and rescue—people I think I can "fix"?

_____   Do I often seem to be abandoned in relationships?

_____   Is it difficult for me to express what I'm feeling—or even to know, myself, what I'm feeling, including feelings of joy and happiness?

_____   Do I feel addicted to excitement?

(Checklist adapted from Melody Beattie,
Codependent No More, page 188.)

Now, any human could answer "yes" to any one of these questions at some point in his or her life. We all know what each characteristic feels like. But the codependency-scarred child of an alcoholic is trapped in these feelings, and is chronically affected by them. It's not easy for the millions of these kids who live with substance-abusing addicts like alcoholics. I know . . . how well I know.

Incidentally, Lori couldn't talk about her own codependency. She just couldn't seem to get around to tell what her experience was like, although she felt very free to talk about codependent problems in general, and mine in particular.

Looking Back

One of the reasons, I suppose, that kids will give me the time of day and listen when I speak on high-school campuses is that I've been where they are. Somehow, out there in the mob of two hundred at Springdale High or in the twenty-two thousand at Reunion Arena in Dallas is a kid who understands that I know what it all feels like. My heart goes out to that poor kid.

I don't exactly have a "straight" past. The Johnston family was victimized by addictions. And almost every one of the friends I hung around with in those days had a mom or dad, brother or sister who was an alcoholic or druggie. A television announcer's son in Kansas City turned me on to drugs. Both of his parents were alcoholics and his brother was a drug addict. You would have never known it, though, passing by their pretty home in one of Kansas City's nice, suburban areas. Weekly he and I, and other friends, flirted with death in the name of fun.

I was perfectly willing to say "yes" to smoking pot, doing downers, and later, to becoming dependent on Valium. At one point when I was fourteen, I realized that I simply could no longer function. I had gotten ill with what our family doctor had diagnosed as bleeding ulcers. I was hospitalized twice—the second time occurred after I had threatened suicide.

I still remember being in the room next to my parents' bedroom, screaming, freaking out, and loudly threatening suicide. I remember, too, that it wasn't my mom sitting on the edge of my bed that day; it was my dad. I remember the strain in his face, his anguished voice saying, "Hold on. . . . We'll do something. Everything is going to be all right." Dad was desperate. But where was Mom that day? I don't even remember if she was in the car with Dad and me when we made the mad dash to the emergency room.

My first cry for help that day had been a phone call to Dad at his office—a call which boomeranged him home to the edge of my bed. Why didn't I call my mom? As an interior decorator at a local department store, she worked closer to our home than my dad did.

But I called Dad instead. Quite honestly, I resented the role alcohol played in Mom's life. Alcohol came first—it always comes first in every alcoholic's life.

Our family at the time was at a critical stage. After my first hospitalization for bleeding ulcers, I hadn't wanted to go back to school. So I didn't—much to my parents' consternation. For weeks, I had vegetated at home, alone. Dad and Mom got up early and left for their jobs, and my brother went to school.

For days and weeks I stayed at the house—unable to function, like a hermit in a cave. This retreat from life continued until that day shortly before Easter when I exploded into suicidal threats, calling Dad at his office. When I was finally released from the hospital after that episode, my sixty-eight-pound frame screamed that something was very wrong; and it wasn't simply that in the hospital I had been on a liquid diet.

I somehow knew that the "party" was over with my friends. And I knew I couldn't cope.

Family Secrets

I deeply resented Mom's drinking. I hated the secrecy. And I disliked the fact that I could never have one of my friends over to spend the night. Why? Because Mom got bombed every night, and Dad didn't want any "outsiders" around. The secrecy galled me.

I needed to talk with someone about our fractured family; but I was committed to the dependent's first mandate: "Don't tell." I strongly believe now that when any teen has a parent victimized by drug or alcohol abuse, that kid needs to counsel with some caring individual. But I had no one. Mr. Alcohol was the only one allowed to spend the night. And he spent every night in our home—and turned it into hell.

It's hard to ever forget what it was like being so close to someone who was transformed dramatically each and every night through a demonic cloud of drinking.

As a teenager, I missed the mom I never really got to know; I mourned for the conversations we never had. In the halls of my memory, there are certain artifacts that remind me of the hell of it all. For example, there are the ice trays.

Mom constantly kept the ice trays full in the freezer. That was important; we *always* had to have ice available. It seemed as if some quiet poltergeist would whisper to each of us boys not to notice as Mom made her recurrent trips to the ice trays each evening. But we did notice. We heard her frequent treks to the freezer, the ice cubes dropping noisily into large plastic cups. We all heard the noise—and we knew what it meant.

Another artifact from the hell of my teenage years is the memory of the cupboard above the pantry.

That was the home of the bottle. After Mom got her glass iced up, there was a pit stop at that cupboard. Then, with her plastic cup filled, she would always take the shortcut out of the kitchen, through the dining room and living room and quickly up the stairs to the vault of her private bedroom. By taking that route, she wouldn't have to encounter us in the family room. But we all knew precisely what was going on. What amazed me was the fact that Mom apparently thought we didn't know she had a drinking problem. Somehow, she thought we were oblivious to the whole matter. But how could we have been? Rarely did Mom ever sit and watch TV with us, or talk with us—or just *be* with us. No, we were put on the back burner. Alcohol was more important.

I resented Mom's absence. Although she was at home, she was almost always up in her bedroom with that white door shut. And that place never changed. I can see it clearly now in my memory, as I recall the few times the door would open, and I would steal a glance into my mom's world. There she sat, always on the left side of the bed next to the TV, the curtains always drawn, a certain wistful look on her face.

My mom must have been more knowledgeable than *TV Guide* or the A. C. Nielsen Company about what television series, movie, or special was to air and when. She was always in her room, watching television—withdrawn from me.

Perhaps that is why I did not turn to her later, when I began to question the existence of life and my own sense of personal worthlessness.

For all the subterfuge and ornamental coverup, I knew a fact that could not be preempted. My mom was an alcoholic. Apart from a miracle, I knew there would never be any change. That was the kind of despair I grew up with—the despair of the codependent.

Codependency and Being the Child of an Alcoholic

What is codependency? Robert Subby writes in the book *Co-Dependency: An Emerging Issue* that codependency is "an emotional, psychological and behavioral condition that develops as a result of an individual's prolonged exposure to and practice of a set of oppressive rules—rules which prevent the open expression of feeling as well as the direct discussion of personal and interpersonal problems" (page 26).

Codependents are people whose lives have become unmanageable as a result of living in a committed relationship with an alcoholic. The definition, of course, broadens easily to describe those who live with any chemically dependent person or any person with a compulsive disorder—from eating disorders to gambling and certain sexual behaviors. Although the condition is incredibly complex, another helpful one-sentence definition might be the one Melody Beattie gives in her book, *Codependent No More:*

> A codependent is anyone who has allowed another person's behavior to affect him or her, and who is obsessed with controlling that person's behavior. (page 30)

Codependents want to fix people, to make things okay, even at the cost of self-sacrifice. It is true, what Claudia Black says in *It Will Never Happen to Me!* Codependency teaches children this: Don't feel. Don't trust. Don't talk.

How does a child begin to react to life as a codependent? He or she begins by experiencing repeated incidents such as Helen Knode's:

> I think it must have been several days before Halloween 1964—my memory of my childhood is pretty bad. My sisters, my mother, and I were spread through the front part of the house cutting out orange cardboard pumpkins and black cardboard witches to tape to the front windows. We lived in a small place where messes developed easily. It was pitch dark outside—Canadian winters start early—and I think it was before dinnertime, because Father wasn't home from the office yet.
>
> When he finally did come home—at this point events get fuzzy—he must have walked in the front door and noticed the mess. But he never would have said anything right away, just smiled and gone tense.
>
> After a while, something minor probably triggered him, something unrelated to the scattered piles of eviscerated cardboard squares and the fact that nobody warned him we'd be having fun when he got home.
>
> I remember being picked up and hurled across the living room against a wall, or onto a couch. My glasses would have flown off, so I probably couldn't see anything clearly after that. I can't remember where everyone else ran to or how long this scene lasted; I don't remember any sounds—just a sick, hot feeling in my head and the pit of my stomach. I remember he ripped some sliding closet doors off their tracks.
>
> My mother got our coats and pushed us out of the house. She drove us down to the shopping mall. I don't remember how long we stayed there or what we did or if we ever ate dinner. I don't remember what happened when we got back home. I don't remember what I was thinking. I only remember that I felt sick.

Helen's account, published in her *L.A. Weekly* article "Sick As Our Secrets" (July 27, 1990, page 16), makes my inner turmoil as the kid of an alcoholic mother seem pretty tame. But the same lessons were there for Helen as they are for any kid having to live with a chemically dependent parent.

In the 1980s, the kids who grew up as alcoholic codependents began organizing for recovery. They began to call themselves "adult children of alcoholics."

"I never thought of life with my father," Helen continues in the *L.A. Weekly* piece, "as anything other than normal. It was normal, I thought, to feel like living in a family was the equivalent of being stuck on an elevator with a monster and your only hope was to get out of the elevator the minute you could."

"Sick As Our Secrets" states that the 1983 publication of Janet G. Woititz's book *Adult Children of Alcoholics* "inaugurated one of the fastest growing self-help recovery movements in a country now bursting at the psychological seams with recovery movements. It is estimated that a new Adult Children of Alcoholics group forms every day in this country!"

Knode reports that Woititz formulated the following thirteen-point characterization of typical adult children of an alcoholic.

Codependency Self-Evaluation. Part II

If you are an adult child who has lived with someone with compulsive behavior such as chemical dependency, think through the following list.

Kids who grow up in hard-core codependency become adults who generally:

- guess at what normal is,

- have difficulty following projects through to the end,

- lie when they could tell the truth

- judge themselves without mercy,

- have difficulty having fun,

- take themselves very seriously,

- have difficulty with intimate relationships,
- overreact to changes over which they have no control,
- constantly seek approval and affirmation,
- usually feel they are different from other people,
- are super-responsible or super irresponsible,
- are extremely loyal, even when the loyalty is undeserved,
- and are impulsive, committing themselves to un-thought-through courses of action, which leads them to confusion, self-loathing, and a loss of control over their environment.

What do we do if too many of these characteristics describe us? We get help. We'll outline some of the organizations battling the curse of codependency later in Part II of this book—many of them are groups that use as their recovery process the famous Twelve Steps developed by Alcoholics Anonymous. But for now, allow me to share with you a heartfelt bit of advice from Melody Beattie, herself an adult child of an alcoholic. In her book, Beattie writes:

> I detest the disease of alcoholism. Chemical dependency and other compulsive disorders destroy people—beautiful, intelligent, sensitive, caring, loving, creative people who do not deserve to be destroyed. The illnesses kill love and dreams, hurt children and tear apart families. Alcoholism leaves in its wake sheared, fragmented, bewildered victims. Sometimes the early death it brings to the drinker causes far less pain than the wretched illness caused during his or her lifetime. It is a horrid, cunning, baffling, powerful and deadly disease.
>
> I unabashedly love Twelve Steps programs. I have great respect for all of them: Alcoholics Anonymous, for people with a desire to stop drinking; Al-Anon, for people affected by someone's drinking; Alateen, for teenagers affected by someone's drinking; and Narcotics Anonymous, for people addicted to drugs. (page 16)

She then lists more organizations—including Adult Children of Alcoholics—which are helping thousands recover from the ravages of codependency. The addresses and phone contacts for these groups are listed in the Resources section of this book. If the questions included in this chapter's self-evaluations hit a nerve, I urge you to consider getting help from one of these organizations, or from a professional counselor, or your local mental health services.

But perhaps you didn't mull through the evaluations very carefully because your parent wasn't or isn't an alcoholic. Or perhaps he or she drank (or drinks now) but you're not sure it's a case of alcoholism.

If there was or is drinking in the home, but it's not clear whether alcohol ruled your family behind the scenes, work carefully through the questions below. They might prod your thinking since they're taken from a Children of Alcoholics Screening Test. (The test is available from Camelot Unlimited in Chicago. Write them at 5 North Wabash Avenue, Suite 1409, Chicago, IL 60602 for more information about their thirty-point survey which can help indicate whether you're just the child of a drinker—or the child of an alcoholic!)

Codependency Self-Evaluation. Part III

_____ Have you ever thought that one of your parents had a drinking problem?

_____ Have you ever lost sleep because of a parent's drinking?

_____ Did you ever protect another family member from a parent who was drinking?

_____ Did you ever feel responsible for and guilty about a parent's drinking?

_____ Have you ever withdrawn from and avoided outside activities and friends because of embarrassment and shame over a parent's drinking problem?

_____ Did you ever stay away from home to avoid the drinking parent or your other parent's reaction to the drinking?

_____ Did you ever take over any chores and duties at home that were usually done by a parent before he or she developed a drinking problem?

_____ Did a parent ever make promises to you that were not kept because of drinking?

_____ Did you ever wish that you could talk to someone who could understand and help the alcohol-related problems in your family?

I knew alcohol was part of my mother's life; but as a teenager, I never really saw that it was part of *my* life too. I now see many codependent traits in my own life, and yet I don't feel overwhelmed by them. I think much of my freedom from bondage to codependency has come through my faith in God's promise that we can be transformed; even emotional scars and the ugliness of the past can be healed. But just to see where I do stand as an adult who weathered an addiction-plagued household during my teen years, I met with one of those rarest of creatures—a warm, happy psychiatrist!

The Joe King Connection

When, as an association geared to helping teenagers in trouble, we established our nationwide toll-free hotline 1-800-SV-A-TEEN (800-782-8336) in the fall of 1987, we soon learned that our office could not handle all the calls from kids in crisis, from kids actually flirting with death. AT&T informed us that we received 3,421 calls from desperate teens in the first six months alone!

I was increasingly convinced we needed trained therapists with special expertise in counseling to answer the calls instead of volunteers. While speaking in Tulsa, Oklahoma, public schools I met Jerry Dillon, CEO and founder of Century HealthCare Corporation. Daily a thousand kids in crisis received valuable counseling and therapy from one of Century's fifty-two programs in seventeen different cities in the United States. With over a thousand full-time staff members, Century HealthCare is the nation's largest adolescent-health-care provider. Instead of charging the highest rates, Century's philosophy has been to offer the best possible form of therapy at the least expense to the young person in need.

I observed Century's program, decided to link up with it, and together reach out to millions of kids needing help.

Part of our rewarding relationship has been having Century's trained professionals answer the phones of our hotline. Another perk has been meeting Joe W. King, M.D., Century's vice president of medical affairs. Traveling with him from Des Moines to Virginia Beach, I sensed in Dr. King a unique blend of impeccable psychiatric credentials and a spiritual commitment to a higher purpose. I knew Joe would be an excellent resource specialist for *It's Killing Our Kids.* As the book developed, Dr. King, the psychiatrist, became Joe, the friend and counselor.

To help me get to the bottom of my own involvement in some of the characteristics of codependency, Joe once interviewed me:

"Why don't you start out by telling me what your earliest memory is about your life situation?" he began. "When did you first realize that there was something amiss with your mom?"

I already felt uncomfortable, just having to think back through the years. "This alcohol thing began gradually until toward the end, she was drinking nearly a quart of vodka a day. I remember that when we lived in Oklahoma City, my mom used to play a lot of bridge with ladies in the neighborhood and that they drank beer. And I remember a few fights that my parents seemed to have that were more than the average argument—they were screaming. Those were about second-grade memories."

I thought back: "When my mom got loaded she really got mean, and so a lot of the connection I have with her being an alcoholic was either acting mean to Dad or suddenly having a totally different attitude, a different personality toward us. It was a dramatic difference.

"When she was sober, she was the nicest person in the entire world. She'd give you anything. Every now and then she made brownies for us or some type of dessert when we came home from school— we were the envy of our friends. For Christmas, she'd make our stockings. I mean, Christmas and every holiday were major productions. At Christmas, our house was loaded with toys of every kind. Our basement was a penny arcade. But then when she got drunk, she was as mean as you could get."

I was surprised at how quickly I remembered so many details from so long ago.

Joe asked, "And what would she do when she was drunk?"

"Well," I said, "I remember her threatening Dad, threatening to leave him, hollering from behind closed doors. She would get inebriated to the point that the least little thing would set her off. I remember one time she just threw coffee grounds around the kitchen—splattered everywhere. My dad always cleaned up the mess. And I guess I had a growing resentment toward my mom. Which is so different in our relationship now since she's been sober. We are best of friends; but we were never that way before."

Joe asked, "Did you talk about it with your brothers? Was there any type of camaraderie between you five boys? Did you feel frightened of her or—?"

"I was frightened," I said quickly. "I remember feeling frightened at night. I mean, it was a scary thing when she really got tanked up and got into one of those fits of absolute anger, screaming."

"Scared for her, or scared for yourself—or both?" Joe asked.

"I wasn't really scared for her. I felt like she knew what she was doing, I was scared more for me. It was kind of a roller coaster, emotionally."

Joe asked, "Were your brothers any support to you? Were you a support to each other?"

"Not really," I said, remembering. "It was kind of 'Shut up; don't talk about it.' Up until Mom got into the midnight hour of alcoholism, we as a family never discussed her problem. It was just a complete unmentionable."

Joe said, "I'm trying to get a feeling about how you coped with the problem. It sounds as if you did it not in concert with but parallel to however your brothers coped."

"I think so," I said. I think all of our coping mechanisms were different. My reaction seemed at first to be resentment that we could never have a friend over; no one could ever spend the night. Anybody besides us five sons and Mom and Dad were called 'outsiders.' Of course, outsiders couldn't know about it. And I felt as if I were locked in a prison in a way."

"Were you isolated from your friends?" Joe asked.

"Yeah, isolated as far as what I thought was normal for other kids—to have friends over, invite people to dinner, you know." I remember the feelings now, just talking about it.

"Were you lonely?"

"I think to a degree. I'd even have a hard time having friends outside of the house. My best friend's mom and dad were both alcoholics, and he was totally messed up on drugs. I guess we both hung around together because we were in similar circumstances. But I must have been lonely because in junior high I came to the point where I was ready to kill myself," I said.

"Do you remember what led to that kind of hopelessness?"

"I was doing drugs and the whole routine, and then I developed a severe digestion problem diagnosed as bleeding ulcers," I said. "I quit going to school. I mean I totally checked out of normal life in the eighth grade. My mom and dad both worked, so about 8:30 every morning everybody was gone—my brothers were in school, my mom and dad were gone. And I sat home all day alone and felt just a total hopelessness. I couldn't talk. I guess part of my problem was I couldn't really talk to my mom because I knew she had her own problem. And my dad has always been the kind of guy who can't handle real heavy trauma, you know. I wasn't able really to begin communicating with him until after I became a Christian and after he did. I think a significant contributing problem was that none of my family were Christians. We were totally out in left field spiritually."

"What do you remember experiencing emotionally when you were home alone and everybody was gone?" Joe asked.

I said, "I remember very clearly watching the clock on the mantle in the family room after everyone had left about a quarter of nine. I got so desperate I'd look in the back of my mom's *Good Housekeeping*-type magazines for those little ads for some religious group where you could send away for a cross or religious paraphernalia. And over the weeks, I actually did send away for some of that stuff."

The memories were coming easily now. "I remember I went up to my dad's closet and I got his big, light-blue bathrobe out of his closet and I wore it every day I was at home. It didn't even begin to fit me, but I think it was my feeble attempt to try and get my parents' attention and say, 'Talk to me. Help me.' The bathrobe had deep pockets on both sides and I carried the pain pills and sleeping pills I'd been given at the hospital everywhere I went. I thought life wasn't worth living. And handling those capsules and pills in my pockets every day, I reasoned that I could probably take them in the morning after everyone had left, and by the time anybody got home about four or five, I'd be dead.

"Maybe that's why it's easy for me today to identify with people who get depressed and can't explain it—because I know what that feels like."

Joe asked, "What *did* it feel like?"

I said, "I think I got to the point that I just didn't want to go on anymore—that was part of the depression. I mean hopelessness. I felt nauseated a lot. Now, as a Christian, I'd say God allowed all that to happen to drag me to Himself. But I just remember feeling really very close to the edge, and my parents didn't even seem to understand it. No one did."

I got lost in the sense of aloneness of those days. "I don't ever remember turning to my mom when I was in this hopeless condition. That's what I was getting at. And these last twelve years as my work with teenagers has grown and as I've been placed at different times under inordinate pressure, I've always called home to talk to my dad. It's only in the last two and a half years that there's been a reversal of that. Now I talk to Mom about some of the struggles I go through."

During our interview, I found that I wanted to talk more and more about what alcohol did to our family. I wanted to explain it all to Joe, this friend who just happens to be a psychiatrist. But I caught myself every once in a while worrying, *I wonder what he's thinking?* Such thoughts must have been vestiges of the old "don't tell" rule. But I bumbled on: "In a sense, we were the American-dream-type family. We had all the cosmetic ornaments of a family that seemingly was happy—with big celebrations at holidays, a nice house, lots of things. But my mom's alcohol problem just continued to get worse and worse and worse, and it was just something we didn't talk about. If we brought it up, we were severely reprimanded."

"So," said Joe, "it was kind of like the elephant in the living room? Just ignore it?"

"Right."

"And the effects of all this now?"

I felt stumped for a minute. Then I said, "Probably the biggest compensation is determination—a drive to help others. I mean I could keep a whole staff busy all the time—probably too busy—working with teenagers' problems. I'm always working on a project. It's very difficult for me to sit down. I am the kind of person who does two or three things at once. If I'm going to watch TV, I'm going to read a newspaper or study while I'm watching TV. I think a lot of my drive now, Joe, is being so mission-oriented. I feel as if I have a calling when I see such tremendous need."

Joe said, "I'm just concerned about your burning yourself out."

"Two years ago I was much worse than I am now. Sometimes I wouldn't go to bed at night; I'd work all night. Or, no matter how late my plane got in the night before, I'd always be in the office at eight in the morning. I spoke 410 times that year. Do you think that kind of drive has anything to do with growing up as a child of an alcoholic?"

Joe simply said, "Do bees be? Do bears bear?"

I guess his answer was yes.

My session with Joe prompted a flurry of memories.

I remembered how my brother's fiancée had invited us to her church, a denomination different from the one we ostensibly and loosely belonged to. Although we went reluctantly, eventually we did go. There, I met a bunch of kids who later asked my dad if I could come to church camp with them. And I went—but only because Dad promised me a professional foosball table for my birthday if I'd go.

I agreed hesitantly. And every day of my life since then, I've thanked God—and my dad—for that foosball incentive that sent me off to spend a week at what I thought would resemble a monastery. Because at that church camp, my life was changed by the message of the speaker during the last evening's program. I came home from that camp a new person, alive in Christ. And when I shared my testimony three days later at church, my dad enthusiastically recommitted his own life to Christ also.

Knowing how my own life changed, I work now to understand and offer help to the youngsters who are still on the struggling side of problems like addiction and codependency.

Codependents seem to be ruled so subtly from childhood by those three slogans: Don't feel, don't trust, don't talk. What particularly hit me after my talk with Joe was my devotion even well into adulthood to that destructive voice of "Don't tell."

Don't Tell the YFC

Everything happened so early for me. I was doing drugs by age thirteen and had rebounded from my suicide attempts by the time I was fifteen. Then, in high school, I worked with an organization called Youth for Christ (YFC) in Kansas City and traveled constantly to similar organizations across the country. Regional director Al Metsker adopted me spiritually; and I cut my teeth learning to speak at YFC's large sixteen-hundred-seat auditorium. Al went way out on a limb in an attempt to launch me into ministry before I headed for seminary—or as he called it, before "cemetery." He allowed me to speak at a highly promoted rally for the first time when I was fifteen, and I enthusiastically shared the message of the Good News.

At sixteen, I started traveling with YFC, speaking to youth rallies, camps, and conventions nationwide. It was clear to me then, as it has always been, that God was using me beyond my abilities. So many doors were opened, simply because God was using me to carry the message that could change lives. A number of times when I would reach a kid who heard me in his high school and attended our evening event, I would end up reaching his entire family. It was remarkable. I was being used to reach so many people—but I could not reach my mom.

The experiences of speaking at a prestigious youth ministry at such a young age were memories never to be forgotten. Al continued to schedule me at least twice a year to speak at the big rally all through my high school years. Each time, I would take weeks to prepare a special message. I called my bedroom at home "The Big D," for no understandable reason, except that it was big. It would be covered with opened reference books, wall to wall, and I would finish off my research by actually practicing my delivery in front of the mirror on my dresser.

How I loved those days! Al and Vidy Metsker, their son Ronnie, and all the gang at YFC became my second family in a home away from home. I didn't just attend the weekly rally, but stayed hours afterward—until the wee hours in the morning—enjoying fellowship with everyone with a cheeseburger and fries in my hand in the adjoining Rainbow Room restaurant. My Saturdays were always reserved for those rallies. Speaking at them was an extraordinary highlight of something already completely satisfying and entertaining to me.

Al's backing and continual promotion of me gave me experience far beyond my years. By the end of my twelfth-grade year, I had spoken over a thousand times from New York to California. It was in those days that I began my embryonic Life School Assembly, which in the years since then has placed me before three million young people in over twenty-eight hundred public-school campuses all over North America.

Al Metsker was the first person who had me speak on television, radio, at conventions, camp (which Al always called a ranch), banquets, and every other imaginable setting. He truly believed in me and the gifts God had given to me.

My dad and mom attended the rally whenever I spoke. It was a big thing to me having them in the audience. This, too, provided Dad with an excellent vehicle to get Mom exposed to more of the Bible. Dad believed Mom was a genuine Christian, even though she struggled with alcohol. He was always praying for her, with her, and modeled for me the perfect example of unconditional love toward a spouse. Dad did not love Mom because of how she treated him. Often when Mom was drunk, she treated him very unfairly. Dad loved Mom because it was the right thing to do. All along he believed God was going to deliver her.

At one YFC rally when I was speaking, Mom was moved. Afterward, I was summoned to the counseling area because Mom had come forward, seeking help. I remember racing to the counseling area, hoping this was the long-awaited breakthrough we were all dreaming for.

"I'm sorry, Jerry, I'm sorry. Pray for me," Mom said, pleading with tears. I wanted so badly to believe this was the recovery we had all been praying for. However, the aroma of alcohol was on Mom's breath. Disappointed, I almost hung my head. Then reluctantly, I forced out a prayer, assured Mom things were going to get better, and helped her find her way back to Dad.

Was I ever low that night! My great message had moved Mom no further than remorse. As humans, we want to blame ourselves when someone so close to us fails. It's part of the codependent's routine. Mom's prolonged defeat by alcohol caused me to question the power and vitality of my own spirituality. As I pillowed my head much later that night in the Big D, my mom just down the stairs in her bedroom sleeping it off, I really wondered if things would ever change.

I had seen God change me from a wasted, suicidal druggie, but I didn't even have the faith that He could transform Mom. As far as I could remember, my mom had always been an alcoholic. And I assumed she would always be one.

At eighteen, I received a seven-year all-expense-paid scholarship to a Christian college and seminary. I accepted, and while I was in school, I was put on salary and turned my honorariums back in to the organization. Monthly, I spoke on the radio network syndicated to nearly four hundred stations nationally while going to school. I was featured with a few others on the television broadcast.

A number of times through the years I would speak in Kansas City and Dad and Mom would come hear me. But apparently nothing I said was revolutionizing Mom's life. I couldn't reach her. Why? I didn't really know, but it deeply bothered me. Shortly after I had become a Christian and my dad recommitted his life to Christ, he wrote in my Bible, "If you can't be a success in the ministry in your home, you will never be outside of the home." What Dad meant was if you don't have rapport with and the respect of those closest to you and who know you best, you will never garner the respect of others.

Many times I failed my family in trying to be a good example. Every time this happened, it grieved me. Several times through the years I was prompted to apologize to different ones in my family and to plead for their prayer support that I could avoid the pitfalls of hypocrisy. My mom respected me, understood my calling, and knew I was imperfect and growing. Nevertheless, my strongest attempt to reach her failed.

Honestly, I almost gave up. Toward the end, when she was at her worst condition, I found myself mentally bracing for the catastrophic. I was afraid we were going to lose her. All along, my dad triumphantly had faith that God could change Mom's life and completely heal her of this wretched addiction. And if you have an impossible case in your family you must believe, too, just as Dad did! You must have faith that God can accomplish the impossible.

In retrospect, it is so easy to see now how God was guiding our paths all along. Even when we were at our most tenuous moments, we had an unseen Person standing next to us, orchestrating all the events for our ultimate good.

But I never really told anyone at YFC about Mom. It seemed strange because they were all so close to me. But it was hard to be that honest. Perhaps they knew, somehow. If they did, they never let on. And under the load of the whole thing, I really wanted to tell someone. But this was such an "unmentionable." It was the Johnston family's closely guarded secret.

Keeping the Secret, Even in Romance

I had a great desire to reach people from the moment I was turned around at camp. I know that only God promotes a man, builds a city, and launches a ministry. Leaving college and returning home was an ideal hiatus to look heaven-ward for divine direction.

After I left college, I had a scheduled engagement in the small town of Holland, Michigan, where I was to speak at a Saturday-night youth rally, and again on Sunday morning. Sunday evening we would wind up speaking in Detroit.

This was a very special time in my life. After leaving college, I determined to pray extensively for God to use me in a unique way. And that's exactly what I did for several days.

The Big D had a large walk-in closet. When the closet door was shut, it was pitch black and very quiet. On my knees in that quiet, private bedroom closet I spiritually glowed like a hot coal. What God was saying to me was inexpressible. In my heart, I knew He was charting my course. A spirit of renewed confidence came over me. I announced to my dad on the way to Kansas City International Airport my firmest conviction that God had some special mission for me to accomplish. We prayed in the car on the way to the airport, as we have done many times since, and I optimistically boarded the plane for Michigan.

Chris Huf was a beautiful nineteen-year-old from nearby, obscure Borculo, Michigan. Her father Al had immigrated to the United States from Czechoslovakia. Escaping his communist homeland in 1949, he met a young woman named Poldi in West Germany. They wed and soon celebrated the birth of Jana, the first of their six children. A faithful, elderly missionary by the name of Lukesh shared the Good News with the struggling young couple, and they turned to God for new life. Stifled by an environment where they felt it was unacceptable to grow spiritually, and aided by Lukesh, the young Hufs left for the United States, leaving family and friends behind.

Hudsonville-Borculo, a predominantly Dutch community nestled under the brim of greater Grand Rapids's religious halo, welcomed the Hufs. Starting from scratch, they began rearing their family and trying their hand at the free-enterprise system.

Because a friend would not stop pestering Al Huf to attend services in Holland where a nineteen-year-old from Kansas was speaking, he begrudgingly agreed to come, more out of loyalty to the man than curiosity for the young upstart.

Al later described himself at that point as spiritually sound— sound asleep. In a sense, that description mirrored the entire community. There was a great deal of exterior show of religion. Attending church faithfully, Bible reading after dinner, and a family prayer or two without fervency from the heart were conspicuous in more than one family.

The two meetings that were scheduled for Holland extended spontaneously for nearly three weeks. They electrified Al Huf. He began to attend every night. And each night, he begged some of his family members to attend. Chris was the only taker. Honestly, I noticed Chris from the platform! Our relationship neatly fit the "love-at-first-sight" category.

People came from all over western Michigan to attend the Holland meetings. By the second Sunday, the building was jammed to capacity! With Chris beside him, Al immersed himself in the meetings and attended nightly. One evening, he waited after the service to introduce Chris and himself to me.

The last night of the meetings, Al invited me to come over and meet his entire family. "Is Chris going to be there?" I asked. "She sure is!" he assured me. From that night on, I began the greatest courtship of my life. Chris was so sensitive, so genuine, and so unassuming. And her dad and mom were just like her.

Early in our relationship, Al and Poldi sat Chris and me down and Al said, "Jerry, we have something we need to tell you. We like you very much. And we are happy Chris is seeing you. But we have made up our minds if Chris would ever get in the way of what you are doing for God, we want this whole relationship stopped."

I could tell from the tone of their voices they meant every word. This was extremely serious to them. "Your reaching kids is more important than dating Chris," Al reasoned.

Well, Chris was it for me. She captured me. Almost any day I had off I flew to Grand Rapids to see her. I didn't want to wear out my welcome, but my time with Chris was priceless. My dad and mom knew I had fallen in love. "When you never came home again, we knew you were in love," Dad later said.

Grand Rapids was an adjustment for me on my visits to see Chris. It was a slower-paced place, not taken to "outsiders," particularly young spiritual mavericks. But when Chris was added into the equation, it was the best city in America. We often went to the malls and always visited the bookstores, my one and only hobby.

Chris's parents became very close to me, mostly because it was so easy to talk to them. They were humble people, and we had great times together.

But I never told Chris or her dad and mom that my mom was an alcoholic. I couldn't. And it was wrong of me not to disclose it.

I planned Chris's first visit to meet my parents in Kansas City. She would come on Halloween, October 31. You would have thought the president was coming to town. I cleaned my mom's house top to bottom, even the toilets. That was a first!

My parents stood back in amazement. I planned everything to a T. I made clear to Mom that she, Dad, Chris, and I would eat in the formal dining room, and we would have boiled shrimp. Mom's picturesque dining room was never used in those days. Mr. Alcohol usually kept Mom far too busy to entertain anyone. Our shut-up house received very few visitors.

Mom rolled out the red carpet for my beautiful visitor. Everything was perfect. Nothing could spoil this great celebration. Chris landed at KCI, I picked her up, and we were off to our delectable dinner. I assumed everyone knew how to eat boiled shrimp! But Chris put a shelled shrimp in her mouth and almost began chomping when, in the nick of time, I sensed her timidity and gave her de-shelling instructions. I certainly saved her indigestion!

There we were, at Mom's dining-room table, getting to know one another—me glowing beside Chris.

Then Mom started crying. *Great,* I thought in disgust. *Not now! What if Chris suspects something's wrong?* Chris seemed to interpret Mom's tears as an indication of her happiness with our union. Now, years later, I find myself still wondering at times why Mom reacted as she did under alcohol; I didn't really know why she was crying.

Later that night, Chris and I walked around the block. I knew she needed some explanation. Why had I waited so long to tell someone so close to me? With my stomach churning, I forced it out: "My mom is drinking. . . . She's an alcoholic.

"But please don't tell anyone, not even your parents," I pleaded. It didn't faze Chris one iota. She pledged her care and love and prayers for Mom. And against my advice, she later returned home and told her dad and mom. And Chris's mom and dad immediately started praying. From the beginning, they cared. Interestingly, they never looked at Mom with condemnation. To them, she was not bad or some type of vile person. She had a problem; it elicited their genuine, heart-felt sympathy.

But I wonder what it says about my tendency toward codependency that I, myself, never officially acknowledged to Chris's parents that my mom was an alcoholic. They learned it from Chris, and then simply responded with love and support.

Later, Chris and I married and were blessed to have Danielle, Jeremiah, and Jenilee. I would learn with much pain that Mr. Alcohol would prevent Mom from being a genuine grandmother. So many times, she wasn't there for my kids. Whenever she attended a birthday party, she stayed only a brief time; the bottle was calling. Chris and I never told the kids until we later intervened with Mom and they wanted to know why Grandma was in the hospital.

In spite of Mom's dependency on the bottle, I loved her. My disappointment, regret, and even at times embarrassment never caused my love for her to dissipate. I always told her I loved her. When Christmas rolled around, I always tried to buy her the best gift. My love wanted her free, not enslaved.

5

An Alcohol Handbook: What You Need to Know

Feel free to quote from, memorize, and generally shout out the tidbits of alcohol facts in this chapter. Sources are summarized at the end of the chapter.

What is alcohol?

Ethyl alcohol, sometimes referred to as ethanol, is the excrement of yeast! As this fungus devours sugars—such as those in grapes, cereals, potatoes, etc.—it releases an enzyme that turns the sugar into carbon dioxide and alcohol. The process, of course, is fermentation.

The yeast feeds on sugar until its alcohol content reaches about 13 or 14 percent. In their book, *Under the Influence,* James Milam and Katherine Ketcham say at this point, the yeast dies, "of acute alcohol intoxication—the very first victim of 'drunkenness'" (page 17).

In beer made from barley, corn, rice, and other cereals, the fermentation process is stopped at about 3 to 6 percent alcohol content. In comparison, wine goes through the full natural fermentation process, and generally contains from 10 to 14 percent alcohol.

Distillation was developed about A.D. 800 in Arabia; and so the Arabic word *alkuhl,* or "essence" became the English word "alcohol." Distillation produces what we call the "hard" liquors such as whiskey, gin, vodka, scotch, rye, rum, and bourbon. Most of these contain between 40 and 75 percent alcohol, since distillation takes over the production of alcohol where natural fermentation leaves off.

The percentage of alcohol in a liquor is sometimes expressed in "proof," which is about double the percentage. For example, a 40 percent alcohol content in a whiskey is expressed as "80 proof." The term comes from the 1600s in England when the alcohol content of a drink could be "proven" by mixing it with gunpowder. If the mixture ignited, it was proven to be more than 49 percent alcohol by weight.

Pure alcohol is added to wines such as port or sherry, which usually have around a 20 percent alcohol content.

Alcohol itself is colorless and basically tasteless, apart from its burning sensation. The different drinks' distinctive flavors come from something called cogeners. Various cogeners include surprising substances such as: aluminum, lead, manganese, silicon, zinc, glucose, fructose, acetic and lactic acids, carbon dioxide, trace amounts of vitamins and minerals, salts, acids, ketones, esters, carbohydrates, other types of alcohol, and by-products called fusel oils.

What does alcohol do?

The Harvard Medical School Mental Health Letter (October 1989), points out some of the effects of alcohol as a drug:

> Alcohol abuse contributes to cancer, cirrhosis of the liver, heart failure, organic brain disease, and other kinds of chronic illness and organ damage. Alcohol, like most drugs, is dangerous to the fetus when used by pregnant women. Thousands of children each year are born mentally defective because their mothers drank heavily during pregnancy; others suffer withdrawal reactions to alcohol at birth. Preoccupation with alcohol is notorious as a cause of violence, broken marriages, lost jobs, legal problems, social isolation, destitution, and pervasive demoralization.

Why do people keep using drugs despite these effects?

According to the Harvard Mental Health Letter, the most recent version of the American Psychiatric Association's diagnostic manual introduces the concept of a psychoactive substance dependence disorder. It is defined as undesirable behavior associated with regular drug use, rather than an acute or chronic drug effect. Persons who have a certain number of the following symptoms are said to be dependent on a drug such as alcohol:

1. Repeatedly drinking more than they intend or for a longer time than they intend,

2. Knowing that they are using too much, but not being able to stop,

3. Spending much of their time obtaining the alcohol, being intoxicated, or recovering from its effects,

4. Being unable to fulfill social, family, and work obligations because of intoxication,

5. Giving up most other activities in order to drink,

6. Continuing to drink, although they know it is damaging their health, capacity to work, or family life,

7. The development of tolerance, which makes it necessary to drink more to preserve the original effect,

8. Sensing withdrawal symptoms, and

9. Constantly drinking to relieve or avoid withdrawal symptoms.

Isn't the really serious problem in our society drug abuse?
Right. And our number-one drug problem is alcohol abuse. About 300,000 Americans are addicted to heroin. But about nine million are addicted to alcohol. It's not even close. When we add alcohol *abusers* to the number of hard-core alcoholics, the number caught in the web of alcohol is estimated at 15.1 million.

As we mentioned in chapter 4, in Canada, about three hundred deaths per year are caused by drugs other than alcohol, while more than eighteen thousand die in alcohol-related incidents.

Aren't most alcoholics skid-row bums?
Only 3 to 5 percent of alcoholics are "bums." Less than half the derelicts on skid row have a drinking problem. About 70 percent of alcoholics are married, employed, regular people. About one in every ten executives has a drinking problem. Many others are students.

Isn't alcoholism basically a male dilemma?

In the 1950s there were five or six alcoholic men to every alcoholic woman. Now the ratio is about three to one.

I don't know any alcoholics. So where are all the alcoholics you're talking about?

Some of your best friends may have a drinking problem. To you, they don't seem "different." They usually try to hide their illness, even from themselves. Actually about one out of every ten drinkers is an alcoholic.

Don't people who drink too much hurt only themselves?

They hurt themselves—and their families, their friends, their employers, their schools, and strangers on the highways. And you.

Drinking and Criminal Activity

What are some of the serious effects of drinking?

The 1987 Alcohol and Health Sixth Special Report to the U.S Congress found a growing connection between alcohol and homicide, fatal accidents, traffic accidents, and suicide. The study revealed alcohol was a key player in approximately 42 percent of the 42,584 traffic accident deaths in 1983 and in 8 percent of the fatal plane crashes in 1981. The study cited measurable blood alcohol contents were found in approximately 40 percent of the fatally injured pedestrians killed by motor vehicles. It also noted that alcohol contributed to home and recreational accidents, as well as occupational accidents.

Does alcohol abuse cause crime?

Studies have linked alcohol to violent acts and criminal behavior, showing that drinking seems to lower inhibitions and allow an individual to commit acts that would be unthinkable under normal circumstances.

Alcohol is a factor in approximately 50 percent of all arrests, 80 percent of homicides, 70 percent of serious assaults, 50 percent of forcible rapes, 72 percent of robberies. Alcohol is present in half of all murders.

Studies establish two links between alcohol and crime. The first is the pharmacological effects—the intoxication—caused by alcohol consumption; alcohol gives criminals a false sense of confidence, for example. The second link connects chronic alcohol abuse with violence. One review of a series of American studies reported alcoholism in 17 to 48 percent of convicted felons.

Is alcohol a major factor in suicide?

Approximately 18 percent of all suicide victims are alcoholics. (And of the seventy-five-thousand-plus Americans who commit suicide each year, more than ten times that number make the attempt.)

Drunk Driving

Just how seriously does drunk driving affect us?

In America, there are more than two million drunk driving collisions each year. In your community between 8 P.M. and 4 A.M. on any Friday or Saturday, one of the next ten vehicles coming your way is being driven by someone under the influence of alcohol. Between midnight and 4 A.M. about 80 percent of the drivers who are killed have been drinking.

Dr. Robert G. Niven, former director of the National Institute of Alcohol Abuse and Alcoholism (NIAAA), reflecting on alcohol's contribution to accidents, said in 1984, "Alcohol is implicated as a significant contributor to a wide variety of accidents resulting in the injury, disability or death of over 200,000 persons annually, as well as the cause of immeasurable psychological trauma to their loved ones."

How is alcohol killing our kids?

More Americans between the ages of sixteen and twenty-four die from alcohol-related accidents than any other cause of death. People in this age group generally are involved in approximately 40 percent of all fatal alcohol-related crashes. The number of young adults so injured is disproportionate to the number of drivers of that age group and to the number of vehicle miles they travel. For example, in 1984, sixteen- to twenty-four-year-olds accounted for 35 percent of all alcohol-related fatalities, while representing only 20 percent of the U.S. driving population.

In 1982, close to 8,000 young adults died and another 240,000 sustained injuries in alcohol-related automobile accidents. An estimated one out of every two Americans will be involved in an alcohol-related accident during their lifetimes.

Media Influence on Drinking

How often is alcohol shown on TV?

According to the Prevention Research Center in California, there are an average of ten to eleven "drinking acts"—defined as ingestion of alcohol or preparation to drink—per hour of prime-time television. So a viewer may witness about twenty drinking scenes per evening of TV viewing.

What are the goals of alcohol marketing?

Regarding alcohol advertising, the marketing strategy of the liquor industry comprises these objectives:

1. Increase the number of occasions on which current drinkers consume alcohol. Michelob Beer's ad campaign began a decade ago with a catchy slogan: "Weekends are made for Michelob." Soon the ad evolved into "Put a little weekend in your week." Then the sales pitch became "The night belongs to Michelob." Michelob moved within a decade from advocating drinking as a way to unwind on the weekend to promoting drinking as a habitual nightly activity. Michelob's campaign represents one of many alcohol industry efforts to stimulate consumption.

2. Increase the percentage of those who drink.

3. Position alcoholic beverages to compete with soft drinks as "thirst quenchers" and "refreshment beverages."

Who is the target audience for alcohol ads?

Almost all alcohol industry campaigns use a variety of approaches which increasingly bombard specific target groups, such as Hispanics, African Americans, and women. College students are another target group, despite the fact the legal drinking age in all fifty states in the U.S. is twenty-one. The alcohol industry saturates the college market with ads in school newspapers and the promotion of special events such as parties and sports competition.

Two factors drive the alcohol industry's involvement on campuses. First, the industry knows that winning the brand loyalty of a young student may result in loyalty for twenty to thirty-five years. If a student becomes a heavy consumer, then the company gains an annuity. Second, the industry knows that the largest portion of beer drinkers are between eighteen and twenty-four, with college students spending two billion dollars on beer annually.

Drinking Habits

What influence does background have on drinking?

The more education and income a person has, the more alcohol the person is likely to consume. More whites drink than non-whites, more men than women.

Who drinks?

About two-thirds of the American population age eighteen and over consume alcoholic beverages at some time during the year. A recent Gallup survey of drinkers was conducted as to the primary reasons for drinking. The most common reasons participants gave were "to be sociable," "to relax," "for personal enjoyment," "for special occasions," and "to add to the enjoyment of a meal." About one-third of the adult population of the United States abstains from drinking any alcoholic beverage.

Are there any signs of change in our drinking habits?

Yes! There has been perhaps a 10 percent downturn in per-capita alcohol consumption in America in the last decade. Yet the largest consumers still remain the young people. A recent Gallup poll found that 64 percent of people age thirty to forty-nine drink and 41 percent of those age fifty and older do. But 66 percent of the younger generation—those age eighteen to twenty-nine—drink.

What has caused this change?

Americans have tapered their drinking and been switching from hard liquor to wine and beer because of their growing interest in healthier, fitter lifestyles and their recognition of alcoholism as a disease.

Youth and Alcohol

What about minors? Are they changing their drinking habits?
The monthly use by senior high-school students declined 8 percent to 64 percent of the students by 1988, and daily use declined from 6.9 to 4.2 percent. But since then, these students' illegal consumption has remained at this still unhealthy level.

How do our youth compare with the rest of the world?
Our high-school students and young adults have outdistanced the youth in the rest of the industrialized world in their use of alcohol and other illicit drugs. Each weekend, 30 to 40 percent of the youth in America use alcohol and drugs. Our children's favorite drug is the same as their parents': alcohol. This generation gap has shrunk as drinking problems for the young have grown.

How do kids get started drinking?
Most teens abuse alcohol at parties with friends in someone else's home when their parents are away. First tries at alcohol are generally between the ages of eleven and thirteen.

When do most youth first get acquainted with alcohol?
While only 9 percent of our sixth graders have tried alcohol, 30 percent of eighth graders and 56 percent of ninth graders have used it. By the twelfth grade, 92 percent of seniors are familiar with alcohol. This is despite alcohol being illegal for all high schoolers and most college students in the United States.

If most seniors have tried alcohol, how often do they use it?
In a one-month period, at least 65 percent of high school seniors admitted some drinking, and about 5 percent admitted drinking daily. That is one in every twenty classmates.
Peer pressure in social environments of heavy party drinking is inescapable for virtually all students. During a typical two-week period, a significant number of our seniors—13 percent of males and

27 percent females—participate in binge drinking of five or more drinks in a row.

The number of girls participating in wild drinking is increasing. Early in 1990, Dr. Louis Sullivan, U.S. Secretary of Health and Human Services, reported, "only a modest decline in binge drinking by high school seniors."

Young alcoholics seem to be increasing. How serious is this?

Statistics vary, but the best estimates seem to indicate that today there could be more than four million American teenage alcoholics under age eighteen.

But do the current statistics reflect the school my youth is in?

Drinking today is so widespread that virtually every student has to face this kind of peer environment. One study reported that all the schools in its survey had at least some students who had drunk five or more consecutive drinks in the last two weeks. In 97 percent of the high schools, at least a tenth of the students had done so. And in 82 percent, more than a quarter admitted they had.

Since no North American schools seem free from student drinkers, what kind of schools tend to be less influenced by alcohol?

In general, the lower the socioeconomic status of the school, the lower the amount of drinking. Monthly use of alcohol by students in high-status schools is estimated at 72 percent. In medium-status schools, it's 64 percent, and in schools of low socioeconomic status, monthly use is estimated at 59 percent. Yet there is a slightly higher *daily* use in schools with lower status. This is explained by studies showing that kids from lower-class neighborhoods drink a little bit each day, while their upper-class peers are more prone to indulge in expensive binge drinking on weekends.

Are schools in some regions of the United States safer from excessive drinking than others?

Among youth, occasional heavy drinking is somewhat less in the South and West than it is in the Northeast and North Central part of the country. In the last decade the Northeast has dropped in heavy drinking so that the North Central area now ranks highest. The religious background of the Bible Belt seems to have a bearing on drinking in the South.

Aren't private and small schools safer from alcohol's influence?

Unfortunately, no. Private school students, on average, use somewhat more alcohol than those in public schools. Also, there is a tendency for more drinking by students of small schools than large ones.

College Drinking

What about college drinking?

One to four years past high school, the tendency to binge increases. Sixty-two percent of college males have an alcoholic binge at least every two weeks. The worst representation of alcohol abuse and its related consequences is on university and college campuses nationwide.

The following are the results from surveys of nineteen- to twenty-six-year-olds conducted for the National Institute of Drug Abuse by the University of Michigan's Institute for Social Research:

	Percentage of Students Reporting Use During Year	Percentage of Students Reporting Use in Past Month
Alcohol	89.4	75.4
Marijuana	24.8	20.7
Cocaine	15.7	6.0
Stimulants	8.7	3.2
Tranquilizers	5.1	1.6
Sedatives	2.5	0.8
Heroin	0.2	0.1

Other findings of the survey show that alcohol is a factor in an estimated 34 percent of academic problems, and 25 percent of the dropouts. In addition, 64 percent of violent behavior on campus is alcohol-related.

For youth in college, alcohol use is slightly less in small schools and in junior colleges. Those students who live in dormitories or live with parents are found to use quite a bit less alcohol than those living on their own off-campus or in fraternities or sororities. The highest rates of drinking are found among students studying social sciences, humanities and arts, business and vocational/technical areas, engineering (occasional heavy drinking), and undecided majors. Lowest imbiber rates are among those majoring in education, clerical fields, and physical sciences.

Students with an A average in high school are less likely to be occasional heavy drinkers in college than B+ students, and B+ students are less likely than B students to drink heavily.

At college age, who drinks more—collegians or non-collegians?

College students are more likely to drink heavily occasionally than those not attending college (43 percent compared with 36 percent). This reverses the high-school pattern of non-college-bound students drinking more than those preparing for college. The "catching up" may be because college students are more likely to leave home and less likely to get married than their non-college peers.

Of all age groups, which has more trouble with alcohol?

The highest proportion of those with drinking problems are males in their early twenties.

Parents' Influence on Drinking

What is the parent/child factor in adolescent drinking?

The highest likelihood of alcoholism occurs in children of parents who are either alcoholic—or teetotalers. Perhaps parental "extremism" is an important factor. And one in three families have someone who abuses alcohol.

Now that many homes have all parental figures working, how does this affect children?

Many young teens come home day after day to an empty house. These latchkey teens (29 percent of those surveyed in one study) had eleven hours or more alone each week and were twice as likely to drink. Lack of adult supervision teaches youth to try being more autonomous and make decisions their parents may not like. A significant number of our youth are left alone far longer than they can constructively handle. These kids need after-school activities such as YMCA or YWCA groups, Scouts, on-campus after-school programs, church activities, etc.

How does growing up with an alcoholic parent affect children?

About half of all alcoholics have an alcoholic parent. Alcohol is a significant factor in 90 percent of child-abuse cases. Frequently, children of alcoholics are victims of incest, child neglect, violence, and other exploitation. Alcoholics often cause their children to be unable to trust, thus having a need to control, an excessive sense of responsibility, and denial of feelings. These children have low self-esteem, depression, isolation, guilt, and difficulty in keeping satisfying relationships. They are apt to have learning disabilities, anxieties, suicidal tendencies, eating disorders, or compulsive behavior.

What is the legacy of alcoholic parenthood?

The majority of those served by employee-assistance programs are adult children of alcoholics. A disproportionate number of those entering the juvenile justice system—courts, prisons, mental health facilities, and referrals to school authorities—are children of alcoholics.

How Alcohol Works

This is quite a bit of damaging evidence against alcohol. How does it work in the body to help bring about such results?

Despite all those beautiful, enticing, promising liquor ads, alcohol is not that wonderful elixir for all your needs. Alcohol acts like a general anesthetic. It slows the brain and the central nervous system. The body doesn't digest alcohol. Instead, it is rapidly absorbed directly into the bloodstream. This happens even faster if the stomach is empty.

Isn't alcohol a stimulant?

It's about as good a stimulant as ether. Alcohol is a drug that acts as a depressant on the central nervous system. Perhaps such facts will help us wake up to the advertising lies we've been promised.

How do authorities define being legally drunk?

In North America, all states and provinces have laws against driving under the influence of alcohol. As we mentioned in chapter 3, most law-enforcement agencies define intoxication at .10 percent blood alcohol concentration (BAC). This is one-tenth of one percent. Such a little amount can have a powerfully dangerous potential. And in California (perhaps elsewhere), driving impairment is seen to be so dangerous that legal intoxication was lowered in 1990 to .08 percent.

I drive better after a drink or two.

Although most states' legal definition of "driving under the influence" is a BAC of 0.10 percent, tests prove that even professional drivers' abilities diminish sharply at levels as low as 0.03 to 0.05 percent. So people may think they're driving better—but they're really driving worse. (See Table 5-1.)

How potent are different alcoholic drinks?

A twelve-ounce beer or a four-ounce glass of wine contains as much alcohol as a shot (1.5 ounces) of liquor.

Table 5-1
Do You Know What Your Blood Alcohol Concentration Really Is?

Your blood alcohol concentration (BAC) is defined as the number of grams of alcohol per 100 milliliters of blood, or per 210 liters of breath. The limit is .10 percent BAC. Use this chart only as a guide to estimate your BAC. Levels may vary with age, weight, sex, and other characteristics.

Body Weight (lbs.)	No. of Drinks (one ounce of 86-proof liquor or twelve ounces of beer)								
	1	2	3	4	5	6	7	8	9
100	.032	.065	.097	.129	.162	.194	.226	.258	.291
120	.027	.054	.081	.108	.135	.161	.188	.215	.242
140	.023	.046	.069	.092	.115	.138	.161	.184	.207
160	.020	.040	.060	.080	.101	.121	.141	.161	.181
180	.018	.036	.054	.072	.090	.108	.126	.144	.162
200	.016	.032	.048	.064	.080	.097	.113	.129	.145
220	.015	.029	.044	.058	.073	.088	.102	.117	.131
240	.014	.027	.040	.053	.067	.081	.095	.108	.121

Caution!	Driving Impaired!	Legally Drunk!
BAC up to .05 percent	.051 to .09 percent	.10 percent or above

(From *Driving Under the Influence* pamphlet. Used by permission of the Kansas Department of Transportation, Office of Traffic Safety, Topeka, Kansas.)

Beer isn't as dangerous as "hard" liquor, is it?

That simply isn't the case. A beer or a glass of wine is about equal to an average highball. (Manhattans and martinis, though, are twice as potent as one beer.) Yes, you can and will get equally as drunk on beer or wine as on "hard" liquor.

Don't people get drunk or sick from switching drinks?

What one drinks shouldn't make much difference. The adverse reaction is usually caused by drinking too much.

What remedies have an effect on blood alcohol to help sober up? Black coffee? Fresh air? Exercise? Cold showers?

Actually none of them do. The only thing that will help the sobering process is time. It takes lots of time for the liver to be able to metabolize all the liquor that's been ingested to the point of intoxication.

How quickly can you sober up?

That depends on how much alcohol is in the bloodstream. If a person drinks no more alcohol, the blood alcohol will drop about .015 percent per hour. That means if someone is legally drunk at .10 percent BAC, then it will take more than three hours to be below the "driving-impaired" level of .05 percent.

Social Drinking

Aren't people friendlier when they're drunk?

Maybe some people are friendlier. But others are more hostile, more dangerous, more criminal, more homicidal, and more suicidal.

But shouldn't a good host never let a guest's glass get empty?

There's nothing hospitable about pushing alcohol or any other drug.

"Ya gotta hand it to Kevin. He can really hold his liquor."

Don't envy him. Often the guy who can "hold" a lot of liquor is developing a "tolerance" for alcohol. And tolerance can be a polite word for need.

"What a man! Still on his feet after a whole fifth."

When we stop thinking it's manly to drink too much, we have begun to grow up. It's no more manly to over-drink than it is to over-eat.

Getting drunk is funny.

Not in real life. Drunkenness is no funnier than any other illness or incapacity.

"I'm just a social drinker."

Plenty of "social drinkers" become alcoholics.

Isn't it all right just to have a few drinks to help you unwind and relax?

Maybe. But if you use alcohol like a medicine, it's time to see your doctor.

What can parents do? Is the time to teach kids about drinking when they reach legal age?

Like it or not, we teach our kids from birth. They learn more from what they see us do than from what we tell them. Sometimes parents of alcohol-abusing children think, *At least my kid isn't on drugs!* But a person who's hooked on drinking, *is* on drugs. With nine million Americans dependent on alcohol, it's time we stopped pretending it isn't a drug.

How can parents tell if their children are in trouble or addicted?

Psychiatrist Derek Miller in a *People* magazine article warned parents to watch out if your "kids become listless, and their school-work goes downhill. They generally become irritable and less pleasant. They also become dishonest, like adult alcoholics or addicts. Insist on a formal good-night kiss, and then you'll know if your child has been drinking."

Unfortunately, many parents are reluctant to take responsibility over their child's drinking. Most parents of today's teenagers were in junior or senior high during the Vietnam War, when authority figures and the establishment were considered "the enemy." Now these parents are uncomfortable with being the authority over their children.

In these permissive times, they are reluctant to face their child's anger such as when denying them alcohol, although it is illegal for them.

Which were America's top ten breweries by volume in 1989?

1. Anheuser-Busch	80,700,000 barrels
2. Miller Brewing Co.	31,900,000 barrels
3. The Stroh Brewery Co.	18,250,000 barrels
4. Adolph Coors Co.	17,698,000 barrels
5. Heileman Brewing Co.	13,050,000 barrels
6. Pabst Brewing Co.	6,600,000 barrels
7. Genesee Brewing Co.	2,363,000 barrels
8. Falstaff Brewing Co.	1,362,000 barrels
9. Lautrobe Brewing Co.	650,000 barrels
10. Hudepohl-Schoenling	500,000 barrels
Total	173,073,000 barrels

Source: Anheuser-Busch, Inc.

Sources of Information

Sources for information included in this chapter's "Alcohol Handbook" are listed below:

"Alcohol and Drug Abuse among Adolescents" fact sheet, National Council on Alcoholism, Inc., no date.

Accident Facts: 1989 Edition, National Safety Council, 1989, pages 22–23.

"Adult Children of Alcoholics (ACoA)" fact sheet, National Council on Alcoholism, Inc., page 1.

"An Outbreak of Teen Alcoholism" (interview with Derek Miller), *People* magazine, January 16, 1989, page 81.

"Drinking Myths," National Institute on Alcohol Abuse and Alcoholism, no date, 24 pages.

Driving Under the Influence: Toward a Drug-free Kansas, Kansas Department of Transportation, no date, 2 pages.

Elias, Marilyn, "Latchkey Teens More Likely To Drink, Smoke," *USA Today,* September 6, 1989, page D-1.

Johnston, Lloyd D., Ph.D., et al., *Drug Use, Drinking, and Smoking: National Survey Results from High School, College, and Young Adults Populations, 1975-1988,* U.S. Department of Health and Human Services, 1989, 339 pages.

Saltus, Richard (*Boston Globe*), "New Temperance Movement: Americans Are Drinking Less," published in the *Kansas City Star,* April 10, 1990, pages I-5–I-6.

Scott, Karen (Source: Gallup Organization), "The Dry '90s?" *Kansas City Star,* April 15, 1990, page I-5.

U.S. Department of Health and Human Services, News Release and Statement by Louis W. Sullivan, M.D., February 13, 1990, 46 pages.

Wallace, Dr. Robert, "'Tween 12 & 20" column, *Denver Post,* July 15, 1989, page F-1.

6

Because It Feels Good, Okay?

Giving my intimate feelings about my own mom being an alcoholic is one of the most difficult things I have done. I've struggled with writing my reflections of my family in this book. It's been difficult to relive the sorrow. Although stable now and respected as a leader for young people, I shudder when I flash back to how addiction-prone I was as a teen flirting with death.

Just fourteen, smoking pot, taking Valium, I was ready to check out on life via suicide.

I'll never forget the fear and weakness I embodied as I left St. Luke's Hospital in Kansas City weighing a grim sixty-eight pounds. I had tried suicide; and my dad had rushed me to the emergency room.

There were reasons I was susceptible and prone to addictive and abusive behavior. An addictive personality runs in my greater family; my mom is an alcoholic, two of my uncles died alcoholics, and both of my grandfathers are remembered as alcoholics. The predisposition was certainly there for me.

And as if I were mimicking a chorus-line routine, I fell into step, into the trap of addiction.

Millions of kids are just like I was—choosing to be victimized by the abuse of drugs, hooked on the high that exhilarates and eventually kills. And for the majority, the risk is worth the trauma. But why?

It Feels Good

After chatting with psychiatrist Joe King, I rummaged through my notes. One of the most obvious factors, Joe says, is that drinking simply feels good. I remember a passage from John Steinbeck's *Grapes of Wrath* that answers "Why drink?" pretty well:

> And always, if he had a little money, a man could get drunk. The hard edges gone, and the warmth. . . . Sitting in a ditch, the earth grew soft under him. Failures dulled and the future was no threat. And hunger did not skulk about, but the world was soft and easy, and a man could reach the place he started for. The stars came down wonderfully close and the sky was soft. Death was a friend, and sleep was death's brother. The old times come back—a girl with pretty feet who danced one time at home . . . ; when was that? . . . Warm here. And the stars down so close, and sadness and pleasure so close together, really the same thing. Like to stay drunk all the time. Who says it's bad? Who dares to say it's bad? Preachers. But they got their own kinda drunkenness. Thin, barren women. But they're too miserable to know. Reformers. But they don't bite deep enough into living to know. No—the stars are close and dear and I have joined the brotherhood of the worlds. And everything's holy—everything, even me.
>
> (*Grapes of Wrath,* New York: Penguin Books, 1976, page 186.)

Even if you've never tasted a drop of alcohol in your life, reading this, you get a pretty clear sense of why some people drink—why some are "driven to drink." It feels good. If we fail to acknowledge that simple fact with teenagers, we're destined to repeat the widespread errors of the '60s, when adults told kids that LSD and marijuana would lead them into escapism, damage their brains, ruin their sexual prowess, cost them bucks, and get them in jail—but never acknowledged that marijuana could also make them feel ecstatic.

So the typical kid, experimenting "just once," decides the old folks didn't know what they were talking about. They had told him grass was all bad; but his first sampling tells him it will help him hit on the most wonderful sensations he's ever felt. So he falls headlong into all the negatives of drugs because it feels good.

Let's learn a lesson as we coach yet another generation on the pitfalls of booze—let's admit that the reason many people drink is that it simply feels good to them.

The Booze Band-Aid: Self-Medication

Self-medication, taking alcohol to feel better, is one of the basic reasons kids drink. They'll try to drown in booze because:

• *Growing into adulthood is complicated.* If you're an adult, take a sixty-second look at your own life—your responsibilities, your relationships, your worries, your schedule, your past. Kids notice the complexity of today's adulthood and often feel unprepared to handle it!

• *Booze provides the false coping mechanism of "magical thinking."* When a youngster feels the need to escape unhappiness or boredom, she or he simply slips into magical dreams, play-acting, and games. As these imaginative activities are no longer "acceptable" in a growing child, she or he finds activities to prolong this mechanism.

Soon magical thinking becomes interest-consuming video games or preoccupation with television or comic books or books or pretending to "cruise" the local mall. But the nearer an adolescent gets to "adulthood," the more these activities are considered immature. Our culture, of course, has no fine line as to when adulthood begins: Perhaps it's at age eighteen when the teen gains voting rights and other new legal privileges. Perhaps it's at age twenty-one with additional legal privileges. Or perhaps it's after marriage, when the responsibilities of independence from family are clearly defined.

Realizing the proximity of any symbol of "adulthood," the teenager who has retreated to magical thinking as a life-long coping mechanism might begin to try drugs and to drink. (Actually, a magical thinker will probably drink and then try drugs. Joe King pointed out to me that, except for the volatile curse of crack-cocaine addiction, a substance-abuse rule of thumb is that everybody strung out on other drugs has used alcohol, but not necessarily vice versa.)

• *Kids are sometimes "trained" to have a low frustration tolerance.* That is, they are allowed to enjoy instant gratification by adults who are too distracted or too unskilled to respond maturely to whining and complaining. Kids who get what they want rarely can associate the fulfillment of their needs and wants with the future. They are not accustomed to putting off gratification, to making sacrifices in favor of a future goal. They are unwilling to put up with frustration until they are satisfied.

When life nearing adulthood doesn't treat him or her with the same indulgence that an immediate-gratification childhood did, the adolescent might turn to booze, which will make the teen feel good right now.

• *Narcissism is also to blame.* Focusing on themselves as the center of the universe can drive kids to drink. Mom and Dad might reinforce the attitude that parents simply exist to please their children and soothe their every hurt.

Society as an Enabler

Wanting to feel good isn't the only factor in why kids take dope, why they drink themselves sick. Joe King tells me the social and cultural backdrop of North America actually encourages misuse and addiction to alcohol and other drugs. These quotes from the book *Not My Kid* are similar to the comments I hear weekly as I speak to high-school and college-age groups:

> "When I was prostituting to get drugs, a lot of respectable businessmen would pick me up. Doctors would even pay me off with drugs."
>
> "I was over at this deacon's house from my church and he had a bunch of ups and downs."
>
> "My counselor told me it was okay to do pot and alcohol as long as I didn't do anything heavier."
>
> "I got high with a Jesuit priest at my school."
>
> (Beth Polson and Miller Newton, *Not My Kid: A Parent's Guide to Kids and Drugs,* page 139.)

We adults live in a chemically oriented culture. We're a consumer society sold out to the magical quick fix. Is it any wonder our teenagers succumb to the notion that life is supposed to be chemically treated?

The ins and outs of our pill-popping culture are regularly expounded on from North America's pulpits, in newspaper editorials from Walla Walla to Washington, D.C. And I don't think we need to add any earthshaking cultural philosophy here on why we are the way we are. Actually, I'm more interested in the fact that we're a society that can change.

We can dump our dependency on drugs so our kids can grow up in a twenty-first century surrounded by more awesome activities than getting stone drunk every weekend or snorting to cope. We can change.

One of the first signs in the United States that we as a society were getting fed up with booze and crack and glue-sniffing and marijuana was the publishing of the 1989 National Institute on Drug Abuse (NIDA) survey. Dan Sperling in *USA Today* (August 1, 1989, page A-1) announced that "drug use in the USA has dropped to the lowest point in a decade, and only half as many people used cocaine last year as in 1985." Besides crack-cocaine addiction, all categories of drug abuse were lower than in the previous three years. For example, the rate of those twelve to seventeen who had ever tried marijuana had dropped steadily since 1979, from 31 percent to 17 percent in 1988!

At the time, the director of the White House Office of National Drug Control Policy, William Bennett, said, "This is the largest drop we've ever seen" since the surveys began in 1972. The basic reason, Bennett said, "is a triumph of changed attitudes. The people who say 'All is lost,' and 'We can't win,' and 'Let's legalize,' have never been more wrong.

"Drugs are potent," Bennett continued, "cheap and available almost everywhere, and yet millions of Americans who once used them regularly appear now to have recently given them up altogether."

Secretary of Health and Human Services Louis Sullivan agreed: "These figures show that we can have an effect, and that what we're doing is working."

Although highly criticized as a politically motivated announcement, the NIDA survey very simply sketched an exciting trend in our society, noting that even former users are tired of the illusions of drugs. In some of the alcohol-related findings, the survey reported:

• Alcohol use in the twelve-to-seventeen age group dropped from 31 percent to 25 percent from 1985 to 1988.

• Fifty percent of those ages twelve to seventeen had tried alcohol at least once in their lives, 45 percent had used it in the previous year, and 25 percent had used it during the previous month. These numbers were all declines—from 56 percent, 52 percent, and 31 percent respectively.

We've obviously still got our work cut out for us to battle for a drug-free America, but the corner has been turned. Plan on being encouraged more as in Part II of *It's Killing Our Kids* we overview a multitude of ways individuals and groups across North America are making a dent in substance abuse. We can change as a society. We don't have to send our kids into a milieu of chemical dependency!

Consentual Validation

Joe King retermed a phrase I'm all too familiar with. He called it "consentual validation." I call it peer pressure.

Again, volumes of clinical and popular reports reveal the hassles of teenage peer pressure—as if it's only a teenage phenomenon! So we don't need to belabor the point here that a kid gets into destructive behavior often because an individual or group expects that behavior. He wants approval from people he admires.

Perhaps a quick look at one of the most revealing experiments in peer pressure will give us some insights into more adequately prepping our teenagers to resist destructive conformity in any form.

In his book *Preparing for Adolescence,* James Dobson relates an interesting study. A team of doctors invited ten teenagers to sit in a classroom to ostensibly study how well each perceived a lesson depending on where he or she sat in the room.

The researchers held up cards at the front of the room. On each card were three lines—line A, line B, and line C. Each line, the instructor said, was a different length. As the instructor pointed to each line on a card, the teenagers were to raise hands as to which they perceived was the longest line on that card. The directions were repeated to ensure everyone understood.

The instructor then raised the first card and pointed to line A.

What one student didn't know was that the other nine had been secretly instructed to raise their hands at the second longest line on each card. Although line A on the first card was clearly shorter than line B, all nine students raised their hands as the instructor pointed to line A. The teenager being studied looked around in disbelief. After the experiment, he recalled that he thought, *I must not have been listening during the directions. Somehow I missed the point, and I'd better do what everybody else is doing or they'll laugh at me.* So, of course as most of us adults would probably do, too, he raised his hand with the rest of the group.

The researchers again repeated the instructions clearly: The students were to raise their hands at the longest line on each card. Holding up the second card, again the nine voted for the wrong line. Dobson reports "the confused fellow became more tense over his predicament, but eventually he raised his hand with the group once again. Over and over he voted with the group, even though he knew they were wrong."

Dobson points out that "more than 75 percent of the young people tested behaved that same way. They sat there time after time, saying a short line was longer than a long line! They simply didn't have the courage to say, 'The group is wrong.'"

A key variation in the study revealed something every parent should remember about equipping a teenager to stand courageous when peer pressure pushes toward destructive behavior. If only one other student voted for the right line, then the chances were significantly improved that the youth being studied would stick by his choice of the correct line, voting against the eight others. Dobson's message to teenagers is clear: "If you have even one friend who will stand with you against the group, you probably will have more courage too. But when you're all by yourself, it's pretty difficult to take your stand alone."

Get realistic about the peer pressure teenagers feel to try dope, to drink alcohol. Remember the old "Candid Camera" sequence on television, when a guinea-pig adult would enter an elevator only to find everyone facing the blank back wall? In every case, the "victim" of the prank slowly, finally would turn to illogically face that back wall as well. The most remarkable peer pressure "Candid Camera" joke I remember viewing was a sketch in which everyone in a doctor's waiting room sat in their underwear as the victim arrived! He would sit uncomfortably and squirm whenever newcomers would saunter in, quickly strip to their BVD's and act as if nothing were unusual. Again, almost without exception, the poor guinea pig would slowly, awkwardly begin to pull off his own clothes until all the planted actors would begin to laugh, "You're on Candid Camera!"

Aren't we all susceptible to peer pressure? Who among us hasn't at some time sacrificed ourselves to save our pride? Consentual validation is one of the major reasons kids try drugs like alcohol. In one survey, nine out of ten kids said their first puffs on a marijuana joint and their first sips of beer were only to impress their friends (Polson and Newton, *Not My Kid: A Parent's Guide to Kids and Drugs,* page 55).

Tom Klaus, author of *Healing Hidden Wounds,* and a youth-worker friend from years back, wrote and reminded me about emphasizing the complexity of the peer-pressure reason for drinking among teenagers. It's not just because they want to fit in and have no choice about succumbing to the rule of the mob. Tom says, "You, like me, Jerry, have read repeatedly about the impact of peer pressure on a teen's decision to use and abuse substances. Every time I read this I get steamed because I believe it misses completely an important link in the chain to addiction—the addictive patterns of the teen's parents."

Tom goes on: "I've met lots of kids who've had their first experience of alcohol or other drug use because of peer pressure. For this reason the role of peer pressure can't be denied. But I can't say that I know any who are addicts because of peer pressure. In every case I've found that the young addict was predisposed to addiction by the composition, structure and experiences of her or his family of origin."

Generally, I agree with Tom. So let's look at another category of the reasons kids get in over their heads in alcohol: the family factors.

All in the Family

I mentioned that my extended family figured into my own teenage flirtations with drugs. Is your family, like mine, predisposed to substance abuse? To addictive behavior?

Experts agree that a family environment which permits or even encourages alcohol and other drug abuse can be a major factor in a teenager's addiction. Carrie, a sixteen-year-old from Arkansas, shook her blonde permed hair away from her face as she said, "Yeah. My friends who get drunk on weekends usually get their beer from older brothers or sisters. I know a few kids whose parents actually buy it for them. They say, 'If you're going to drink, we'd rather you drink at home instead of out on the road or in some sleazy place.' So they buy liquor for their own kids! It's like they're ordering them to go ahead and get drunk!"

Unfortunately, the kind of families that actively encourage each other into substance abuse are not the families that bother to read books like *It's Killing Our Kids.* So let's not bother analyzing the extremes of how a family can push teenagers to alcohol and other drug dependency. Let's look instead at subtler indications that a family is providing a "drug-pushing" atmosphere right at home. Think carefully through the following checklist. If several of the items describe your family life, perhaps it's time to rethink your family's dependence on chemicals:

Is Yours A Drug/Alcohol-Pushing Family? A Quiz

_____ Do you regularly use medications, prescriptions, or over-the-counter drugs to lose weight, gain weight, to stay awake or relax?

_____ Does your family doctor prescribe pain or mood-altering medication for you for minor illnesses?

_____ Does your family find drug-culture humor entertaining?

_____ Does your teenager listen to pro-drug, satanic, or music with violent themes, particularly as an "escape" alone in his or her room?

_____ Do you allow your teenager to regularly attend rock concerts or drug-oriented movies?

_____ Do local stores in your area sell drug paraphernalia? If so, is your teenager allowed to frequent such stores?

_____ Does your family avoid talking openly about the use of alcohol and other drugs?

_____ Do you allow your teenager large blocks of unaccounted-for time, particularly on weekend nights?

_____ Do you mostly ignore changes in your teenager's behavior—in school grades, in sleep patterns, in moods?

_____ Is there usually alcohol in the house? If so, is your family policy on its use clearly stated?

You may have scored cleanly in that little evaluation. But your family can still certainly work at not being one of the factors that allows your kid to slide into substance abuse. Make some definite plans as a family to counter these general reasons why kids get into alcohol and other drugs:

• *Lack of information drives some kids to drink.* Is your house a place where facts about booze and alcohol, and consequences of substance abuse are discussed?

• *Lack of clearly defined values, personal beliefs, and appropriate behaviors allows some kids to bumble into substance abuse.* Are you as a family honest and clear on your values and standards?

• *Discomfort in social situations prompts some teenagers to feel that it's only proper to walk around with drink in hand.* Do you as a family talk about how to refuse alcohol politely? How to resist peer pressure to drink and do drugs?

• *Boredom and thrill-seeking hook lots of teenagers into substance abuse.* Is your house a fun, stimulating place to live, or are you simply surviving?

• *Rebellion, difficulty in coping with problems, and depression invite kids to escape through drugs.* Are you dealing with these serious warning signs? Are you getting help for the problems in your family?

There is mounting evidence that families with a history of alcoholism and substance addiction pass on a genetic proclivity toward addiction from generation to generation. We'll look at that disturbing idea shortly. But even if a family's contribution to a kid's drug dependence is merely environmental, it is sometimes especially revealing to plot the actual ancestry of the family. What sort of family environments were the teenager's parents, grandparents, and even great-grandparents raised in?

Go ahead. Take a deep breath of honesty and plot out your family tree in what's called a genogram. Follow the sample diagram shown in Figure 6-1, adapting and expanding as necessary for your own genogram following the outline provided in Figure 6-2. Plot natural parents' and stepparents' families. Mark clearly any occurrences of:

• alcoholism and heavy drinking,

• any other substance abuses or addictions,

• any criminal characteristics,

Figure 6-1
Sample Genogram

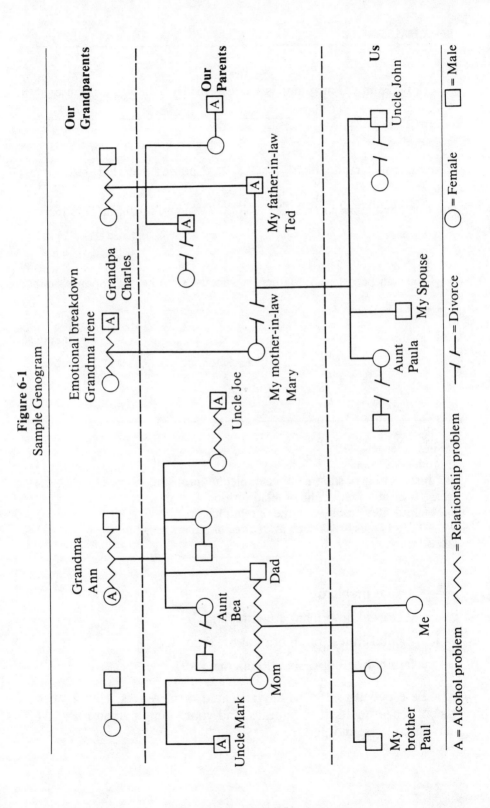

Our Grandparents

Our Parents

Us

Grandma Ann

Emotional breakdown
Grandma Irene

Grandpa Charles

My father-in-law
Ted

Uncle John

Uncle Joe

My mother-in-law
Mary

My Spouse

Aunt Paula

Uncle Mark

Aunt Bea

Dad

Mom

My brother Paul

Me

A = Alcohol problem   ⋀⋀⋀ = Relationship problem   ⊣⊢ = Divorce   ◯ = Female   ☐ = Male

Figure 6-2
Your Family Genogram: Is There a History of Substance Abuse?

- -

Your maternal grandparents ○ □ | Spouse's maternal grandparents ○ □

Your paternal grandparents ○ □ | Spouse's paternal grandparents ○ □

- -

○ Your mother | □ Your father | ○ Spouse's mother | □ Spouse's father

- -

You | Your spouse

- -

Your teenager

○ indicates female
□ indicates male
"A" inside circle or square indicates alcohol problem.
——— Indicates family line of relationship.
⋀⋀⋀ Indicates problem in line of relationship.
—/ /— Indicates break such as divorce or "disowning" in line of relationship.

- sexual problems,
- distorted emotional attachments,
- mental illness or emotional breakdowns,
- family breakups, abandonments, etc.

Be especially alert to any repeated occurrences. History has a way of repeating itself in families, and your young person isn't invulnerable to those old patterns.

Be as honest as possible to determine what sort of behavior patterns, coping mechanism and values have been being passed down to your youngster. If you're unaware of any particular dysfunctional factors in a distant relative's history, chat with trusted family members who know the facts.

If your family genogram provides more revelations than you can sort out by yourself, be sure to seek a professional counselor who can help you through a more formal genogram exercise and assist in understanding some of the ancestral patterns you've inherited.

As interesting as a genogram is in its own right, remember that what you're looking for is an answer to: Is it possible that my teenager has some built-in proclivity for substance abuse?

What does your family genogram reveal as far as your offspring's vulnerability to patterns that might encourage substance abuse? Be sure to think carefully through chapter 9 on what a parent can do to raise drug-free teenagers.

But it isn't just occurrences, habits, and patterns in family life that can affect a kid's tendencies to fall into addictive behavior. Research is increasingly suggesting that addictive proclivity is passed genetically through family bloodlines.

The Genetic Factor

The April 18, 1990 *Wall Street Journal* had an incredible announcement on page B-1. "Alcoholism is Linked to a Gene," the headline said.

I had an interesting discussion with an older fellow a few weeks ago on the controversy of "Is alcoholism a genetic disease?" His point was that if it were, then addicts of every genre would be playing the old rationalization game that they weren't responsible for their actions.

"But what if it's true?" I had asked the old man.

"It's not true." He was adamant. "If they wanted to quit drinking, they would. Thousands do. Just like smoking or drugs. If the person decides to quit, he can."

"So if he doesn't quit, it just says he's not trying hard enough —that he really wants to keep on drinking or smoking or taking drugs?"

"Of course." Somehow, some button was being pushed in the old guy. "It's this whole generation's problem of not taking responsibility. An excuse for everything is 'My parents didn't raise me right.' Did you know a kid sued his parents a few years ago in Chicago for not raising him right? He was getting in trouble at college and in trouble financially and legally; and who was to blame? His parents, of course! This whole business of addiction being a disease, of being born an alcoholic is just another hustle at blaming anyone or anything but the one who's really responsible for the problem! Alcohol has nothing to do with genetic disease."

Three weeks later, I was carefully cutting the *Journal* article out to send to the old guy. I don't think it'll change his mind, but it does suddenly force us to face the question: Are addicts destined genetically to be addicts?

The article is careful to explain that the UCLA and University of Texas researchers involved in the study do not claim to have found a gene that forces a person to become an addict: "The findings could lead within five years to the availability of a blood test to detect the presence of genes associated with the condition [of alcoholism]. Such tests, the scientists say, could help divert children predisposed to alcoholism from situations that increase the chances of becoming an alcoholic." *Predisposed* seems to be the key word.

The article says that researchers report finding a link between the presence of the receptor gene for dopamine (a neurotransmitter in the brain associated with pleasure-seeking behaviors) and alcoholism. With about 100,000 genes in the body, the article by Sonia Nazario says, it is remarkable that 77 percent of the individuals with this gene are alcoholics.

The *Journal* article reports that UCLA-based researcher Ernest Noble says the research ". . . more firmly establishes alcoholism as a disease and adds to evidence that genetic factors are as important as environmental factors in predisposing people to the disease."

Interestingly enough, the article mentions another researcher who disagrees with the conclusions of the study. David Comings, director of the City of Hope Medical Center Department of Medical Genetics in Duarte, California, seems to feel the announcement of finding a single gene link to alcoholism is a bit ambitious:

"There might be another gene more important than this one," Comings says. The article cautions that many genetic experts say that "unlike genetic diseases such as . . . cystic fibrosis or Down's syndrome, for which one gene is thought to be the cause, alcoholism is considered to be tied to several genes. That means no one genetic marker can tag all individuals at risk and other genes must still be identified and studied."

But the excitement over the study is hardly dampened by these criticisms—mostly, I think, because so many people want to believe in the "magic" of finding in one gene a red-flag warning to families that their children are predisposed to alcoholism. We want to believe scientists might find a means to end hereditary alcoholism by chemically blocking that one gene's effects.

A final paragraph in the article bothers me in the same way the proliferation of weight-reduction programs in our culture bothers me. I just hope alcohol treatment isn't getting to be big business the way weight-loss is. The *Journal* sums it up this way: "The estimated $4 billion-a-year alcohol treatment industry hopes the study will help convince more alcoholics that theirs is a disease requiring medical care. 'Most families still don't really believe this is a disease. They feel ashamed and embarrassed by it,' says Frank Picard, who counsels Portland, Oregon alcoholics on getting treatment. 'This will help them see alcoholism as a health problem. It will help them get help.'"

An "Addictive Personality"?

While the verdict is still out on the accuracy of selecting a specific gene that is linked to alcoholism, a broader controversy rages in many scientific circles as to whether addiction itself is physiologically "caused" or is flatly a symptom of upbringing.

Either way, there's certainly no controversy that we as a culture are suffering from a contagion of addiction.

Again, the *Wall Street Journal* profiles the amazing addiction phenomenon in our culture with an article headlined: "Baffling Plague: As Addiction Crisis Mounts, Experts Delve Into the Root Causes" (page A-1, August 1, 1990). The subtitle on the article by Joseph Pereira rambles on: "Scientists Probe Personality, Brain Chemistry; Genetics May Hold Vital Clues."

The article begins: "From cigarettes and prescription drugs to cocaine and heroin, virtually every American knows personally someone who suffers from addiction." It continues: "Scientists don't yet understand whether the key to addiction lies primarily in personality traits or in some chemical predisposition. Some researchers believe there are those who are destined to become addicts the moment they begin consuming an addictive substance because of the chemical makeup of the brain; others believe the answer lies with the state of mind of the user, and still others believe it is a combination of these forces."

Pereira says that recent studies suggest people with a shortage of endorphins, those tranquilizing neurochemicals in the brain, have a greater tendency toward addiction than others. Additional findings reveal that about 5 percent of the population is "immune" to the effects of caffeine because of their bodies' chemical makeup. So it would seem that addictions could be physiologically determined.

On the other hand, scientists note no drug addiction, and no alcohol abuse in the nation's Amish and Mormon communities, regardless of biochemistry and personality. These findings suggest, say researchers, that "the prime component in addiction is upbringing and environment."

What some people are calling an "addictive personality" may be no more than a condition resulting from an untreated mental disorder. The *Journal* piece continues: "The National Institute for Drug Addiction says . . . that many young addicts—those generally under the age of 21—were led to drugs or alcohol by some form of clinical mental disorder that had gone untreated. 'The early recognition and effective treatment of psychiatric disorders should be able to prevent a sizable portion of the drug problem among the young,' the federal drug agency said in a recent report."

I asked Joe King about this phrase I've heard bantered about— addictive personality. He's already pretty well analyzed me as a codependent in my role as an adult child of an alcoholic. But do I have an addictive personality? Does anybody?

"Not really, Jerry," he said. "Now, there is an obsessive-compulsive disorder that some folks might misname as addictive personality. This particular disorder, when surrounded by certain experiences, is seen as an obsessive-compulsive personality.

"There are about thirty centers around the country studying this condition," Joe said. "But no, I don't believe we could say even with the recent announcements about genetic links to alcoholism that there is such a thing as an 'addictive personality' a predisposition to become a substance-abusing addict without choice. There can be a proclivity toward addictions; but there is always the factor of choice."

The World Health Organization, reports *L.A. Weekly,* defines compulsive/addictive behavior as "a pathological relationship to any mood-altering experience that has life-damaging consequences" ("Detox America," August 2, 1990, page 22).

So kids drink, whether they're addicted or not. Pathological or not, they want the mood-altering experiences of booze regardless of its possible life-damaging consequences. They sniff model-airplane glue. They jab themselves with dirty needles full of heroin. They ignore the future. Why? "Because," a kid leaning against a chain-link fence once slurred to me, "because I want to."

And that's what we're up against—a fascination with booze whether they or we understand exactly why. A much clearer point is: What can we do about this age-old phenomenon we barely understand? As we'll find out, we can do plenty!

PART TWO

The Solutions

An old farmer in the Ozarks told me this life-long story of hope from his own childhood:

"As a boy, a fellow named Jackie lived down the hill a ways. Whenever his dad would get real drunk and beat him about something, Jackie would come on up to our house and have supper or sleep overnight.

"One summer night, I heard the noise of the ruckus down at Jackie's, and pretty soon here he'd come to sleep over on our sleeping bags out in the back yard.

"About midnight, Jackie was telling me about how his pop was probably right: Jackie was no good, would always be a nobody—couldn't ever do anything right.

"Then he pointed his finger like a gun up to the black sky and whispered "Bang" as he pulled the imaginary trigger.

"A star fell.

"Without missing a beat, Jackie glanced over at me, put his gun barrel finger up to his lips and blew away the smoke.

"I told him that a kid who knew how to shoot a star could do anything.

"And from that day on, he could."

People *can* change; we *can* win the war against alcohol and other substance abuse—if we acknowledge alcohol as North American teenagers' drug of choice. And if we work together!

7

We *Can* Change Our Communities!

We can change the alcohol-abuse picture in North America. We're on the upswing of winning the war on substance abuse, and the trend will continue if we acknowledge alcohol as the substance-abuser's drug of choice and if we work together.

One of the obvious targets of activism against alcohol abuse is in the arena of laws. And it's amazing the strides that have been taken in alcohol-abuse problems such as drinking and driving. For example, most states in the United States have passed laws mandating that all those who are caught driving drunk will immediately lose their driving licenses for thirty days. In 1982, twenty-two of the states enacted that law, and that year the death toll from drunk driving dropped 11 percent nationally—that's a saving of five thousand human beings, perhaps including you! The raising of the national drinking age to twenty-one prompted similar drops in fatalities—in 1982 the highway death toll for the New Year's holiday was the lowest since 1949.

People are changing their drinking habits because of these new, tougher laws. The U.S. Supreme Court's recent approval of sobriety checkpoints is bound to continue the trend of making drinkers think twice about drinking and driving. In a six-to-three ruling, the court said that checkpoints do not violate the Fourth Amendment protection against unreasonable search and seizure. Studies have shown that these highway fatalities have dropped in at least one state where checkpoints have been used.

Let's look at a few other examples that just might prompt you to check out your local, state, and national laws on this horrendous problem.

A Virginia Federation of Communities for Drug-Free Youth poster warns: "New Laws Hit DUIs [Driving Under the Influence] Where It Hurts—The Pocketbook." The poster spells out quite clearly the new "get-tough" approach some states are taking toward drunk driving, and particularly toward those under the drinking age:

> One sip of alcohol can impair your motor skills for a full year. There's a new law. Get caught under age with alcohol and you'll lose your license. You don't have to be drunk. You don't have to be driving. You don't even have to have your license yet (your privilege of getting it will be suspended). It's not a threat. It's the law.

In Ohio, a Department of Highway Safety pamphlet reads, "Those convicted of DUI are subject to the minimum penalties of time in jail, driver's-license suspension, and $150-$1,000 in fines. (NOTE: Juveniles are subject to varying penalties, depending on the juvenile court.) Some judges may give you the option of serving time for a first offense in a driver intervention program for traffic safety education and the assessment of alcohol and drug dependency, and may make undergoing treatment part of the sentence.

"For your first offense, you will serve at least 3 days in jail, and your license will be suspended from 60 days to 3 years.

"For your second offense, you will spend at least 10 days in jail, and your license will be suspended from 120 days to 5 years.

"For your third offense, you will spend at least 30 days in jail and your license will be suspended 180 days to 10 years."

Another brochure published by the state of Missouri Department of Public Safety, Division of Highway Safety, promises, "Missouri Will Show You Drunk Driving Is a Crime." The following facts and figures are taken from this brochure. The costs are based on a 1986 arrest of a drunk driver with no previous record.

Step 1: Arrest
If a Missouri law-enforcement officer has reason to suspect you are driving while intoxicated and pulls you over, he may administer

field sobriety tests. If you fail these tests, he will place you under arrest for DWI (Driving While Intoxicated) and take you in to have your blood alcohol concentration (BAC) tested. This is usually performed at a law-enforcement facility. If your BAC tests between .10 percent and .12 percent, you will be charged with DWI and booked into jail. If your BAC tests at .13 percent or above, the officer will take your driver's license on the spot, and book you into jail.

Cost: Your car may be impounded and you will have to pay a basic towing fee, plus a daily storage charge. $50.

If you want to get out of jail, you will have to post bond. If you use a bailsman, you might pay a flat fee plus 10 percent of the bond, or you might pay a minimum fee up to a certain amount. Average, $60.

Step 2: Attorney

You may decide to hire an attorney to represent you in court. If the judge deems you cannot afford a private attorney, a public defender may be appointed for you.

Cost: An average of $400 if you hire an attorney and plead guilty.

Step 3: County Court

Your case will first be presented to the judge for arraignment, and then will go to trial. You will end up paying court costs, a fee to the Victim's Compensation Fund, subpoena fees, and sheriff's department fees. In addition, you will be assessed a fine which will vary from court to court (usually from $250 to $500 for a first-offense conviction).

Cost:	Fine for a plea of guilty	$300
	Crime Victim's Compensation Fund	$ 36
	Subpoena fee	$ 2
	Sheriff's department	$ 3.80
	Basic court costs on misdemeanor	$ 42.95
	Total	$384.75

Step 4: Auto Insurance

In many cases, your insurance may be canceled. If not, premiums will increase.

Cost: Premium for one year on a 1985 Tempo with no prior tickets or accidents (a "high risk" premium that will be in effect for five years), $2,046.00

Step 5: Driver's License Bureau

If your license was suspended by administrative action, or if the judge conditioned an Alcohol-Related Traffic Offenders' Program (ARTOP) course, you must bring proof of satisfactory completion of the ARTOP to the license bureau. In addition, you must file a form to show proof of financial responsibility.

Cost: Reinstatement fee, $20

Step 6: Alcohol Education

If required, you must attend a state-certified ARTOP for ten hours of classroom instruction. If your license was suspended by administrative action, you must have proof of satisfactory completion of the ARTOP in order to have your license reinstated.

Cost: ARTOP schools range from $50 to $125, with the average being $80 to $100.

Total cost to you: $3,020.75

Keep in mind that most of these figures are minimums. Additional costs are incurred if:

- You hire an attorney, plead not guilty, and take the case to jury trial.

- Your attorney requires depositions from witnesses.

- You plead not guilty, require a jury trial and lose; then you may pay more in fines and court costs.

- The judge sentences you to treatment. Then you will also have to pay these treatment costs, which can be extremely expensive.

Hidden costs include time lost from work for your trial, meetings with your probation officer, attorney, and insurance agent, and treatment. Many people lose their jobs, especially if their work involves driving. Some people end up selling their vehicle to meet costs and because they can't afford insurance. You'll have to pay for alternate transportation or bear the burden of asking family and friends to provide transportation for you.

The brochure winds up with this reminder: "If you use a little sense, you could save big dollars. . . . Don't discover your drinking limits by accident!"

On the national level, strong measures are being suggested, as well. For example, former Surgeon General C. Everett Koop launched a sweeping campaign encouraging the enactment of these provisions for reducing alcohol-impaired driving:

• Increase the federal excise taxes on alcoholic beverages to at least five cents a drink. Increasing the price of alcoholic beverages through taxation delays under-age drinking and reduces heavy drinking. The revenue should be earmarked for impaired-driving programs.

• Reduce the legal blood-alcohol limits for automobile drivers from .10 to .08 percent. For drivers under twenty-one, the level should be 0.00 percent.

• Provide funds for public service advertisements for pro-health/ pro-safety messages to counter the two-billion-dollar annual alcohol advertising and promotion budgets of alcohol producers.

• Eliminate "happy hours" and other reduced-price promotions of alcoholic beverages.

• End voluntarily the alcohol industry's official sponsorship of sports events.

• Halt voluntarily the use of celebrities who have strong appeal to young people in alcohol advertising that implies a link between drinking with athletic, social, and sexual success.

The *Nashville Tennessean* reported in its June 25, 1989 edition, "The American Academy of Family Physicians, American Heart Association, Center for Science in the Public Interest, Association of Junior Leagues, and numerous other groups have all endorsed Koop's plan . . . and have urged President Bush to back this groundbreaking initiative."

Find out your state's laws against drunk driving, public drunkenness, selling alcohol to minors, serving inebriated customers, etc. And if what you find isn't to your liking, get radical. Get active in a group that's changing things—a group like MADD.

Getting MADD

One of the most astonishing successes in grass-roots activism in recent years is the Mothers Against Drunk Driving (MADD) story.

MADD was founded in California in 1980, and its aggressive campaign resulted in California's passage of the toughest drunk driving laws in the country at the time.

Shortly thereafter, MADD erupted into a nationwide, nonprofit corporation. Numerous successes have fueled the MADD operation, both at the national office in Texas and in communities throughout the United States. Since 1980, more than one thousand drunk driving laws have been enacted nationwide. The rights of victims and survivors of alcohol-related crashes are now being viewed more equitably in the criminal justice system.

Youth programs, both cooperating with and sponsored by MADD, have sprung up in almost every state, providing young people with a sound background in alcohol awareness and education.

I interviewed Micky Sadoff, president of this organization that has set the pace for doing something about substance abuse. Join with me as we talk with the head of this remarkable organization:

JERRY: Micky, what is MADD up to these days? Are things working?

MICKY: I don't know another organization that has been responsible for changing social attitudes about drinking and driving so radically. We are very proud of the work we've done—grass-roots work all over the country, changing attitudes, saving lives, helping victims. Sadly, we are not ready to go out of business. We're looking ahead at the things that need to be done. We have a full slate of areas that we work in: legislation, victim assistance, monitoring the justice system, education.

JERRY: What about helping a victim? Exactly what does MADD do?

MICKY: MADD is the leading victim-assistance organization in the country, and probably the world, barring the Red Cross. Unfortunately, we have an unending supply of victims. Daily, new victims are drafted into this war and the majority of them have never had any contact with the criminal justice system. They aren't used to dealing with devastating grief in which there is no time to say goodbye.

We can be there with support, peer counseling, attending court with families if they wish, distributing literature and so on. We are very proud of our victim assistance. We sent in three crisis teams to Carrollton, Kentucky, during the Kentucky crash and are continuing to work with those families, because the grief goes on.

JERRY: How large is your network?

MICKY: We have four hundred chapters across the country, as well as chapters in New Zealand, Australia, Canada, and England. Altogether, we have 2.95 million members and supporters.

JERRY: Tell me the difference for a drunk driving offender now as compared to before MADD began.

MICKY: Before, it was commonly thought that a drunk driving crash was not a crime; it was an unfortunate incident. The general attitude was that drunk drivers don't mean to hurt anyone; they have a drinking problem and we need to address that problem. It was a slap on the wrist, a point-reduction school where you went in and went to a few classes and got it expunged from your record. There might have been a fine. The attitude was that this is no big deal, and if you killed or injured someone, it was still no big deal because you didn't mean to do it.

JERRY: Offenders were generally not put behind bars?

MICKY: Rarely was anybody ever going to jail for killing or injuring with a car. Multiple offenses were ignored. It was not a priority for the judges or law enforcement. But things have changed. I think that people are looking at drunk driving now as a violent crime—as the leading cause of death for our young people. I think society is realizing these deaths and injuries are preventable, that driving drunk is deserving of punishment.

Laws are changing. I am not sure that every drunk driving conviction gets a form of punishment, but punishment is now at least considered in some way. For example, the record can't be erased in most states. If you contract multiple offenses, it's all there on the record. A third offense penalty will be stiffer than a second offense because the second offense isn't erased, isn't bargained down to a crime unrelated to alcohol or a lesser charge. Driving drunk is taken much more seriously than it was even ten years ago.

But we are definitely not there yet, because I don't think it's taken seriously enough. My best example of this problem is the Carrollton bus crash of Larry Mahoney, who killed twenty-seven people, injured fourteen severely, and received a sixteen-year sentence from the jury in Kentucky. That sixteen years, eligible for parole in eight, is less than a few months for each one of the victims that he killed—which is absurd. Absolutely absurd. So we are not there yet.

On the other hand, we have seen more drunk-driving homicides get charged with second-degree murder; people who have terrible records of multiple offenses have been incarcerated for thirty or forty years. I'm sure they are out in ten or fifteen; but we're getting somewhere. Too often in the past we've seen somebody who is a repeat offender, who has killed, or killed repeatedly, and the penalty is a six-month or one-year sentence. I'm sure that still happens, and it is appalling. But on the whole, there are some stiffer sentences being handed down out there.

JERRY: What is the typical sentence for minors who kill under the influence?

MICKY: I think it is getting stiffer. The sad part is that if a young person is the drunk driver in a crash in which there is injury or death, the killed or injured person is often a close friend of the driver! It's a difficult situation when you have a parent whose daughter was killed by a drunk driver saying, "Well, I know Tim, and I don't want him to go to jail." The victim's voice often has a strong influence in sentencing, so you may find young people getting probation or several hours of community service. And yet these are drunk drivers who have killed with their cars. There was, however, a boy in my community who went to jail for killing. He went to jail for a year and served the full year.

JERRY: What penal response would MADD be satisfied with for those who injure or kill while under the influence?

MICKY: Actually, it's a case-by-case evaluation. You can't say that everyone who kills with a car deserves to be put away for life. And more important than what I personally think or what MADD thinks is what the victims think. When we go into families we do not say that you must tell the judge that, for example, since this is a maximum five-year penalty, we demand five years. It is important that the victims, if they get to speak in the courtroom at all—which is another victims' right we're fighting for so families can be heard in this whole process—it's important that they themselves talk about their own ideas of the sentence deserved.

So, what MADD wants is generally what the victims want. Again, the Kentucky bus crash is a good example in which the victims' ideas of punishment deserved should have been carefully considered. MADD would want to know the victims' viewpoints; then that is what we would pursue as a sentence in a particular case.

JERRY: Do some families of victims want the death penalty?

MICKY: First of all, MADD has no position on capital punishment. Also, the death penalty isn't even an option in most states, because the charges are not murder charges but are generally "homicide by intoxicated use." These are lesser-degree felonies. There is not even a question in some states of a charge of second-degree murder, regardless of how many were killed by the drunk driver.

In the Kentucky case, Mahoney was originally charged with a capital crime offense, and that was reduced when those elements needed to convict him on that charge were not met. That's the only case in which it has ever come up for me that the victims might want the death penalty. I'm sure a lot of victims don't want to have to see that person in the courtroom, and might wish that person dead. But I've never had a victim come to me and say, "I'd like the death penalty."

JERRY: What do they generally want, life in prison?

MICKY: No, not necessarily. It varies. There are victim families who feel that that person should not go to jail. They feel imprisonment is not going to serve the public, that the drunk driver should do community service perhaps in a hospital where they'll see other victims of drunk driving crashes and see what they suffer.

I think what victims want—and I was a victim and went through the court system—is some voice. They want to be heard saying that this is what happened, this is the person who caused it, and some form of punishment is deserved because this is a crime. Victims want the justice system to know who it was that was killed or injured, what that person meant.

It's a cliché with us, but we say, "Until the victim's voice is heard, the truth, the whole truth, and nothing but the truth has not been heard."

It has been our fight to get the victim's voice heard in the courtroom, to allow somebody to get up at sentencing and say, "This is my beautiful daughter, who was eighteen years old, who was killed needlessly, who will never be with us again, and this is what she was like." That sounds very simple to you and me; but a lot of judges in many states, until MADD came along, wouldn't allow it. They wouldn't allow a picture to be shown in the courtroom of this child. They would not let family members get up and speak; and to this day often do not let family members get up and speak. Some judges wouldn't accept a letter from the victims until the person had been convicted.

Those are the things that I think frustrate victims most, that no one cares about what happened to this one human being or how the family has been devastated.

So sentencing is a state-by-state thing and a family-by-family situation. We do have recommendations, a menu of sanctions that are modeled for a state to look at, to work on, particularly regarding death and injury.

JERRY: Are the courts still too lenient with drunk driving offenders?

MICKY: It has gotten better. But in some cases it's still a situation of reducing charges down to lesser offenses. Why does that persist? Maybe because judges or prosecutors may be drinkers and know they themselves have driven after a few drinks now and then. Or instead of thinking *There I am, like the victim,* they think, *There I could be as the drunk driver too.* Besides, the jails are overcrowded and we really need to look at our alternative forms of sentencing. And MADD certainly agrees with that—let's impose alternate sentencing such as a weekend offenders program or sentencing in which drunk drivers get education along with incarceration.

But with the serious injuries and fatalities, I don't know what is going through the judges' minds. Many of them do give what I call stiff sentences, or maximum sentences, especially with repeat offenders.

I think judges need to send a message to the community that this crime is taken seriously. But judges actually only see a very small portion of the drunk-driving problems. There are almost two million arrests, and yet that's a small piece of the pie. There are people out there driving drunk every day who won't ever get caught until they kill or injure and get into the court system. Something needs to deter them—either news about strong sentencing or losing driver's licenses, or realizing that insurance costs will go up after drunk-driving convictions, or having a friend who cares enough to take the keys away so drunk drivers don't get behind the wheel.

JERRY: Has MADD had any input on alcohol advertising?

MICKY: We have a position about responsible marketing and advertising. And we certainly have gone to bat against those ads that show people who look as if they are under age—also against ads that portray someone sitting with a can of beer on a motorcycle or in a boat or some other form of transportation.

We find the marketing on college campuses very distasteful because a majority of college students are under age, although there's a long argument about campus ads for alcohol. The argument is that if you look at the total population of a college campus, the majority of students are over twenty-one. This is the total of those registered. But those who live on campus in dorms and fraternities are the ones who are targeted with the marketing, and most of them are under twenty-one. I have a nineteen- and a twenty-three-year-old, and I know.

The spring-break marketing on Padre Island, Texas or at Daytona Beach, Florida is amazing, considering that the majority of those kids are not only under-age college kids, but many of them are high-school kids as well. The actual commercial advertising on television—beer advertising, wine advertising—we have not taken a stand on.

JERRY: Isn't there a larger problem, that even if we got the penal response desired, alcohol is still the socially accepted drug of choice? What does MADD have to say about all that?

MICKY: We do a tremendous amount of education about drinking, itself. Raising the U.S. drinking age to twenty-one was one of our coups. We worked strongly in Congress to get the sanctions in place so states which didn't have twenty-one as their legal age would lose highway funds. And we worked to make those sanctions permanent so no state, after a period of time, could change the law and revert to a lower drinking age without loss of the highway funds.

Not only has it saved a tremendous number of lives in the past several years as it was implemented state by state, it also has slowed drinking in general, we believe.

JERRY: What else is MADD doing?

MICKY: We have a prom and graduation program, and educational materials for kids; we have a student library which goes to kids with drunk driving statistics, and we have a poster and essay contest about drinking and driving which had fifty thousand entrants this year.

Our members work with schools all the time at all ages. For example, my chapter developed lessons for three- and four-year-olds about seven or eight years ago which are still in use.

The problem in my mind is that I know beer is the drug of choice for kids and for their parents. I think a major part of the problem is parents who buy alcohol for parties like sixteenth birthdays and think it's fine because the child isn't using cocaine, heroine, PCP, marijuana, or whatever. I have horror stories in my community of parents who live in affluent suburbs leaving their sixteen- and seventeen-year-olds on weekends. That home, of course, is where the party is. The parents come home, the house has been trashed, and things have been stolen, and they don't understand why or how.

Every weekend, kids are looking for alcohol and finding it, and parents are looking the other way. They think it is fine; they know where the kids are. And many feel there is nothing they can do about it anyway because they, as parents, drink too. They think, *I drink myself, and I have no problem with having a party here.*

JERRY: It's as though they think it's a double standard to tell their kids not to drink when they do. As if kids should be able to run for president because adults can, or sign a billion-dollar engineering contract because adults do.

I think too many parents are bamboozled about feeling sheepish about "double standards." If nothing else, they must know that teenagers who drink are in a different legal standing than an adult who drinks, since the laws say drinking before age twenty-one is illegal!

MICKY: I am really angry at parents who don't think this is serious, who don't think they can have an impact—because they can. Parents are not giving them rules with regard to alcohol because they seem to remember back to their own high-school days of beer parties.

But it's not the same at all. The level of use is broader and the age of users is younger. It's really sad because I think the parents can make a difference by drawing a line and not turning the other way. We can give kids alternatives, or help fund alternatives, because not all these kids, I know, want to drink. They are just in situations where there is virtually nothing else to do. There is nothing wrong with being in somebody's house and watching MTV or something; but they need to know they can do that without having to have a beer while they're there. We've got to quit encouraging drinking.

Let me give an example. A friend's son was in Padre Island last week and he really thought that the drinking age there was eighteen because he was allowed as an eighteen-year-old to be in the bar with kids who could drink. Well, the law in that community was that eighteen-year-olds can be on the premises, but they are not supposed to drink.

But, of course, they were drinking; there is probably no realistic way that you could segregate ages after you allow them into a place. We have been fighting that in Wisconsin—they want to allow eighteen-year-olds on premises without letting them drink. And you know that is just a joke.

There are too many people who are breaking the law, winking at it. There are establishments that don't care—package stores and restaurants selling to kids. They don't take this seriously and they don't look at the devastation.

And the devastation is obvious. Besides drunk-driving crashes, you know very well from your research on suicide and family breakups that on down the line the alcohol-abuse problem is enormous. But I think too many people brush alcohol-abuse problems aside because we are in the middle of what they think is a drug war that somehow doesn't include the drug of alcohol.

JERRY: How do you maintain your communication network with victims of alcohol-related tragedies? Do they seek you out, or do you find them?

MICKY: We did not solicit victims at all for years, and then many would come to us six months or a year later and say, "I wish I had known you were here; thank goodness I saw something about you on television." Now what is accepted and allowable is we send a card which says we are here, we care, and here's our local telephone number. We also have a toll-free number in some areas, and we have a national toll-free number for victims. It's 1-800-GETMADD.

JERRY: What about the total number of employees, and how are you funded?

MICKY: There are about two hundred employees at any given time at the national office and out in the field as chapter administrators, state administrators, secretaries, and a few hired volunteer coordinators.

The majority of our funding comes from one-on-one contributions from individuals. On the average last year, I believe it was about thirteen to fourteen dollars per contributor. We do get some funding from corporations, and some from grants; but they are a very small portion of our budget. Local MADD groups raise money at the chapter level through whatever means they choose to. If they choose to use telemarketing or direct mail or a 5K run, as we have in our community, they may.

We don't get any compensation from anybody for any of the work we do with victims. On the other hand, we do not give any financial aid to victims at all. If a fund is started in a community, for example, MADD may help publicize it to buy a wheelchair or something, but we don't directly give or hold those funds.

JERRY: Do you receive grants from any of the beer or wine makers? Would you accept any?

MICKY: No. We stopped accepting any money from the liquor industry in '83 or '84. We now don't take any money from the alcohol industry due to the sensitivity of our victims; but that doesn't mean we don't work with the alcohol industry or restaurant associations or people that serve or sell alcohol. We promote, for example, the designated driver program with the National Restaurant Association. We do work with them, because obviously without their help, we are never going to change anything. We need to work with everybody.

JERRY: Why are you doing this? I mean, a schedule like this is grueling and it has to interrupt your family life. What is your personal motivation?

MICKY: I think the fact that my husband almost died in a car crash with a drunk driver is my motivation. I know it shortened his life. MADD really began for me after the crash.

It was January 16, 1982. He had a head injury. He still needs further surgery on an arm. He had a concussion and about a month later contracted bacterial meningitis. He almost died from infection in the brain because of the concussion. If he had not gotten to the hospital that day, he would have been dead that night. He was in ICU for ten days and it was touch and go.

JERRY: And the driver was . . .

MICKY: The driver was a repeat offender who lived five blocks from us, and was out driving because we didn't have a law then that took away his license. The trial was a year and a month after the crash. He was sentenced to, I think, one of the stiffest sentences at the time—to four and a half years in jail. He served two and was released to go back to school. He went to AA meetings and had every opportunity to clean up his act. I hope he did, because after all he went through and all the suffering he caused, I hope he turns his life around, and we'll have one less drunk driver on the road. So I really do wish him well.

His first offense was drunk driving. In his second offense, he crossed the center line in a pickup truck and hit us head-on. He had had twenty-two to twenty-five drinks in a bar within a three-hour period, and no one gave a thought about what happened to him when he left that bar.

He was in the bar from three to six o'clock in the afternoon; there were nine people in the bar. He almost died in the crash, and if the bartender had cared about him, or thought about the consequences, maybe none of this would have happened. That's what we are asking bartenders to do—to care. Without them changing their attitudes about what they can do to change the picture, we are not going to change that picture. So that is why we need to work with the alcohol industry.

My husband had heard of MADD, although it did not exist in our state. I tracked it down, and literally ended up calling the founder, Candy

Lightner, and getting some information. I think what shocked me into action was looking at the fact in a brochure that this was not an isolated incident—in fact that it *wasn't* an accident, or a freak accident as we called it. This is happening every day. I had children, loved ones, who it might happen to again; and I figured we had to get involved to change things in our community.

We went through a terrible, terrible time. We are, thankfully, healed and not in the same situation as somebody who has lost a child or who is permanently disabled. But that was our motivation.

I had never given a speech, I had never been on television, I had never been involved with criminal justice. I was just a person who said, "I want to do something." It's very corny, but when I stepped out as president locally, my basic theme was that one person can make a difference—one person can change things. I said that sometimes change is very easy when people care.

One person really can make a difference. I've helped changed laws, and I hope I have helped victims. People don't come up in the street and tell me "Thank you for saving my life." They often think that I only tally the fatalities, sadly. But I know there are people out there who are aware of what I'm doing, and that helps. I'm not special; I don't wear a halo. And yet the exciting part is that I know if I keep working, there will be people out there tomorrow who might not be alive if I didn't. It's not noble martyrdom at all; I get much more than I give.

What also keeps me involved is that MADD workers are terrific people. They are working all across this country—people from all backgrounds, men and women at all levels of education. The amount of work they do is just amazing. So I'm very proud to be a MADD spokesperson and represent all these terrific people. I just wish we could have prevented these tragedies in the first place.

Organizational Activism

There are literally hundreds of fired-up organizations fighting alcohol and other drug abuse across North America. Let's look at just a couple of them: SADD, a students' group patterned after MADD, and Alcoholics Anonymous, the famous alcohol treatment group. SADD—Students Against Driving Drunk—is an international citizen-activist organization founded by Robert Anastas in 1981. Its goals are:

- To end under-age drinking
- To eliminate alcohol and drug abuse

- To encourage students, parents, and community leaders to join together in a triangle of care in which drug abuse, under-age drinking, and death due to drinking and driving are eliminated

Robert Anastas founded SADD, which is known for its Contract for Life, an agreement between parents and children to build a safety net of caring. This contract delivers a strong, no-use message and has been signed by an estimated four million students!

The Contract for Life between Parent and Teenager reads:

Under this contract, we understand SADD encourages all youth to adopt a no-use policy and obey the laws of their state with regards to alcohol and drugs.

Teenager:
I agree to call you for advice and/or transportation at any hour from any place if I am ever faced with a situation where a driver has been drinking or using illicit drugs. I have discussed with you and fully understand your attitude toward any involvement with under-age drinking or the use of illegal drugs.

_____

Teenager's Signature

Parent:
I agree to come and get you at any hour, any place, no questions asked, and no argument at that time, or I will pay for a taxi to bring you home safely. I expect we would discuss this at a later time.
I agree to seek safe, sober transportation home if I am ever in a situation where I have had too much to drink or a friend who is driving me has had too much to drink.

_____

Parent's Signature

AA

Alcoholics Anonymous is an international fellowship of men and women who once had a drinking problem. It is nonprofessional, self-supporting, nondenominational, multi-racial, apolitical, and available almost everywhere. There are no age or education requirements. Membership is open to anyone who wants to do something about his or her drinking problem.

Alcoholics Anonymous and related programs such as Al-Anon, Alateen, and Adult Children of Alcoholics all are Twelve-Step groups, and have excellent records for helping victims of alcoholism. Codependents and children of alcoholics are helped to find a new sense of serenity in their lives—by emphasizing acceptance, self-care, forgiveness, confession, and trust in God.

The Twelve Steps are based on scriptural principles identified by an Episcopal minister, Dr. Samuel Shoemaker, who developed a ministry to alcoholics during the 1930s in New York City. In 1934 an alcoholic businessman named Bill Wilson attended Shoemaker's group, known as the Oxford Group. During his detoxification effort, Wilson became deeply depressed. In the midst of this depression he experienced an amazing conversion-like experience.

Wilson later left the Oxford Group and put together a collection of writings that outlined his theories about alcoholism. He called his book Alcoholics Anonymous. It included the Twelve Steps, which alcoholics and other addicts have learned to follow through their support groups.

The Twelve Steps of AA outline a plan of recovery for alcoholics, and have been adapted—with permission—for programs dealing with drug addicts, overeaters, and addicts of other compulsive behaviors. The steps are:

1. We admitted we were powerless over alcohol—that our lives had become unmanageable.

2. Came to believe that a Power greater than ourselves could restore us to sanity.

3. Made a decision to turn our will and our lives over to the care of God, *as we understood Him.*

4. Made a searching and fearless moral inventory of ourselves.

5. Admitted to God, to ourselves, and to another human being the exact nature of our wrongs.

6. Were entirely ready to have God remove all these defects of character.

7. Humbly asked Him to remove our shortcomings.

8. Made a list of all persons we had harmed, and became willing to make amends to them all.

9. Made direct amends to such people whenever possible, except when to do so would injure them or others.

10. Continued to take personal inventory and when we were wrong promptly admitted it.

11. Sought through prayer and meditation to improve our conscious contact with God *as we understood Him,* praying only for knowledge of His will for us and the power to carry that out.

12. Having had a spiritual awakening as the result of these steps, we tried to carry this message to alcoholics and to practice these principles in all our affairs.

(From *Alcoholics Anonymous,* "The Big Book,"
published by Alcoholics Anonymous
World Services, Inc.)

Alan Sverdlik of Alcoholics Anonymous explains how the Twelve Steps works:

Rarely have we seen a person fail who has thoroughly followed our path. Those who do not recover are people who cannot or will not completely give themselves to this simple program, usually men and women who are constitutionally incapable of being honest with themselves. There are such unfortunates.

They are not at fault; they seem to have been born that way. They are naturally incapable of grasping and developing a manner of living which demands rigorous honesty. Their chances are less than average. There are those, too, who suffer from grave emotional and mental disorders, but many of them do recover if they have the capacity to be honest.

Our stories disclose in a general way what we used to be like, what happened, and what we are like now. If you have decided you want what we have and are willing to go to any length to get it—then you are ready to take certain steps.

At some of these, we balked. We thought we could find an easier, softer way. But we could not. With all the earnestness at our command, we beg of you to be fearless and thorough from the very start. Some of us have tried to hold onto our old ideas and the result was nil until we let go absolutely.

Remember that we deal with alcohol—cunning, baffling, powerful! Without help, it is too much for us. But there is One who has all power—that One is God. May you find Him now!

Half measures availed us nothing. We stood at the turning point. We asked His protection and care with complete abandon.

("Comparing Philosophies," *The Atlanta Journal and Constitution,* February 5, 1990, page C-5.)

MADD, SADD, AA, and other groups pushing for justice in drunk-driving cases, trying to educate the public on the problems of alcohol, and serving as support groups for alcoholics or victims are only a few of the powerful forces crisscrossing our society that are saying they've had enough crime, disease, irresponsibility, and pained families from substance abuse. In unprecedented ways, organizations, government departments, and whole communities are working together to win the war against the booze blues and other drug problems. With strategies and teamwork, we can give our next generation the option of choosing to rebuild a drug-free North America.

What Can City Government Do?

Although battles are lost daily, we're winning the war. It may be mired in red tape and warrant no front-page headlines, but the battle your city or town is waging against substance abuse just might surprise you.

No matter where I travel in Canada or the United States, I find town and city leaders who care about local alcohol abuse and other drug problems. And they're doing something about it. Check with your city or town mayor to find out what's going on in the war against substance abuse—and to volunteer to help!

Across the North American continent, we're fighting substance abuse. Although battles are lost daily, we're winning the war. One battle is being fought in Toronto, where this statement by Mayor Art Eggleton was published in the newspaper:

"The struggle against substance abuse is everyone's business. If we want to keep our city the safe, livable place it is, we have to firmly reject drug and alcohol abuse and the horrible human price they exact."

Listed below the mayor's statement were the names of these "Toronto community groups concerned with drug issues":

Toronto Mayor's Task Force on Drugs

Kensington Residents' Association

Blake-Boultbee Residents' Association

Streets Are For Everyone—S.A.F.E.

200 Wellesley—Vertical Watch

Communities Against Drug Abuse

Bloor-Crawford Working Committee

Bloor/Lansdowne Community Against Drugs

EEDAPT—East End Drug Awareness Program of Toronto

Regent Park Residents' Association

Tenants Against Drugs (TAG)—North Regent Park

Danforth—We Care Too

Alexandra Park Residents' Association

P.O.I.N.T.—People and Organization in North Toronto

Parents in Transition

Gladstone Residents' Association

Parkdale School and Community Association

Seaton Street Residents' Association

Hundreds of other cities and towns have comparable programs aimed at informing, preventing, treating, and offering support in the fight against alcohol and other drug abuse. Find out what your city is doing. Then get active.

What Can a Citizens' Action Group Do?

Grass-roots activism against substance abuse is making a difference. Doris Aiken, president and founder of RID (Remove Intoxicated Drivers), chronicles in her foreword to Peggy Mann's book *Arrive Alive* the fact that "the most important factor in controlling drunk driving is the activity of concerned citizens at the local level, watching the operation of their criminal justice system, showing interest with public praise for officials and, when deserved, public criticism."

Regional advertising against the tobacco and alcohol industries in California is "another chapter in the growing clamor of public opposition to the marketing of alcohol as well as tobacco. The emotional groundswell . . . is fueled by a powerful combination of health consciousness, consumer activism and community pride," according to an April 23, 1990 article in *Time* magazine titled "Volunteer Vice Squads" (page 60). The article reports that in New York, Dallas, and Chicago, local neighborhood groups have been whitewashing billboards advertising such products as cognac. Members of the Abyssinian Baptist Church in Harlem, New York, regularly patrol their neighborhoods armed with whitewash and paint rollers to cover over ads for booze.

The article further reports that in its 1990 advertising contract with CBS television, the National Collegiate Athletic Association reduced its alcohol advertising to just sixty seconds per hour. An association spokesperson reported, "We had gotten widespread feedback from parents, school administrators and the general public that alcohol was the No. 1 problem."

You can make a difference through grass-roots insistence on sensibility about booze. The 1990 U.S. law mandating warning labels on alcoholic beverages against alcohol's effects on the unborn, etc., basically came about through simple consumer complaints. Several bills have been introduced—and eventually one will probably pass—to force the alcohol industry to announce the same warnings during beer and wine commercials on radio and television.

Public activism against alcohol abuse finds champions these days in the American Congress: "The timing is right [for what's called 'beer bashing']" an aide to Representative Joseph Kennedy, D-Massachusetts, said in an April 9, 1990 *Adweek* article headlined, "Alcohol Ads Draw More Fire" (page 6). "The issue is getting a lot of attention right now, and people are angry about it. It has a lot of grass-roots support and momentum right now." This continent-wide cry for social responsibility in advertising alcohol, according to Joe Culligan, management supervisor for Jim Beam brands advertising, "is like a big stone going downhill and gathering no moss" (page 1).

Sacramento, California, is the site of some of that snowballing community resolve to make a difference. Sharon Jarvis reports in the Summer 1990 *Friendly Exchange* special report by the Farmers Insurance Group that "In Sacramento, we're working together to steer our teens away from the disease of drinking and driving. I've become involved, and I think I can make a difference" (page 10). In an innovative city-wide program called Friday Night Live, teenagers are encouraged to live free from alcohol and other drugs. Friday Night Live also offers adult-supervised teams of youth who will drive other teenagers home from parties as an alternative to riding with drivers who've been drinking. A twenty-four-hour events hotline lists local alcohol-free activities for teenagers.

The U.S. Department of Health and Human Services Office for Substance Abuse Prevention challenges communities to help themselves fight alcohol and other drug abuse. Its "One By One" pamphlet announces that "the Office for Substance Abuse Prevention is asking for your assistance in creating drug-free communities across the United States. To combat alcohol and other drug problems one by one, each community must make a commitment."

The commitment is, "Yes, I am committed to alcohol- and drug-free lifestyles for our children. I want to join with the Office for Substance Abuse Prevention to create a protective and drug-free environment within my community."

If you want to sign such a bold declaration, contact the National Clearinghouse for Alcohol and Drug Information, Box 2345, Rockville, MD 20852.

You can make a difference as you join with others in your community to fight drug abuse, including alcohol abuse. A little activism can even transform your local schools.

What Can a School Do?

The *Tulsa Tribune* blared the story:

> Seven players from the 1990 Jenks High School baseball team missed about half of the season following their six-week suspensions from extracurricular activities. The suspensions of the seven players—along with two others who received shorter suspensions—came as a result of drinking, which is against Jenks school policy. The drinking was discovered during a trip to Tempe, Arizona during spring break to watch major league baseball players practice and play exhibition games.
>
> Athletic Director Joe Hollowday said, "We will be hurt this year as far as talent on the field, but we are into more than just winning baseball games. We support school policy." (*Tulsa Tribune,* April 25, 1990, page B-5)

Jenks students participating in extracurricular activities sign a contract vowing not to use alcohol, drugs, or tobacco. Your local school could implement the same program. The contract reads, in part:

> Participation in extracurricular activities at the Jenks School district is a privilege, not a right. . . . Participation shall be subject to the following restrictions. A student's use or possession of alcohol or illegal drugs between the first and last day of classes of the school year, including evenings, weekends, and holidays shall result in . . . two stages of disciplinary action.

The second stage, as the baseball players found, results in complete suspension from participation in all Jenks extracurricular activities.

Based on drug testing at school, the Jenks plan is working, as administrators, faculty, parents, and students are striving together to "establish," according to the district's policy statement, "an educational environment free of alcohol and illegal drug use."

We *can* change our families, our schools, neighborhoods, towns, and nation!

8

The Church and Alcohol: Stained-Glass Beer Mugs?

Imagine the scene: Sunday dinner after church.

John, the new preacher, thought it was water. He and his wife shuffled around the gingham-covered table and grinned at their hosts, the Harmons.

"How about here?" Mr. Harmon waved at a chair for John. "Chair of honor for the new preacher, hmmm? We hope you like trout."

John smiled; his wife smiled. The Harmons smiled, too, as they all sat down. John suddenly realized that Mr. Harmon reminded him of a hard-boiled professor at seminary—the one whose last advice to the graduating preacher-boys had been to beware the first people who clamor for attention in a new church. He had warned that those people would want the new preacher to "be someone"; and if you weren't the someone they wanted, they'd stone you—maybe with real stones. Remembering those words, John nervously licked his lips.

Mr. Harmon asked John to bless the meal. John prayed, felt his throat constricting, squeaked a quick "Amen," and reached for a deep gulp of water.

It was wine.

John squawked and coughed, spewing wine across the table, pawing at his lap for the napkin. His wife pounded him on the back as John choked out, "I . . . I—" The veins bulged across his forehead.

"Well!" Mr. Harmon pronounced triumphantly to his wife. "I guess we found out what we wanted to know." He reached over and slapped John's shoulder. "Not a wine drinker, huh?" He slapped again. "We just wanted to make sure, Pastor. Some of you new boys coming out of those seminaries, you know—winebibbers, everyone of them. Sorry, Pastor, it was the only way we could tell if you'd practice what you preach. You all right, Pastor?"

John wiped tears off his cheeks and croaked, "How about doing a Bible study on it sometime, Mr. Harmon?" He coughed again. "I'd hate to think how you'd test my biblical view of. . . ." He blew his nose. ". . . Capital punishment!"

What can the church do about alcohol abuse? First, it can solidify its position on the use of alcohol. Second, it can minister honestly to those individuals and families affected by the curses of substance abuse. And third, the church can serve as one of the vocal forces and rallying points in a community to fight alcohol abuse.

The Church—A Place of Healing?

A thorough overview of booze and religion in North America should incorporate every religious tradition. And with the incredible influx of religious groups from other parts of the world, a thorough review would include North America's nontraditional religions' views on alcohol, as well. But detailing every religious opinion on the subject isn't the point of *It's Killing Our Kids.*

So let me apologize right off: With my Protestant evangelical background, I won't be presenting every other religious group's perspectives on alcohol. But if you're from another religious persuasion, stick with me through this chapter; it might be particularly interesting to see what the seventy million evangelical Christians of North America are thinking these days about booze.

And they *are* thinking about it. There are too many alcoholic connections in these Christian churches to let their members think that the ravages of booze abuse will magically pass them by. In my first few phone calls asking for some denominational views on alcohol, I talked with a secretary in a Baptist church who was personally wrangling with the problems of teenage alcoholism in her family. Her teenage son is now in a treatment program; and she is still in shock, since they discovered his problem only a year ago. She told me, "A big percentage of church kids are involved in alcohol use."

In another call to the home of a Wesleyan Methodist pastor, the pastor's wife shared that her niece had become an alcoholic after getting involved in drugs as a teenager—even though she had been raised in a church that held strong views about total abstinence from alcohol.

Tom Klaus's book *Healing Hidden Wounds: Ministering to Teenagers from Alcoholic Families* suggests that the church "can do more for alcoholic families than any other institution." He says this because the church's emphasis is spiritual, and, according to Alcoholics Anonymous, alcoholism is something "which only a spiritual experience will conquer" (*Alcoholics Anonymous,* page 44). Also, Tom points out that the church is to be a place of healing and a community that can deal deeply and lovingly with the personal struggles of an individual's or family's life.

But, Klaus says, "With the exception of the liquor industry, probably no other institution has done more harm to alcoholic families than the church!" (page 87). The fake "Life is Great!" mask too often worn at church is the very worst burden that can be placed on children in alcoholic homes who already are cursed with the rules of "Don't feel, don't trust, and don't talk." He says most churches just can't handle the "gut honesty" alcoholics and children of alcoholics have to learn as part of the recovery process.

For example, a friend of Tom's named Claudia was in a Sunday school where she was asked for her ideas on how God is like a loving parent. "When I imagine God as a parent, all I can think of is my drunk mom screaming and swearing at me," Claudia responded. The group froze, said Claudia, and the teacher said, "That's pretty negative, Claudia. And it's not fair to God. Can you think of a more positive comment?"

So here's hoping the church will rise to its role in the healing processes as we work together to win the war against substance abuse. But for now, what do churches think about alcohol usage, itself?

Even among evangelical Christians there is quite a difference of opinion on the rights and wrongs of using alcohol. I took a totally unscientific survey of random denominations, simply asking their positions on alcohol. If your religious affiliation isn't represented, be sure to let me know about your group's policies on the use of alcohol. If you happen to disagree with the position of your denomination, let its leaders know.

Here's a review of my findings:

Denominational Survey on Alcohol

Some denominations set down specific policies, while others have no official statement, but encourage their constituents along one path.

The Lutheran, Christian Reformed, Church of Christ, Catholic, Christian, Congregational, United Church of Christ, Southern Baptist, Unitarian, and Unity churches all have no official statement prohibiting the use of alcohol.

The Lutheran Church does offer alcohol counseling. A pamphlet titled "Pastoral Counseling and the Alcoholic," published by the Division for Mission in North America, states that "Alcoholism affects one family out of every five in the average Lutheran Parish. This means that alcoholism is all around us; we don't have to look far."

The Southern Baptist denomination has no official position on alcohol use, but according to Robert Parham of The Christian Life Commission of the Southern Baptist Convention, Southern Baptists "have historically opposed the use of alcohol. We have favored a position of abstinence."

An "Issues and Answers" pamphlet offered by this commission states:

> Human society has never succeeded in removing alcohol from people or in removing people from alcohol. Nevertheless, Christians should work concertedly and consistently to solve the problems caused by beverage alcohol.
> Since drinking is many issues in one, varied approaches are required. The ideal solution to the alcohol problem would be the development of a society in which people would not feel a desire or a need for drinking.

Short of that solution, however, there are some important continuing actions which need to be made, particularly in the areas of education, legal controls, and rehabilitation. . . .

The *aim* of the alcohol education to which many Christians are committed is to help persons build firm convictions against alcohol abuse and for total abstinence from alcohol based on sound moral and theological reasoning. In addition to factual knowledge of the effects of alcohol, successful alcohol education requires a broad comprehension of the problem. Christians should understand how certain emotional problems drive people to search for an escape through drinking. It is also important to learn how drinking is encouraged by such community factors as housing, leisure, unemployment, or a sense of meaninglessness in work. Above all, alcohol education should impart the biblical view of personhood as the basis for decision making about drinking.

David Lawson of the Executive Council of the Church of God reports that members of that group "have recorded no specific official stance against the use of alcohol . . . , [yet] it is widely held among us that alcohol and drugs, including tobacco, those addictive substances, are not acceptable for Christian witness. . . . Our local pastors would be solidly in support of this position and I'm sure are vocal about it. I regret we have no official supported vote to set forth this teaching."

The Episcopal Church has no abstinence policy stated, but it, too, has recognized the problem in its midst. A resolution passed by the General Convention states, in response to the desire to minister healing to its constituents and clergy, that the Convention will "provide a written procedure for treatment of clergy and Diocesan employees and members of their families who suffer from the illness of alcoholism. . . . [and] include in its policy a statement covering the use of alcoholic beverages at Church functions and/or on Church property, with particular emphasis on the provision of nonalcoholic choices."

The Church of the Nazarene in its Special Rules of the Church prohibits "the use of intoxicating liquors as a beverage, or trafficking therein; giving influence to, or voting for, the licensing of places for the sale of the same; using illicit drugs or trafficking therein; using of tobacco in any of its forms, or trafficking therein. The Holy

Scriptures and human experience together justify the condemnation of the use of intoxicating drinks as a beverage. The manufacture and sale of liquors for such purposes is a sin against God and the human race. Total abstinence from all intoxicants should be the Christian rule for the individual, and total prohibition of the traffic in intoxicants the duty of civil government. (Only unfermented wine and unleavened bread should be used in the sacrament of the Lord's Supper.)" (Paragraph 34.5, page 49.)

An independent church in Shawnee, Kansas states in its "Church Covenant, Confession of Faith, Constitution" that its members "believe that the Bible is to be the guiding principle in faith and practice," adding that there are general principles that apply to the use of alcohol, thus allowing the individual members to make their own choice whether to consume alcohol or not.

Wesleyan Church Special Principles contains "Special Directions" which are "official admonitions to the members, ministers, and officials of the Wesleyan Church." Regarding substance abuse, it states: "The Wesleyan Church is opposed to the production, sale, purchase, and use of alcoholic beverages, tobacco, narcotics, and other harmful drugs." It also states that members should "abstain from using or trafficking in substances known to be destructive of physical and mental well-being, such as alcoholic beverages and tobacco, and from using drugs for other than proper medical purposes."

The Book of Discipline of the United Methodist Church includes this statement:

> We affirm our long-standing support of abstinence from alcohol as a faithful witness to God's liberating and redeeming love for persons. We also recommend abstinence from the use of marijuana and any illegal drugs. As the use of alcohol is a major factor in both disease and death, we support educational programs encouraging abstinence from such use.
>
> Millions of living human beings are testimony to the beneficial consequences of therapeutic drug use, and millions of others are testimony to the detrimental consequences of drug misuse. We encourage wise policies relating to the availability of potentially beneficial or potentially damaging prescription and over-the-counter drugs; we urge that complete information about their use and misuse be readily available to both doctor and patient. We support the strict administration of laws regulating the sale and distribution of all opiates. We

support regulations that protect society from users of drugs of any kind where it can be shown that a clear and present social danger exists. The drug dependent person is an individual of infinite human worth in need of treatment and rehabilitation, and misuse should be viewed as a symptom of underlying disorders for which remedies should be sought.

The Mennonite Brethren Church's stance is:

> The Christian [voluntarily] abstains . . . in the face of the staggering problems of alcoholism, love to the neighbor, and in particular love to the weaker brother. . . . His freedom to indulge moderately is therefore restricted by the necessity of using his freedom responsibly to help others and thus to serve and glorify God. We accept and endorse [the following statement] as the basis on which we covenant together to practice total abstinence: We can say that while the Bible does warn against the use of alcohol, it does not explicitly forbid the use of beverage alcohol. We believe that this best expresses our divine calling as disciples with responsibility to God and man."

There are obviously other stances we could review. But instead, let's return to people who are the real focus of this book—the kids. What do church teenagers think about alcohol?

The Church Kid Survey

Since some of my involvement with teenagers takes place in church settings, I'm always interested in what church kids, themselves, think about booze. Invariably, they know their local religious groups' feelings about alcohol. Responses I got just last night as I visited with kids from several different Protestant churches included: "Yeah, the adults can drink, but of course kids can't, because we're not legal yet," and "Yeah, they make a big deal about never touching a drop of demon rum as if it'll send us straight to hell—Do not pass 'Go'—Do not collect two hundred dollars."

In a survey I took at a Christian youth get-together of 127 senior-high girls, some of the findings indicated:

- 116 claimed to be Christians

- 68 said they had never drunk alcohol

- 17 said they had fewer than two drinks monthly
- None drank on a weekly basis
- 3 claimed to be alcoholics
- 23 said a drinking problem exists in their families
- A majority—51—said friends were the strongest influence on them to drink. Next came advertising and third came family influences.

In a similar survey of guys, I found that out of 109 senior-high boys:

- 78 claimed to be Christians
- 29 claimed they had never drunk alcohol
- 18 said they had fewer than two drinks monthly
- 4 drink on a weekly basis
- 3 claimed to be alcoholics
- As with the girls, friends were noted as the strongest influence to drink; family influences came next, then advertising.

Are the kids in your church drinking? Probably. Maybe not much or often, but more than likely they're trying it. If you're a local church member, why not find out? Do an anonymous, informal survey. Find out if your Sunday school kids are breaking the law now by drinking; and be prepared to realize that if drinking is important enough to them now to do it illegally, it could get to be a serious driving force in their lives when it's legal for them to drink! Whether or not a church cares if its young people are messing around with alcohol, it should care that they are equipped to make choices about drinking. When they get to the legal drinking age, is it right or wrong for them to use alcohol?

Usually church kids know their church's position on drinking alcohol. But I find few teenagers who can articulate *why* their church takes the position it does. Many of these religious bodies' forefathers wrestled through the alcohol issue as an ethical and even moral quandary; then they set down their conclusions in black and white. Some decided, as we saw in the denominational survey, that alcohol in moderation lies perfectly within the realm of Christian liberty.

Others set down the conclusion that alcohol was to be off-limits to the Christian. These conclusions have been passed down to today's church kids; but unfortunately the mechanism by which the conclusions were decided have not been so diligently passed down. Sunday school kids generally know what their convictions about booze are supposed to be, but they're often not helped to work through how that personal conviction is reached.

Here are two exercises that youth—or adults, for that matter— can work though to determine the why of their convictions about alcohol.

The Bible and Booze. A Study

If there's a basic standard for these Christian convictions, it's got to be the Bible's teaching about booze. But what does the Good Book actually have to say about alcohol? The passages listed here comprise an inductive study—which means I don't give you conclusions; those are to come from the study itself.

Think through Genesis 9:21; 19:32–35; Deuteronomy 32:32; 2 Samuel 13:28; Esther 1:10; Psalm 78:65; Proverbs 4:17; 23:29–35; Isaiah 28:7; Hosea 7:5; Joel 3:3; Zechariah 9:15; 1 Corinthians 5:11; 6:10; 11:21–22; Galatians 5:21; and Ephesians 5:18.

Don't form your conclusions yet! There's more: Exodus 29:40; Leviticus 23:13; Numbers 15:5, 7, 10; 28:14; Deuteronomy 7:13; 11:14; 14:26; 28:39, 51; Judges 9:13; Psalm 104:14–15; Proverbs 3:10; 31:6–7; Isaiah 62:8; Luke 7:34; John 2:1–11; 1 Timothy 3:2–3; and 5:23.

A careful word study would reveal that the Hebrew word *yayin,* "wine," is used in Genesis 9:21; 19:32–35; 1 Samuel 25:37; Esther 1:7, 10; Isaiah 28:1, 7; and Jeremiah 23:9, as well as in Genesis 14:18; Deuteronomy 14:26; 1 Chronicles 27:27; 2 Chronicles 11:11; and Nehemiah 5:18.

The Hebrew word *tirosh* for "new wine" is seen in Hosea 4:11 as well as in Genesis 27:28, 37; Numbers 18:12; Deuteronomy 7:13; 11:14; 14:23; and Proverbs 3:9-10.

The Hebrew word *shekar* is translated "strong drink" in Numbers 6:3; Leviticus 10:9; 1 Samuel 1:15; Proverbs 20:1; Genesis 9:21, 43:34; and Isaiah 49:26, as well as in Deuteronomy 14:26.

The word for wine (Chaldean *chamar*) of Daniel 5 is also used in Deuteronomy 32:14.

The Hebrew *asis* for "sweet wine" is used in Isaiah 49:26, Joel 3:17–18, and Amos 9:13.

"Mixed wine" (in Hebrew, *mesek*), probably mixed with spices, is mentioned in Proverbs 23:30 and Isaiah 65:11.

Wine-soaked lees or dregs (in Hebrew, *shemarim*) is found in Isaiah 25:6 and Jeremiah 48:11.

The "blood of grapes" is mentioned fourteen times in the Old Testament in Genesis 40:10–11, Leviticus 25:5, Numbers 13:20, Deuteronomy 34:14, Nehemiah 13:15, and Amos 9:13.

The Greek word *Oinos* is used in the Septuagint (the Greek version of the Old Testament quoted by Jesus and used by early, Greek-speaking Christians) in passages such as Genesis 9:21; 19:33–35; Leviticus 10:9; Numbers 6:3; 1 Samuel 25:37; Proverbs 20:1; 23:29–35; Isaiah 49:26; Deuteronomy 14:26; 32:14; Judges 9:13; Psalm 104:15; Proverbs 3:9–10; Ecclesiastes 9:7; and Isaiah 25:6. *Oinos* is the word used throughout the Greek New Testament as "wine."

The command "Do not be drunk" (Ephesians 5:18) uses the Greek word *methusko* (translated as "to become intoxicated," or "grow drunk"), which in various forms appears in Matthew 24:49; Luke 12:45; 21:34; John 2:20; Acts 2:15; Romans 13:13; 1 Corinthians 5:11; 6:10; 11:21; Galatians 5:21; 1 Thessalonians 5:7.

An exhaustive concordance will exhaust you further in gaining an overview of the subject of booze in the Bible!

Booze and the Christian—Right or Wrong?

As much as I have read, studied, and listened to leaders of every evangelical persuasion, I have to admit that the Bible does not absolutely, explicitly, and unquestionably say "Thou shalt not!" about booze.

Incidentally, the last thing I want to do is offend any reader who is not sympathetic with what the Bible says. But since churches can be such lighthouses in the war against substance abuse in each of our communities, bear with me for a bit while I address my evangelical

Christian family on this critical topic. Alcohol is something the church doesn't talk about much, unfortunately. But all North American teenagers—especially those in church—deserve to be helped as they work through the basic question of "Should I drink at all?"

Since the Bible doesn't explicitly command, "Thou shalt not drink alcohol," does that mean the local Sunday school kids can start having keg parties to attract newcomers?

There's more to be done in equipping Christian kids to make their choice about drinking. The Christian who wants to understand God's direction about something not covered by an explicit command then gauges it against the more general principles of the Bible—which isn't always easy because the process takes some real thinking—and which we Christians are not famous for. Usually Christians want their leaders to simply tell them what to do in areas not covered by a clear "thus saith the Lord" edict. But the Bible demands individuals to be responsible for wading through this type of issue personally, and become people who "because of practice have their senses trained to discern good and evil" in their lives (Hebrews 5:14).

Christians are to consider what the Bible says, to think about how that truth applies, and then to decide "Should I drink alcohol or not?"

But this God-given responsibility to think and choose what is right and wrong in our lives is an uphill battle because:

• *We're relativists.* We're firmly ensconced in an age that insists there are no black-and-white absolutes. The idea that "everything's relative" has grown like crab grass from a philosophical speculation to a reason not to look for what's true. Even Christians tend to slur "everything's relative" to all of life—as if it's impossible to determine whether an action does or does not violate a biblical principle.

The truth is that much of life is *not* black or white (people are neither wholly humanly good nor bad; fault in divorce cases rarely belongs to one party; etc.). But everything is not muddled in gray relativity. In true, Christian, Spirit-guided thinking, you'll often find that the notorious gray areas of ethics are only—in the context of your own life—intricate variations of blacks and whites. An individual Christian *can* come to a definite right-or-wrong conviction about whether it's right or wrong for him or her to drink alcohol.

• *We're mechanistic.* Since Sir Francis Bacon's *Novum Organum* was written in the early 1600s, we humans have competently trained ourselves to think left-brained scientifically—to trust only what can be verified and cross-verified by human senses, and better yet, by instrumentation. So we're nearly hopeless utilitarians; a theorem is true only when it's proven to work. We therefore tend to mistrust an idea that can't be quantified and empirically proven—such as an ethical principle from the Bible.

• *We're not used to thinking.* Most of us have fallen into ambitious or respectable or just plain frantic schedules that have virtually left us no time to think about anything personal—beyond problems and escapist fantasies. How would your maturity be affected if, as many of our great-grandparents did, you spent nearly every evening thinking and talking with others in your family? What if you spent that time discussing drinking or not drinking—or any other quandaries of life? Imagine the hours of staring into the fire, the books you'd read, the winter days of thinking long, long thoughts. (Sounds strangely like the vacation you're dying for, right?) No, I don't think our ancestors were more educated or smarter than we are; ignorance of facts is dangerous and limiting. But I do think they were deeper people; the life-texture of today's One-Minute Thinker is ultimately sawdust.

Christians need to challenge themselves to think, deliberate, and choose. As only C. S. Lewis could put it, your right-or-wrong choosing is at the core of who you become:

> Every time you make a choice you are turning the central part of you, the part of you that chooses, into something a little different from what it was before. And taking your life as a whole, with all your innumerable choices, all your life long you are slowly turning this central thing either into a heavenly creature or into a hellish creature; either into a creature that is in harmony with God, and with other creatures, and with itself, or else into one that is in a state of war and hatred with God, and with its fellow-creatures, and with itself.
>
> (*Christian Behaviour*, page 23.)

How can Christian teenagers know whether God—not their parent, not their Sunday school teacher, not the preacher—allows them or prohibits them from drinking alcohol? The same way they can know in every moral and ethical quandary not covered by the explicit commandments of the Bible. I advise Christian kids to:

1. *Get straight with God.* Make sure that as a born-again believer you're controlled by the Holy Spirit (Ephesians 5:18 and 1 John 1:9).

2. *Study the truth.* Pray for guidance to know the truth (John 16:13) as you study what the Bible says on a questioned activity.

3. *Study the situation.* Pray for wisdom (James 1:5) as you research the facts of the situation surrounding the quandary in the Bible and other sources. (In our question of "Should I drink?" the research would involve days at the library studying pamphlets and books about booze. It would involve talking with experts, and recovered alcoholics. It would mean doing some slow, serious thinking.)

4. *Decide.*

Sound too simplistic? It's not, when you consider the meaning of each of those steps. If it seems too simple, however, isn't that exactly what you'd expect when God knows every human, regardless of intellect, has to determine rights and wrongs?

Undoubtedly you've got some good questions on the validity or rationale of this simple system. But I think the best way to crystallize those questions and to work through answers is by putting the pattern to work. So let's get practical.

Study the following discussion guide yourself—regardless of your religious opinions. Then consider going through it with a young teenager who needs to know his or her own answer to the question: "When it's legal for me to drink, should I?"

Whatsitgonnabe?
A Four-Part Study/Discussion Guide for Youth Groups

"Is it right or wrong for you to drink alcohol? What does God say?"

1. Answer this tough question first: If you stumbled into the cosmic throne room of God and He told you nose-to-nose whether (when you are of legal age) you can or can't drink, would you go along with His statement? If not, don't bother with this study.

2. What does the Bible say about booze?

- Look up the references listed in the section titled "The Bible and Booze" earlier in this chapter.

- Jot down the words used for booze in these references. You can think of yourself as a budding Hebrew and Greek scholar, okay?

- Beside each scholarly term, jot a phrase describing that word for booze. For example:
Hebrew word *shekar*—"strong drink"

3. Research the topic.

- Read through the Alcohol Handbook in chapter 5.

- Pick out the two most impressive facts about booze and explain to a partner why you think those points are important.

4. Read/scan/discuss the following principles from the Bible that can apply to questions not covered by commandments.

- Pray about all that's in your head related to you and God and booze. Then work through the "God, Should I Drink?" checklist at the end of this chapter.

Youth Leader's Commentary

Study through the following principles, decide how much your youth group can handle, then present the information before your teenagers work through the checklist "God, Should I Drink?" at the end of the chapter.

Principle 1—Weight!

Imagine the coliseum, the grandstand crowd, the well-marked cinder track, and the taut muscles of a sprinter kneeling into the starting blocks. The apostle Paul equates the Christian life to a race (1 Corinthians 9:24–27) in which every believer is hot-footing it toward the finish line to become like Christ (Romans 8:29). Contemporary Christian singer Twila Paris sings, "Runner, when the race is won, you will run into His arms." The allusion, of course, is to Hebrews 12:1: "Therefore, since we have so great a cloud of witnesses surrounding us, let us also lay aside every encumbrance, and the sin which so easily entangles us, and let us run with endurance the race that is set before us."

When you enter a race, you don't put on anything that'll slow you down and make the race harder. Did you ever see a race participant with extra weights strapped to his or her ankles?

If you're a believer, you are in the race. And it's serious; it's your life. You don't need and eventually will regret anything that makes it harder for you to run—any weight that slows you down from becoming more like Jesus Christ. (See 1 Corinthians 9:24–27; and see

Matthew 19:16–24 as an example of something that is like a weight that slows you down in becoming all you can be.)

Principle 2—Usefulness

"All things are lawful for me," the free-thinking apostle Paul wrote, "but not all things are profitable" or useful (1 Corinthians 6:12). Christians have among their favorite buzzwords terms like "just" ("Just thank You, Lord, for just helping us to just. . . .") and "truly" ("It's truly a joy to be with you today because truly. . . .") and "purpose" (". . . bring such purpose into my life that. . . .") The definite "purpose" we can find in Christ shouldn't be just another buzzword, however. Look at it this way: Everything I do in life should contribute in some way to the overall purpose God has for me—the purpose of being restored to the image of God, of becoming more Christlike.

Don't get weird with this profitability factor; even physical rest and emotional refreshment can be part of my growth toward Christlikeness. So don't twist this principle into the old adage that "Idle minds and hands are the devil's tools!" or "Churchwork busyness is true spirituality."

I used to be a boob-tube addict as a kid. I watched hundreds of hours of crackly old "Little Rascals" episodes and "Leave It To Beaver" reruns and "George of the Jungle" stories until my eyes were chronically bloodshot and my skin was a lovely shade of television-gray. But as every tube addict must eventually realize, TV was mostly a wonderful time-waster. Most of my viewing time was spent hoping that something really captivating would come on next, so I'd hang on for another program, flipping through the channels with something of an ache for excitement or laughs. As much as I hated to admit it, those daily hours of canned laughter and faked punches could easily have been spent doing something that would have challenged me more, taught me more about real life. It hit me in high school that often for months at a time, the most interesting things in my life were television shows!

Are you much of a chess player? If you're on my level, I sit down to a match and figure, move-by-move what could happen if I moved here or here. A master chess player, they say, sees the pattern of a game and doesn't worry about step-by-step moves. The master simply rejects the moves that don't fit. Is there any rational reason to take a step in a direction other than toward your race's finish line? To put into your life a habit or practice that's useless?

That's the principle of usefulness. Even innocent activities that don't fit into God's plan for you aren't part of your best possible life.

Principle 3—Control

"All things are lawful for me . . . but I will not be mastered by anything" (1 Corinthians 6:12). If something enslaves me, takes away my ability of choice, the activity violates the control principle.

An explicit command reflecting this principle is, "And do not get drunk with wine, for that is dissipation" (Ephesians 5:18). A drunk gives up the control of his or her body and everything in it—soul and spirit—to wine, which is "dissipation" or a definite waste. It's the waste of time and energy encapsulated in the hung-over question, "Did I have a good time last night?"

Principle 4—The Body Principle

If you're a Christian, ". . . your body is a temple of the Holy Spirit who is in you, whom you have from God, and . . . you are not your own. For you have been bought with a price: therefore glorify God in your body" (1 Corinthians 6:19–20). Your body and everything in it is God's.

Don't minimize your body because it's only physical: religious sects throughout history have made the mistake of discounting the importance of the physical or branding the body as evil. A little Spirit-guided Bible-digging will reveal that God values your body—so much so that He planned for you to live in your perfected body forever (1 Corinthians 15). Being trustworthy in taking care of your body (1 Corinthians 4:2) is an ever-present learning activity in your growth as a whole person.

Principle 5—Conscience

God wants us to enjoy a clear conscience (see Acts 24:16, 2 Corinthians 1:12, and 1 Timothy 1:5). Even a believer who is "weak in the faith" (Romans 14:1), who is "not accustomed to the word of righteousness" (Hebrews 55:13), can enjoy a clear conscience in the "gray areas" of right or wrong.

Let's spend a little time on this to help our teenagers understand that as long as we don't feel conscience-stricken about an activity, it's perfectly right for us. Or if we feel even a false sense of guilt about an activity it is definitely wrong in God's eyes. Condense the sense of this important principle according to the level of your teenage study group.

A "gray" area—an activity about which there are no explicit commands—in apostle Paul's time was the eating of meat which had been offered to idols (and was therefore sold at bargain prices!). It was an issue that's pretty similar to our question today about drinking alcohol.

Paul writes:

> Let each man be fully convinced in his own mind. . . . I know and am convinced in the Lord Jesus that nothing is unclean in itself; but to him who thinks anything to be unclean, to him it is unclean. (Romans 14:5, 14)

Some early Christians couldn't shake the premise that the idols they had earlier worshiped actually had mystical power. Paul wrote:

> . . . We know that there is no such thing as an idol in the world, and that there is no God but one. However not all men have this knowledge; but some, being accustomed to the idol until now, eat food as if it were sacrificed to an idol; and their conscience being weak is defiled. (1 Corinthians 8:4, 7)

Notice the clarity of the principle as it relates to a person's knowledge of what God has said:

> The faith which you have, have as your own conviction before God. Happy is he who does not condemn himself in what he approves. But he who doubts is condemned if he eats [meat offered before idols], because his eating is not from faith; and whatever is not from faith is sin. (Romans 14:22–23)

Now go back over those passages and replace the question of "eating meat offered to idols" with "drinking alcohol."

The obvious exhortation here is to grow in faith, to find out the truth of what God says and decide to trust it. But in the meantime, if a believer isn't sure what God says about an activity or, because of past experiences, can't shake a conviction that the activity is just flat wrong for him or her, God's principle is: Maintain a clear conscience.

Paul fiercely protects the integrity of those who lack knowledge or haven't lost past associations. He asserts their right to conclude that a certain activity is wrong for them, even though other believers seem to find it an innocent expression of their freedom (Romans 14). Yet he still encourages the strong to help the weak toward understanding God's truths (Romans 15:1–2).

In the meantime, his practical advice on the meat-eating issue is almost tongue-in-cheek:

> Eat anything that is sold in the meat market, without asking questions for conscience' sake; for the earth is the Lord's, and all it contains (1 Corinthians 10:25–26).

The use of this principle in our transformation to Christlikeness is pretty simple: Don't violate your Spirit-controlled conscience. The implications of the principle are profound: The same activity can be solidly, biblically sinful to one believer and solidly, biblically clean for another. We're not to enforce our convictions—our gray-area conclusions—on others as if they're God-given commandments.

Final Exam Time

So far we've outlined five basic principles related to avoiding extra weight, seeking usefulness or profitability, maintaining Spirit-control, taking care of your body, and keeping a clear conscience.

Before concluding this exercise with the "God, Should I Drink?" checklist, first read through the instructions below:

1. Make sure you're under Spirit control (see 1 John 1:9).

2. Ask the Spirit's wisdom (James 1:5) to guide you (John 16:13) in studying and reviewing each principle.

3. Visualize the activity as an actual situation in your own life; don't imagine the activity as an abstract or as someone else's experience. If understanding the topic or the situation requires still more information, do some Bible research and/or fact-finding.

4. Check the True or False blanks as you answer the statements. If your questioned activity just doesn't seem to apply or register a definite true or false, leave that particular response blank.

If even one "False" check appears among your answers, you know that God is saying to you personally that this activity isn't the best way for you to live. It would violate a scriptural principle in your case; it would be wrong. If only a string of "True" answers results, there's a healthy chance that this activity is right for you; but observe the note below as you begin the exercise.

Note: These obviously aren't all the principles in the Bible; five is a pretty slim representation of the principles covering the "gray areas" of living. So don't presume that the results of this checklist will be the final say on everything. But it'll be a good start.

Remember, if you and God disagree on the rightness or wrongness of something, it's your problem—not His. Review your belief system to determine what needs to be readjusted to His way of thinking, of valuing. Regardless of how you feel about drinking (and feelings are sometimes strong in these areas), no matter how you may try to rationalize, you can trust God that He knows whereof He speaks. He's been around.

Also, remember that our question of "Is it okay for me to drink alcohol?" can only be asked when drinking is legally permissible. That is, if you're under age, drinking alcohol in any setting (regardless of family, friends, rationalizations, etc.) is off-limits. God says to "be in subjection to the governing authorities" (Romans 13:1–7). The only times you can biblically disobey governmental authority is if it demands that you disobey God's explicit commands (see Acts 4:5–20). So if you're not of legal drinking age, think of this exercise as good preparation for the future. Right now, God's direction to you is that it's wrong for you to drink booze because of the government's law prohibiting under-age drinking.

Finally, notice that the question isn't "Can I get drunk?" God already said, "Do not get drunk" (Ephesians 5:19)!

Now, using the wisdom of the Spirit, ask the questions:

God, Should I Drink?

A. Is my public drinking of any alcohol right or wrong?

Principle	Reference	True	False
Weight: It doesn't slow me down spiritually.	Heb. 12:1		
Usefulness: It can be profitable, useful.	1 Cor. 6:12a		

Control: I can be Spirit-controlled in this.	1 Cor. 6:12b
Body: I can take care of my body in this.	1 Cor. 6:19–20
Conscience: My conscience can be clear.	Rom. 14:5

Therefore, at least at this stage,
this activity is: _____ right _____ wrong for me.

B. Is my private, nobody-knows drinking of alcohol right or wrong?

Principle	Reference	True False
Weight: It doesn't slow me down spiritually.	Heb. 12:1	
Usefulness: It can be profitable, useful.	1 Cor. 6:12a	
Control: I can be Spirit-controlled in this.	1 Cor. 6:12b	
Body: I can take care of my body in this.	1 Cor. 6:19–20	
Conscience: My conscience can be clear.	Rom. 14:5	

Therefore, at least at this stage,
this activity is: _____ right _____ wrong for me.

If you're a teenager, how did you do? If you're just a few years past those teenage years, do you do any better now than you would have as a kid in trying to figure out exactly what is right or wrong for you and why?

Fortunately for most teenagers, there's almost always a decrepit old adult to help them work through some of these ethical quandaries. The next chapter gives the teenager and a parenting adult an interesting chance to communicate on a variety of subjects—including this hot topic of "Should I drink?"

9

Keeping Kids Safe from Booze by Teaching Them How to Talk

They now seem to love luxury; they have bad manners and contempt for authority; they show disrespect for adults and spend their time hanging around places gossiping with one another. They are ready to contradict their parents, monopolize the conversation, eat gluttonously, and tyrannize their teachers.

Socrates

Booze abuse on the part of teenagers is only one of the myriad of abuse-problems that have to be confronted at home. And the most effective prevention program parents can implement against these problems is called, quite simply, communication.

Communicating with your teenager is such a critical point in the war against substance abuse that we'll focus on it in two ways. First, let's kick around some of the basic principles I've developed during my years of communicating with millions of kids. Then let's get practical with all this communication-with-teens theory: Play the communication game of "When I Was Your Age." Teach your teenager to listen and show him or her how to talk. Then, when the specter of substance abuse invades your teenager's life—and it does

147

and it will—your kid will have a safe person to run to for empathy and advice: You.

My Kid's a Stranger to Me!

Living with a new person takes some understanding. Ask newlyweds.
Or new roommates. Or teenagers and whoever's parenting them.
Somehow in our society, thirteen-year-olds and their parents (we'll
use the term for whoever is parenting—whether it's a guardian, stepparent, foster parent, etc.) become new people.

"My kid's a stranger to me these days!" wails the adult. And
a disgusted "I never knew what adults were really like. . . ." comes
pretty easily to the teenager. So face it: You're new people to
each other. You need to make some adjustments, to reach some understanding, right? You need to communicate—on a nitty-gritty-gym-
socks-and-car-keys-and-curfew-and-best-friend-and-career-worries-and-
sex-and-zits-and-school-and-grades-and-dope-and-booze level.

It takes time for people who are new to each other to communicate about important issues. But it's worth it. Learning now to communicate with a person they have to live with gives teenagers the vital
skills they need to enjoy satisfying social relationships, effective career relationships, and dazzling love relationships later on. And communicating on the issues raised in James Dobson's book *Preparing for
Adolescence* gives the parents an unexpected joy of developing a new
person-to-person friendship with somebody who's more than just-
another-mouth-to-feed responsibility.

Of course, some people think communicating is too much like
work. Millions of teenagers figure they're the hottest thing since
jalapenos, and that all advice-spewing adults hit senility at about age
twenty-three. So when young people determine to learn nothing about
twenty-four-hour-a-day relating at home, they often begin practicing
that "nothing" in relationship after relationship.

And parents are often just as mush-minded. Some adults never
catch on: When you're obnoxious or distant or uncaring to kids, they
become obnoxious and distant and uncaring right back. Refuse to
communicate with your child or teenager, and you'll simply and
dreadfully multiply the drags of parenting. Instead of "working easy

in the harness" through your youth's dynamic teenage years, you'll have to wait like millions of other fine American parents until the kid moves away to start building your relationship on an adult-to-adult basis.

It's either/or: Work now to communicate—to respond to each other as persons and reap the rewards—or pay later. Dearly.

Problems and Platitudes

Communicating is tough business. It's hard to find time in our *allegro* schedules for little extemporaneous instructional chats on the meaning of life:

"Morning, Dad."

"Morning, Son. Can you give me a ride to work? Bring back the car for your sister?"

"Swimming practice in twenty minutes. Sorry."

"No problem. How're the Supercorn Sweeties? How's your sex life?"

"Okay. Is there a God?"

"I'll just grab this honeybun. Messed with dope yet?"

"Coming to my swim meet Saturday?"

"Maybe, Son. See you. Remember, it's better to give than to receive."

"Right, Dad. 'Bye"

It's hard to work your way into heavy discussions. Teenagers don't want to ask leading questions, and parents sometimes feel awkward carrying on a monologue or asking prying questions just to get to talk about an important topic.

Talking, itself, is often tough for young adults. Teenagers' verbal skills are generally not developed until they near the end of their teenage years. Although they can spit out buzzwords—one-size-fits-all slang—a teenager often doesn't have the verbal skills to find the right words to express deep feelings and ask meaningful questions.

Finally, real communication is often stuffed with problems from years-old habits. See if any of these comments sound familiar:

"We always end up fighting about the same old things. I just don't want to talk anymore."

"Yeah, they're just trying to make me agree with their point of view. This communication stuff is just another ploy to manipulate me."

"We know what's best and we tell her so. And as long as she's under our roof. . . ."

"That's the end of it. There'll be no more discussion."

Communication Myths

Yes, Virginia, there really are problems in communicating. And there are also misconceptions to clear up such as:

- *"Yes, my teenager will reveal all to me since we'll be real buddies."*

Your teenager doesn't need an old buddy who always thinks and acts on his or her own level; he or she needs a mature adult who's open and willing to talk. Kids see an adult who tries to be a fellow teenie-bopper as either a fool or a spy. So don't expect your teenager to reveal everything to you as if you're a best buddy. You're not.

- *"Parents are supposed to have it all together. And if they don't, why bother listening to 'em?"*

Nobody has it all together, your parents included. They have made mistakes; they could have lived more successfully. So now you get to learn from their shortcomings without getting burned. Since they're not perfect, you can get to know them as real people—which isn't exactly the way you knew them when you were a child. You get to watch them as they work to handle problems like the ones you'll face. You'll have a chance to think about whether their solutions are going to be your solutions or not.

- *"Fortunately, we have a good relationship; and with effort at communication, we'll never make mistakes or embrace the horrors of teenage rebellion."*

Wrong. Your teenager needs to become his or her own self, and that involves breaking away from (and experimenting with breaking away from) who you are. Normal teenage rebellion is healthy. Disagreeing with parents' views, testing the rules, learning from mistakes, abandoning civilized decorum are to be expected. (See the "Persevere" section under "The Care and Feeding of Teenage Communication," later in this chapter for a discussion of *abnormal* teenage rebellion.) If teenagers don't rebel normally between the ages of thirteen and sixteen, they'll probably go through "teenage" rebellion in their twenties, when the consequences are more serious.

• *"We might as well not talk. We just always end up disagreeing anyway."*

So? Imagine: Somebody might have to say, "Well, I'm afraid I disagree with you. But I'll respect your opinion and I love you anyway!"

• *"Times have changed. Everything's different since adults were my age."*

Half right. Many of the surface issues have changed, but the deeper feelings and fears and problems and stages of growing up haven't. Although Dad felt pressure to take up swearing at the same age Junior feels pressure to chug a beer, peer pressure is still peer pressure. Maybe Mom rolled her long, straight hair on tin cans while her daughter dyes her hair blue; but the dog-eat-dog competition for popularity and eye-catching attractiveness is as healthy as ever. The fantasized finale to a date might once have been a long kiss, while now it might be jumping into bed; but the basics of sexual curiosity, fears of sexual inadequacy, and quandaries about the morals of it all are the same.

Make sense? You'll be surprised how much is still the same after all these years. The awesome generation gap—as most survivors of the sixties now know—thrives on superficial issues and invariably is "ungapped" at deeper levels of life.

• *"What's best for me will be best for my kids. There's no need to discuss things."*

Who says? Just because your kids inherited a few of your genes, aren't they like any other human? And surely you don't think that what's best for you is always best for every human being on earth, eh? You're not always right—even if you really think so.

• *"All this communication schmaltz doesn't work."*

If by "doesn't work" you mean that a teenager can't get a parent to agree to all his or her demands or that a parent can't produce a teenage clone who'll never wonder about getting drunk, you're right. But the point in communicating with each other is not to rig up a system for manipulating each other.

Everyone knows that pleasant living arrangements are not the result of 5,739 rules or hard-won power games or who can whine or nag the loudest and longest. Good living arrangements come from good relationships. Values-learning comes from good relationships, not from behavior-modification brainwashing. Peace and understanding are found in good relationships, not in don't-rock-the-boat silence.

The point of parent-teen communication is to build an adult relationship that's big enough to accommodate differences and disagreements, and is honest enough to work out problems without cheap manipulation. And for that kind of real relationship, real communication does work.

Bringing Up Your Past

"It's useless to bring up my past—especially my teenage years," you might say. "What I want to communicate to my youngster is how life *should* be, not how it was for me."

If that sounds like something you'd say about your involvement with alcohol and other drugs, consider the following ideas.

The good, the bad, and even the ugly of your life . . .

• *traces your education in life.* Giving teenagers only the conclusions of what you've learned in life doesn't tell them how you reached those conclusions. Learning how to think—not just what to think—will help teenagers decide wisely about issues *you* never faced.

• *gives you credibility.* On your trek across the Gobi Desert, you'll listen to a guide who's "been there." When your teenager realizes the two of you have been through nearly all the same internal struggles, he or she will tend to listen to you. Don't expect your teen to swallow everything, but he or she will usually at least listen, because your experience gives you credibility. You might even be trustworthy!

• *breeds confidence in a teenager.* If you're honest in revealing problems you faced when you were a teenager, your teenager will see that he or she, too, can overcome obstacles. Your kid can learn from your mistakes and successes.

• *explains a lot.* Your own upbringing and the traumas you've endured affect your parenting. Knowing that background can explain

volumes to a teenager. (*Oh, that's why she's so paranoid about. . . .*)
In your close adult relationships, you give explanations for your
quirks, hobbyhorses, and personal idiosyncratic rules. Those explanations allow your friends to understand you. You'll be amazed at how
accommodating teenagers can be when they understand even irra-
tional reasons for your behavior.

• *sharpens your parenting effectiveness.* Seemingly overnight,
you're having to shift from practical parenting ("Get out of that
tree!") to relational parenting ("Can I trust you when you're out
with those kids?"). As you recover from the shock of the shift, remembering your own teenage experiences and feelings will heighten
your empathy. Getting in touch with your past will help you focus
your parenting emphases: You'll remember what was—and still is—
the deep, important, *major* stuff to focus on. You can avoid the
curse of so many teenagers' parents who major on minors and minor on majors.

Recalling the old days will refine your stance on issues. You'll
get a chance to fine-tune your opinions, standards, values, and expectations: Are you just mimicking or reacting against your own parents'
quirks? What exactly are the reasons behind your personal and parenting axioms?

• *solidifies your relationship.* Do you know adults who constantly mutter judgments and platitudes about your life? ("You
should know better than to mess around with those stocks." "After
all, a woman's place is. . . ." "Anybody who drives a foreign car
deserves. . . ." and on and on.) If that's the focus of your acquaintance, you no doubt resent their attempts at manipulation, their as-
sertions of superiority. You know they want you to do things the way
they do things, to admit your own stupidity. But meaningful adult
relationships aren't based on an exchange of judgments, platitudes,
and opinionated conclusions. They're based on an exchange of self—
of what went on in the past, of why you've reached certain conclusions, of who you were and are.

Sharing the good, the bad, and the ugly of yourself will make
you a better parent. The risk is worth it. Share even your old traumas with your teenager. Believe it or not, your pre-teenager is becoming an adult. And he or she needs to learn how to develop
meaningful adult relationships. Starting with you.

The Care and Feeding of Teenage Communication

> Times are different for them today than they were for us at that age. Yet many values of yesteryear retain their timeliness and appropriateness and still serve as the basis for the standards of behavior we expect of our adolescents. It's just that we should relate our values to the present time, rather than rely on repeating what our parents said to us.
>
> (Dr. Louis L. Fine, *After All We've Done for Them,* page 167.)

Some of us parents never catch on. If we give the kids the silent treatment or verbally humiliate them or come across as hard-nosed despots, they'll become miserable, obnoxious kids—kids who aren't any fun to be around. Or they will become the kind of kids who miraculously amplify the miserable aspects of parenting. So, parent, do yourself a favor: practice the basics of parent-teenager communication. Nurture a kid who'd be great to know if you were his age. Here are some suggested how-to's:

• *Minor on the minor stuff; major on majors.* If you major on minors ("If you clear your throat one more time, I'm going to kill you!" or "No, Tammy and I haven't talked since I insisted she wear socks with her tennies,"), you'll never get to the stuff of life that really matters. Try something tough: Write out a list of the major issues of life that your teenager needs to know about. Then set a schedule— perhaps monthly—for talking over each of those topics. (The next section of this chapter outlines a "When I Was Your Age" communication workout for bringing up such subjects.)

• *Persevere.* Keep listening and talking right through the unsettling traumas of normal teenage rebellion—blatant disobedience about a specific thing, surliness, groans and moans when giving in to your orders, thoughtlessness, forgetfulness, laziness, time-wasting, general craziness with friends, bizarre outfits, and makeup.

Keep listening and talking, and get some counseling help and support when you see signs of *abnormal* teenage rebellion such as:

—harmful actions or threats toward you or your property,

—constant, verbalized disrespect to you or other authorities,

—actually running away (not threats to run, or staying at a friend's house for a day or two, or the usual call-for-attention announced attempts to run away),

—more than one incident of illegal behavior involving dope, alcohol, theft, vandalism, driving, fighting. . . . (One incident may be a powerful lesson that truly was a foolhardy teenage adventure. More than one incident spells trouble.)

And keep listening, talking, and getting counseling help when you see other serious problem signals such as

—sudden weight loss or gain,

—sudden drop in school grades,

—constant depression,

—preoccupation with suicides, catastrophe, the occult,

—inexplicable hyperactivity or inactivity

—frequent unaccounted-for blocks of time or wads of money.

• *Show a little respect.* I know you don't get much or any in return, but you can *give* some respect, right? After all, you're the parent. And eventually respect breeds respect. Respect excludes cheap putdowns calculated to hurt, embarrass, motivate, or conquer. Respect includes talking *with* your teenager, instead of talking *at* him or her.

• *Separate who your teenager is from what your teenager does.* This will help you, for instance, direct constructive criticism at mistakes and wrongdoing rather than at the individual. ("So, since you got another F in geometry, what're you going to do about it?" rather than "Look, you must be stupid; you're never going to amount to anything.") Avoid personal attacks.

• *Practice communication-enhancing phrases* such as:

"If you can show me what I can do, I'll give it some serious thought."

"Is this making any sense?"

"I feel . . ." rather than "You make me feel . . ."

Say "all right" and "okay" and nod a lot to emphasize shared points.

"I'll help you if you need help. . . ."

"I'm not an ideal parent and I don't expect you to be an ideal kid."

"Want to talk about . . .?"

"What do you think about . . . ?"

• *Be prepared with facts and information when you need to talk about something serious like alcohol and other drug abuse.* Pretend you're a consultant on the subject who needs to give concise, logical information. Evaluate carefully your own values before you recommend them to your teenager. (Is sleeping with the light on really wrong? Is coming out as a debutante really vital? Is it right or wrong to ever drink alcohol?)

• *Don't force your teenager to share deep feelings with you.* You'll either push him or her into stubborn silence or to lying, thus damaging possibilities for future communication. Your one-way chat with a nonresponsive kid may mean that you have either now or in the past overstepped his or her privacy. "I don't want you to ever hide anything from me," and "Tell me everything that happened on your date" are the badges of insecure or vicarious, thrill-seeking parents.

When your kid just seems to remain obstinately silent, remember that in every relationship there are times when two people just can't seem to communicate. Of course, if the matter is disciplinary, feel free to expect obedience in giving you information you need.

• *Kids aren't possessions.* Is it hard to admit that your little one is growing up and away from you? Remind yourself that independence comes with the territory. Then work hard at not smothering your teenager. A smothered kid will be:

a) overly dependent for life,

b) a blatant rebel,

c) a person who does what he or she wants and gets very good at lying about it.

• *Periodically, when you're upset or humiliated about an incident, step back and ask yourself,* So what?

• *Treat your teenager as you would an adult.* Your days of practical parenting are ending as your child becomes a teenager. The challenge now is relational parenting, with precepts such as, "Power games don't work with teenagers." Eventually teenagers get big; or they have too much time away from home for you to control every aspect of their behavior. Ever heard the taunt, "You can't *make* me!"? A parent's power trip or provocation guarantees resentment and retaliation, just as a boss's power play at work promises resentment on the part of the employees.

Think of your parent-teenager interaction as if you're relating to another adult. You're *not* relating to an adult yet—otherwise the kid would be long gone on his or her own. But try to think of your communication as conversations with an adult. In other words, the respect, cooperation, negotiation, and contract-setting necessary in every successful adult relationship does work with teenagers. Power doesn't.

• *You can't order their feelings* ("Now, don't be mad"), *relationships* (Do you really think you could talk your daughter out of being in love with her boyfriend?), *or values* ("Our family has always stood for total abstinence from liquor"). You can't *make* a kid like patriotism or your idea of a "nice friend" any more than you can make him or her like eggplant quiche. (Rules and values aren't the same thing, right? Enforce your rules for behavior, but forget about trying to enforce values, relationships, and feelings.) However, a teenager's values *can* change over a period of time when he or she is influenced by a person the teenager likes, and who has wisdom, facts, experience, and demonstrated competence. Be that person!

• *Don't work harder at parenting teenagers; work smarter.* For instance, as preadolescents mature:

Set aside time to spend with them alone.

Be alert for hints that they want to talk.

Determine to be shocked at nothing. Teenagers know they can goad, hurt, panic, and get lots of attention by pronouncing shocking statements they themselves know are nothing but baloney. ("Mom, how do I become a nymphomaniac?)

Give praise.

Don't depend on all-verbal communication; smile, nod, pat an arm.

Give reasons for your dictums; if you have no coherent reason, don't issue an order. (And remember that the answer, "Because I'm your mother/father/ whatever" and "Because I said so" are reasons for their *obedience,* not rational reasons for whatever behavior you're ordering.)

Use resources (books, movies, TV shows) as discussion starters.

Role-play tough situations.

Discuss your basic, bottom-line rules (such as not talking back, letting you know where he or she is, not physically abusing the family) with your teenager. Presume nothing.

Take your teenager's problems seriously.

When discussing a disagreement, use questions to help your teenager develop ideas to their chronological and logical conclusions. Youth sometimes have trouble seeing beyond the present or the immediate future, and will actually appreciate your longer-range (not to say older, of course!) perspective.

When I Was Your Age: A Communication Workout for Teenagers and Adults

Now let's put you to work in a communication exercise that'll surprise you by providing a fun, comfortable forum for discussing topics like alcohol.

Adults' Instructions

I'll begin the instructions for using this communication workout by listing the don'ts:

• Don't worry about what to do. Just stick with the program and follow directions as they come.

• Don't think that nothing you say to your teenager is getting through. It may take years or decades, but your teenager will someday show you how much this sharing of your self means.

• Don't worry about sticky subjects—those areas in your own life where you feel regret or inadequacy. In the first place, you can be as general or specific as you choose about past problems. Second, all you ever need to say about your own current problems is that you're working on them. If you don't want to elaborate, don't.

• Don't dump current emotional problems on your teenager. Kids have enough pressure on their own. If you're not handling a problem, find a professional counselor; they're paid to get dumped on.

• Don't get tense over "results" of perfect behavior. Your budding teenager will still make mistakes. Glorious ones. But in the painful consequences of mistakes, the security of your open relationship will be all the "results" your teenager needs right now.

• Don't worry about having to be always right. Name one person over the age of six in the universe who expects you to pop up with the right answer every time.

• Don't take yourself too seriously. If a question reminds you of some mistake you've made with your teenager, go ahead—apologize.

It's tough for your preadolescent to love you when you have done and can do no wrong.

Now, the do's:

1. Determine what year you were your teenager's age.

2. Check out that year's almanac or yearbook or magazines or stone tablets; rummage through old scrapbooks, photo albums, and diaries. Talk with family members to get your bearings on what happened that year.

3. Get a good, thick spiral notebook and start writing the questions and answers. Tackle one section at a time, writing out some kind of answer to each question as if your teen had asked it. (If you can do this orally with your teenager, great!)

4. Write in specific details, using sensory descriptions that evoke what was seen or heard or smelled or touched. Avoid vague abstractions; stick with actual, concrete things and actions— not "I was lonely that year," but "One morning in December I got on the schoolbus and while some kids sat three to a seat, nobody sat next to me." Feel free to be general on some questions according to your teenager's needs—the doctor's anatomical diagnosis of which metatarsal was broken is boring stuff. Visualize actual scenes; then write about the pictures in your mind. Don't bore.

5. Glue photos when suggested or wherever a picture would be worth thousands of words.

6. Don't feel you have to stick exactly and only to that specific year.

7. Jot down as much as you want on each item. If there's just too much to write, give the juicy parts; then write, "I'll just tell you the rest. When's a good time? Maybe you and I could sneak out for pancakes Saturday morning. . . !"

8. Answer one section at a time (each section will take you ten to twenty minutes), mark the section with a note saying something like, "Read and weep!" (Keep the exercise game-like.) Then leave the notebook for your teenager. Don't push it as to when you expect the notebook back, but after a few

days feel free to ask, "Had a chance to look through the notebook yet? If not, can you do it now? I want to get on with the next section."

9. Go ahead. Get crazy and enjoy writing your life story. It might not seem like it, but your teenager needs to know you.

Teenagers' Instructions

Now that I've spelled out the adults' directions, here are the instructions for teenagers:

• Have a good time with this communication exercise. Humor the old folks.

• After your parent (or stepparent or grandparent or warden or whoever's raising you) fills in a section, read through it, and if you feel like it, jot down comments, responses, or questions you have. Then hand the notebook back. If you're wondering about something that wasn't asked in any section, write out your question or just ask it if you don't feel like writing.

• Remember, this will probably be like liver-paste sandwiches: a little slow going down, but incredibly good for you. Practicing these back-and-forth exercises will develop your skill in communicating—the main adult skill you need for successful career/social/love relationships. Think of it as practice for the big time.

P.S. When you comment on something, don't snap or be smart-mouthed (smart-penciled?) about it. Yes, you know by now you can really hurt and anger them with well-placed one-liners—especially when they're trying some meaningful new parenting trick like this. But that doesn't help you learn to communicate about touchy stuff— a communication skill you have to have since you will encounter touchy areas in your adult relationships. Keep up the smart-mouthed comebacks and you're signing your life away to isolation, a rocky career, and fair-weather-only love relationships.

So at least for this exercise, work at not provoking them. It ain't worth what it does to *you.*

Now, simply wait until whoever's parenting you gives you the razzle-dazzle of his or her life in the notebook. It could be spicy! Or extremely dull. So be kind.

Questions

Section 1

What century, uh, er, year was it that you were my age?

What was your favorite song? What were some of the words?

Do you still have the record or music to it?

What would somebody your age have worn then to look really wild?

Did you wear wild outfits? If so, what did they look like?

How did you look—your height, weight, complexion, hair?

Were you considered attractive, unattractive?

Any old photos of yourself?

Now, write: "Any comments?" and give your notebook to your teenager.

Section 2

Who was your favorite music group or celebrity? Why?

What was your birthday like that year? (or Christmas, if you can't remember that many birthdays ago!)

What did you get?

What was school like? Who was your best/worst teacher?

How did you feel about English, history, other courses?

Got a yearbook I can see?

What kind of stuff was generally said about your generation when you were my age?

What was the craziest thing you ever did that year? Did you get in trouble for it?

Now give your notebook to your teenager.

Section 3

What did you want to be when you became an adult?

Did you feel you were overweight? Underdeveloped? Skinny? Just right?

What did you like/hate about your appearance?

What would you do to make yourself seem really "with it" or "in"?

Did you ever try dope or alcohol to be "in"?

How late did you usually stay up? When did you have to get up on weekdays? weekends?

Now, give the notebook to your teenager.

Section 4

Did you ever sneak out of the house at night?

What was important to you? Rank in order of importance things like clothes, job, free time, God, athletics, friends, etc.

What was important to you that wasn't to your parents?

What was important to them that wasn't to you?

What was your ideal plan for your life—your big dream?

If you ever drank alcohol, did you ever worry that you'd become an alcoholic?

Now, give the notebook to your teenager.

Section 5

Where'd you go when you wanted to be alone?

Did you think you had enough privacy? Did anybody else ever read your mail or diary, listen in on your phone calls, or go through your drawers?

Did you think about suicide, or know anybody who tried or succeeded at suicide?

Did you believe in love? How—back then—would you have defined it? How about now?

Now, give the notebook to your teenager.

Section 6

Ever beat up anybody? Get beaten up? Ever watch a fight?

Were you made to go to church or temple? How often? How'd you feel about going or not going?

How did you imagine God—or did you?

Did guilt about what God thought about your activities ever keep you from trying alcohol or other drugs or cigarettes?

Did you have any personal contact with death?

Did you believe in heaven? Hell? Why or why not?

Now, give the notebook to your teenager.

Section 7

Did your parents (whoever brought you up) hug you much? Did you want them to?

Were you afraid of your parents? Why or why not?

Were you too sheltered? Allowed too much freedom?

Did your parents tell you specifically not to drink, or did they allow it?

Describe the worst emotional hurt you had to go through.

Now, give the notebook to your teenager.

Section 8

What was your biggest problem—the worst thing about your life then?

Did you ever run away? Why or why not?

Name two things you usually were disciplined for. How were you disciplined? Grounded? Hit? Yelled at? Did it work?

Were there limits on where you could go and when? If so, what were they?

What did you do (or what would like to have done) to make your parents proud of you? Was making them proud important to you?

Did you have friends your parents didn't like? How did or should you have handled that situation?

Now, give the notebook to your teenager.

Section 9

Did you lie to your parents? If so, what did you lie about? What happened?

Were your friends good influences on you? Were any of them bad influences?

Did your parent(s) ever embarrass you in front of your friends or others? When? What happened? How did you feel?

Did you have a temper? Regardless, what things made you really mad?

Ever feel really depressed? About what?

Now, give the notebook to your teenager.

Section 10

Who was the most important person in your life? What made that person so important to you?

Did that person use alcohol or other drugs? Who did you hate? Why?

Did you feel obsessed/scared/disinterested/etc., about sex? Explain those feelings.

Did you feel unsure or confident about dating? Describe the date you remember most.

Now, give the notebook to your teenager.

Section 11

List your parents' three most-used phrases.

How did you feel most of the time? Were you happy? Sad? Explain why you felt that way.

It'll probably take too long to write, but tell me sometime about our family history—stuff I don't yet know, any family secrets that might someday affect me, such as any alcoholics or other addicts in the family?

Did you feel you knew enough about sex? Where did you get information on it?

How long did it seem until the world would end?

Now, give the notebook to your teenager.

Section 12

Did you "own up to" your mistakes, or mostly try to blame somebody else? Tell about a time you made a mistake and how you handled it.

Did you want to grow up? Why or why not?

Did you often feel romantic? In what ways?

How'd you feel about authorities—parents, police, teachers? Did any of the authorities in your life drink much or use drugs?

Now, give the notebook to your teenager.

Section 13

What did you need that you weren't getting—emotional support, material things, practical help, etc.?

Did you swear? Why or why not?

Did your parents trust you? Why or why not?

Who did you get advice from? Who did you talk with about your feelings?

What were your parents like? (Do you have a picture of your parents when you were my age?)

Now, give the notebook to your teenager.

Section 14

What was your philosophy of life then—how you thought life should be lived, how the world worked?

What did you try (cigarettes, swim team, Zen, stamp collecting, marijuana, etc.) that you either stuck with or didn't pursue?

Describe the biggest argument you had with your parent(s). Was it a win, a loss, or a compromise?

What did you appreciate most about your parents? Appreciate least?

How did you feel then about your (birth) mother? Your (birth) father?

Did you often feel as if people didn't understand you at school, work, home, or when you were out socializing? If so, why did you feel that way?

Now, give the notebook to your teenager.

Section 15

When you were my age, in what ways were you like me? Not like me?

Did your parents want you to be the same kind of person as they were?

Did they want you to be different from the kind of person they were? How did you know? Did you ever feel that you were unwanted? If so, why?

Were you told not to do something your parents did? Did you understand that rule or did it just seem like a double standard?

Did your parents love you or not? How did you know?

Now, give the notebook to your teenager.

Section 16

Did your parents ever apologize to you? What's something you've never quite forgiven them for?

Were there taboo subjects you couldn't discuss at home? Other subjects that always caused arguments?

How did you handle disagreements with your parent(s)? With brothers, sisters, or friends? Did you get violent, pout, carry a grudge, laugh it off, yell, etc.?

Now, give the notebook to your teenager.

Section 17

What were your attitudes then about sex? Did you:
—think it was "dirty"?
—fantasize much about it?
—think sex before marriage was damning, or okay?
—feel powerless against your sex drives and sexual pressures?
—separate between love and sex?
—other attitudes?
What did you know about incest?

Did your parents set specific limits on your sexual activity?

Did you have your own limits on how far you'd go sexually?

Did booze have anything to do with the sex stories your friends would tell?

Now, give the notebook to your teenager.

Section 18

If I were a teenager when you were my age, would we have been friends?

If you were a teenager today, how would you fit in?

Would you like to be my age these days?

What did your family teach you about alcohol?

What did you know about other drugs?

Did your parents tell you they loved you? *Did* they love you? Did you tell them you loved them? *Did* you love them?

Now, give the notebook to your teenager.

Section 19

Was there violence in your family? If so, describe.

Did you care about a "cause" of some kind? If so, what?

What part did religion have in your inner life? Did you pray much?

Did you believe in occult stuff? Ever dabble in it?

What was the saddest thing that happened that year?

Now, give the notebook to your teenager.

Section 20

Were you ever promised something and it never happened? What was it?

In what ways do you feel yourself wanting to live your life through me (for example, making sure I get to do the things you missed, or getting the things you never got, making sure I avoid your mistakes, etc.)?

Did you ever get punished for something you didn't do? What was it?

Were conflicts with your parent(s) mostly their fault or yours?

What regrets do you have about your teenage years?

Are you worried I'm heading for those same regrets? If so, is your worry based on my behavior or on your experiences?

Do you love me? Do you think I love you?

Now, give the notebook to your teenager.

Don't stop with this section's questions! Make up your own. Or move ahead in your communication workouts. Have the teenager write his or her own questions. Allow a few days for your recollections from those stone-age days to re-surface; then share answers face-to-face. Or get crazy: Just start discussing things using these ground rules.

Ground Rules for Discussion

A discussion is a time to talk something over. The word suggests there is room for negotiation on an issue. So if a parent and a teenager get together to issue edicts to each other ("You will not grow science-project pizza mold in the bathroom!" or "So cut my allowance! I'm not gonna wear that space-cadet headgear with my braces!"), it's not a discussion. Save the words "discuss" and "discussion" for discussions in which compromise and negotiation are the names of the game.

Here are some basic guidelines both discussers need to agree to before launching into a session:

1. *A compromise solution will be okay.* Focus on needs and how to fill them in creative ways, not on one solution or the other. There's no such thing in human relations as only one workable solution. The compromise solution is one in which nobody loses.

2. *We'll be honest about whether what we say is fact or is just our opinion.* Be prepared with real facts about the issue. And nothing's wrong with expressing personal opinions as long as they're not pushed as facts.

3. As far as the logistics of the discussion, we'll:

—*remain seated and keep our voices conversational.*

—*set a time limit.* Keeping the discussion to around twenty minutes will keep it from getting either out of hand or borrrinnng.

—*write down and stick to set topics.* Discuss three at the most; this'll keep you from bringing up old, tired issues.

—*define the problem* in terms of who needs what, *brainstorm* for possible solutions, **decide on a solution** acceptable to both of us or put the issue aside for another discussion. If a solution is chosen, set a time for evaluation; expect that first-time solutions don't always work.

4. We'll try our best not to use any of the following low-budget clichés:

"You're just worried about what the neighbors/your friends will think."

"As long as you're under my roof, you'll. . . ."

"I hate you!"

"I don't have to have a reason; it's because I said so. . . ."

"You're crazy if you think. . . ."

"I didn't ask to be born (into this family, etc.)."

"You're just like your brother (or father/mother/sister or any other disreputable relative or friend)."

"You just care about yourself."

". . . get it through your thick skull. . . ."

"This is a free country; wait till I'm eighteen," etc.

"Look at me and straighten up when I'm talking to you."

"Everybody else is. . . ." or "Nobody else is. . . ."

"If it was good enough for me, it's good enough for you."

"You always. . . ." or "You never. . . ."

"The subject is closed," or "I don't want to hear another word about. . . ." or "There'll be no more discussion of it, and that's final."

"You make me so. . . ."

"How many times do I have to. . . ?"

"You're ruining your life/my life."

"How can you be so stupid?"

"If I've told you once, I've told you a thousand times. . . ."

"Don't do as I do; do as I say."

"Where have I failed? I tried to raise you right, and now. . . ." or " I sacrificed the best years of my life for you; and now. . . ."

Well, how did it all go? Perhaps you got so caught up in teenage nostalgia or the rush of actually communicating with your teenager that you missed the point of our communication workout as it relates to alcohol. The very best you can do to keep your kids safe from the problems of alcohol is to teach them how to talk and how to listen.

Now, let's fit together all these elements of substance-abuse prevention—legal toughness on alcohol issues, community and organizational activism and education, spiritual input, and well-oiled parent-kid communication. With all the avenues we have for influencing teenagers, we can form a prevention matrix to ensure that the next generation coming of age in the twenty-first century can live drug-free!

10

We Can
Win the War

Prevention, support for abusers, and treatment are all steps in the battle to end alcohol and other drug abuse in your community. City governments, neighborhood action groups, parents, and teenagers, themselves, can construct a veritable maze, a matrix of influences to curb substance abuse. It's working in city after city, town after town. And a combined-forces approach can work in your city, too.

Think through the Prevention Matrix diagram shown in Figure 10-1; evaluate and adapt it to your own community. How many beams of influence affect the kids in your town, your neighborhood? Is anyone working to coordinate the efforts of these influential points, to encourage them in curbing substance abuse among your teenagers? If not, why not you? As I've been told time and time again when I visit city after city: We're all in this together; everybody can do something to help win the war against substance abuse—from officials to kids on the street.

Use your imagination to focus on what the families on your block could do together to squelch substance abuse in your school, your neighborhood, your town, your country. But be sure to keep your main thrust of activism targeted right at home. The best preventive factor to discourage substance abuse in a teenager's life is a communicating, aware parent, and the teenager's own growing sense of maturity and responsibility.

Figure 10-1
The Alcohol-Abuse Prevention Matrix: How to Evaluate Your
Community's Fight Against Substance Abuse

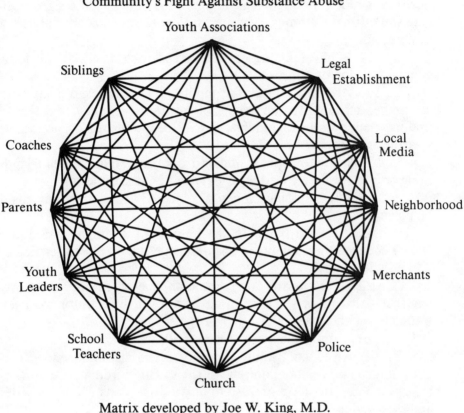

Matrix developed by Joe W. King, M.D.

Is My Kid a User? What Do I Do?

Drug abuse is rampant among teenagers, even though the percentages of users are inching downward. From any of the mental health organizations in your nearest city, you can get more information than you can probably handle on what to do about drug problems with your youth.

Much of that general information will help if you suspect your kid is sliding into alcohol use. What can you do specifically about your teenager's involvement with booze?

Watch for clues—danger signals such as:

_____ Has my teenager's disposition changed noticeably—beyond the usual teenage hormonal ups and downs? Unprovoked hostility, sudden mood swings, depression? Any of these signs indicate something is wrong—whether in the area of substance abuse or other areas.

_____ Is he or she especially irresponsible lately about doing chores, arriving on time, etc.?

_____ Are school grades dropping? Have I checked lately with his or her teachers for any signs of tardiness, truancy, a series of undone homework assignments, discipline problems, or noticeable weariness at school?

_____ Is my teenager losing or dropping an old circle of friends in favor of a rowdy crowd that is or may be into drinking?

_____ Am I missing money or objects in the home that might be pawned?

_____ If I keep liquor in the home, is the supply dwindling? Have I checked the contents to ensure bottles haven't been refilled or diluted with water?

_____ Have I heard any comments or even rumors about my teenager—that he or she is running with a rough group or has been associated with drinking or other drug use?

_____ Is my teenager in trouble with the police?

_____ Although I know much of his or her independence is normal teenage rebellion, does he or she spend inordinate amounts of time alone in a bedroom, refuse to answer questions about activities and destinations?

_____ Has my teenager's family relationships—especially ones that were once close—deteriorated?

_____ Does my teenager change the subject or refuse to talk openly about alcohol, or about his or her peers' involvement with booze and other drugs?

You might be one of the parents who think their kid would never imagine getting involved in alcohol. Or a parent who thinks that it's no big deal if the teenager is drinking a little. Or you may be relieved that it's "only" alcohol that's being abused and not "harder drugs." Think again. If you came up with more than two "yes" answers to the above warning list, your kid—and you—could be in trouble with a serious booze problem that needs to be acknowledged, confronted, and treated.

What can you do? I asked Joe W. King, M.D., the psychiatrist who deals extensively with adolescents who are courting addictions. What follows in the next pages is the advice he generously shared:

What do I do with a drinking teenager?

Whenever a problem of substance abuse (alcohol or other drug) is suspected, parents should:

- Recognize the problem.

- Evaluate the seriousness.

- Intervene at one of four levels.

1. *Recognize the problem.* Think about *communication* in trying to catch on to substance abuse on the part of your teenager. (Review regularly the "When I Was Your Age" communication tips in chapter 9.)

And don't be afraid to watch for warning symptoms. If an adolescent develops a fever, for example, most parents would take a temperature, give some early symptomatic treatment, get further evaluation of the problem, talk to the kid with the fever, and call in outside professional help if their own interventions did not cause the fever to subside or if the fever got worse.

Often parents become indirect and sneaky and instantly behave as detectives in dealing with the suspicion that their youngsters may be on drugs. The initial step should be to sit down and talk with the teenager in a very straightforward manner. We do not have to have proof of anything to express concern—just as we might not know the exact cause of a fever—but we can take a course of action when we recognize certain symptoms.

Concern represents our feelings or perceptions about a situation. Our feelings, perceptions, worries, and concerns cannot be repudiated even if an attempt is made to do so.

On the other hand, if the initial step in trying to ascertain a substance-abuse problem is to accuse, then the accusing party, the parent, can be refuted on the basis of multiple "technicalities" as the youngster defensively attempts to cover his or her tracks. For example:

Parent: "Your clothes started smelling funny and we thought it might be marijuana. So we went through your things and found this bag of stuff in your dresser drawer, and we want to know how much you're smoking and what other drugs you're using. And which one of your sleazy new friends is responsible for getting you started on this stuff?"

Now, in that one little speech I've condensed several "cardinal sins" to make my point. A response to such an intervention might be:

Adolescent: "It's not my stuff. I'm keeping it for a friend; and besides that, what are you doing going through my stuff? You tell me all the time that you want me to trust you and you want to trust me. How can I trust you if you're sneaking around in my stuff? My new friends aren't sleazy and they're more interested in how I feel than you are! I'm not using drugs—and do you think I'd tell you if I was?"

Obviously, from the very onset, we have an almost complete breakdown of communication, trust, and understanding. We've bungled the opportunity for empathic intervention.

As an alternative, I would suggest the following type of intervention:

Parent: "Bob/Mary, we're concerned about you. We've noticed some changes in you which worry us. Your clothes and your room smell funny to us. You seem to be less available to us emotionally and physically and not as interested in doing things with the family. Your schoolwork has fallen off. We're worried about what has happened to your old friends; we don't seem to know your new friends very well, and that worries us, too. You seem to have money and we don't know where it's coming from. You've lost interest in being on the track team, and physically you look tired and your eyes are often bloodshot—especially on the weekend. We are really worried about you and want to know if you are all right, if you're okay. You don't seem as happy to us as you used to."

Obviously, this kind of approach needs to be utilized when the parents and youngster are not dealing with any hot issue. It should be a time when both parents and youngster are emotionally "in neutral gear," are available to each other, and have ample time to pursue any discussion which might follow.

Also, a parent should not wait until all the symptoms that I have identified in the example above come forth. Hopefully, only one or two of those symptoms would be recognized before parents would sit down and express their concern to a youngster.

Parents need to be prepared that the youngster might respond in a very defensive, hostile, and "show-stopping" way. If the situation is not so urgent as to warrant an emergency type of intervention, I would suggest that within the next twenty-four hours or so the parents once again express their concern to their youngster, telling the teenager that his or her storming out of the room or in any way stopping the discussion is not going to alleviate their fears, but in fact it reinforces them. Parents might want to sit down a second or even third time to present their concern about the changes they are seeing in their son or daughter.

The key elements in recognizing the problem are a genuine expression of concern and the pursuit of understanding—not the establishment of "proof" and the identification of guilt.

If the situation is one of real urgency—that is, if the youngster is coming in drunk or staying out all night or running away or skipping school—if things have gone to that degree, obviously this early stage must be expedited quickly in the interest of the youngster's physical and emotional safety.

Having expressed a sincere desire to deal with their son or daughter in an honest and straightforward way, parents should then continue to seek to intervene over a reasonable period of time—and what is reasonable depends on the urgency of the situation.

If things look serious, then parents must turn to being detectives. However, investigating should be a clear "Plan B." Parents should become familiar with what is in their youngster's room, seek information from anyone who knows the teenager, especially his or her "old" peer group, coaches, teachers, etc.

Talking it out ("Plan A") or a "Plan B" detective investigation should give parents some clarity as to whether their adolescent is using drugs such as alcohol. At that point, it becomes important to confront the situation—warmly, firmly, but directly—and then to determine how to evaluate the seriousness of the situation.

2. *Evaluate the seriousness of the youngster's substance abuse.* Sometimes the use of drugs is simply that—a use of drugs. In that situation, the youngster may need some type of intervention in an

outpatient counseling program which helps the person understand the significance of substance abuse, its potential in terms of its impact on his or her own life, and so forth. This program should contain a strong cognitive component. It could be through some group sessions at schools. Many schools are now having peer-run and/or professionally run after-school sessions for kids who have been into booze and other drugs, or are worried about getting into drugs.

At this level of intervention, parents should familiarize themselves thoroughly with the many services for both evaluation and treatment available on an outpatient basis in their community.

If the youngster starts running away from home, staying out at night, or becoming more defiant or oppositional, then obviously outpatient counseling will not be sufficient, because the teenager will probably not show up for sessions on a regular basis. So parents at this time often get professional help in evaluating the problem.

I urge parents to seek psychiatric or professional substance-abuse help at this level, just as they would if their child had a physical symptom that persisted that they didn't understand. If a youngster had persistent, frightening asthma attacks, no caring parent would give in to "I don't wanna go see a doctor," under those circumstances. In the same way, a parent doesn't need to give in to "I won't go see a counselor; I won't go see a shrink!"

Parents need to communicate that they support their son or daughter's getting help and that they are willing to participate in the whole process. This reassurance just might be spit back in a parent's face; but it is laying the foundation for potential growth in the future of the parental-youngster relationship.

This evaluation stage is a time when parents, if they haven't done so yet, must thoroughly educate themselves with the signs and symptoms of substance abuse. Educational resources are available by contacting any local mental health agency or the organizations listed in the Resources section in Appendix B.

3. *Intervene.* The level of intervention will, of course, be mostly determined by the degree of psychopathology the youngster demonstrates.

To glimpse that psychopathological state, I do a mental-status check on adolescents—that is, I determine through exploratory psychiatric interviews the type and level of functioning that the youngsters are experiencing internally: Are they oriented to time, place, and persons present? Do they seem to have any disruption of the thinking process? Is their thinking appropriate to their current life situation? Are their judgment and intellect intact? Are they able to utilize their ability to read, write, and do arithmetic? What level of psychological maturity or development do they seem to be utilizing? Do they deal with stress or a difficult life situation in an age-appropriate way, or do they respond to such a situation like a much younger child?

Next, I evaluate how the youngster is coping with the four areas of responsibility that we all have as individuals: 1) the family, 2) the "job," which for most kids is primarily school, 3) the peer group, and 4) the community in general.

1. *The family.* I attempt to determine what the youngster's relationship with the family is and especially if there has been a significant change. In doing this, it is very important to remember that a normal developmental process of adolescence is to emancipate psychologically from dependency on the family and become a free-standing individual by late adolescence or young adulthood. So all of this has to be very carefully put into perspective. I would especially look for any marked differences or changes in the relationship with the family—and particularly areas in which the youngster used to derive pleasure and satisfaction with parents, siblings, and even extended family members.

2. *The job.* The vocational aspects of the youngster's life need to be evaluated again, especially looking for changes. Obviously, the primary vocational interest for most youngsters is school, although many kids may have jobs. This area of how they productively engage in vocational or educational pursuits is an important area to evaluate.

3. *The peer group.* The youngster's relationship with peers also needs to be very carefully evaluated. Has there been any change in peer relationships? Has the youngster pulled away from former peer relationships that used to bring him or her pleasure? Have the activities with the peer group become less planned and more aimless—not necessarily destructive, but at least not constructive? It is normal adolescent behavior to do some "cruising," and it can be done nondestructively. This is a way that adolescents deal with desires for an increased sense of mastery over the huge responsibilities of being "on their own," and can be a very important time in teenagers' development. On the other hand, if there is a sense of aimlessness, if the

wandering around means that the youngster misses dinner time, doesn't do homework, comes in too late or not at all, this can signal a problem.

4. *The community.* The adolescent's general relationship to the community can be evaluated in two major areas. One has to do with the youngster's basic respect for community standards: Is the teenager under arrest, repeatedly speeding, etc.? The other major area is his or her participation in whatever opportunities the community offers. Is she part of the local Scout troop or is he a member of a motorcycle gang? Is his best friend a friend from school or church, or is his friend his favorite pusher? There are multiple opportunities in the community to become involved, and it is important to see to which of these the youngster in question is drawn.

Another major determinant in the evaluation process is to determine how cooperative and available a youngster is for an intervention process. Obviously, if the youngster refuses to come into the observation session, if he refuses to come in on time, if he refuses to go to school, then we are dealing with a situation that will probably involve the need for inpatient intervention where external support and structure can be provided for the youngster until he or she can provide those structures and supports independently from internal resources.

Almost any youngster who comes in for evaluation will do so with some degree of defiance or resentment. This is understandable, especially if he or she has never been involved in any kind of evaluation process by a counselor. After all, some kids think, *Psychiatrists only see people who are crazy, so they must all think I'm insane.* That's why it is very important that the initial evaluation processes involve the parents and the patient, and sometimes even siblings, so that everyone can start on a basic level of understanding—which does not always mean a basic level of agreement.

I emphasize strongly that it is not important that the family agree, but that family members understand how each of them experiences the current life situation. Mom may be concerned about the grades dropping off, Dad may be concerned about the kid getting kicked off the football team, and the kid may be concerned about the parents being "screwed up." Those are all important points of view.

But often, understanding is preceded by resistance and fear; I have worked with outpatient teenagers who have very quickly expressed a sense of relief when they understand they are not in trouble in terms of a punitive approach. Relief is sometimes obvious when they see that, in fact, their parents, myself, and others are concerned about them, that we are seeking resolution and understanding and not "proof and guilt."

Having then determined the degree of disruption of the youngster's internal state, shown outwardly in his or her interactions with family, peers, school, or vocational area responsibilities, and within the community, a level of intervention should be chosen that is appropriate to the disruption of functioning. It is a cardinal rule to remember that the primary concern is the youngster's safety and the family's safety—physical, as well as emotional. If I am torn between having a youngster participate on an outpatient or inpatient level of treatment, I choose the safe route and openly admit I am doing so. If I have overcompensated, that will become apparent early in the inpatient treatment process and gradually the treatment will be moved to an outpatient level of intervention.

The youngsters who are able to be treated on an outpatient basis are ones:

- who have a strong family support system with which they are still engaged,

- whose substance-abuse problem is fairly new,

- whose ability to function in any of the areas mentioned previously remains intact, and

- who feel a degree of displeasure with their drinking or substance abuse.

It is terribly important to emphasize that kids often use drugs as an expression of intense underlying discomfort, unhappiness, and so forth. These youngsters frequently fall into the category of being "dual diagnosed"—they have a substance-abuse diagnosis, but they also have a legitimate psychiatric diagnosis. This psychiatric diagnosis can be anything and everything that non-substance-abusing youngsters endure, as well, including psychosis, behavioral or adjustment problems in adolescence, and/or depression in childhood or adolescence. Unfortunately, this is a growing child problem. So it is very important that between evaluation and intervention an intense effort is made to understand the "total kid," and not just look at the surface behavior of substance abuse. It is important to understand the meaning—I like to call it the "psychological economy"—of any surface behavior for a given person, including the surface behavior of alcohol and/or other substance abuse.

At any level of intervention, it is important that the parents really know something about the program that they would engage their youngster and themselves in; they must make a commitment to be right in there with the youngster all the way.

The cardinal rule that I use is to try at all times to recommend what is best for the youngster and the family. That's the only promise I ever make to a patient or the patient's parents: I will do or recommend what I think is best for their child, and/or for them. I am concerned with two things: 1) what is safe psychologically and physically for the identified patient and for the family, and 2) what is fair and reasonable to ask of the identified patient and the family.

Levels of Intervention

I generally think in terms of four levels of intervention:

1. acute-care hospital inpatient,
2. residential treatment center,
3. partial hospitalization, and
4. outpatient level of intervention.

The *acute-care level* of intervention is appropriate when the safety of the patient is paramount—when the patient is clearly behaving in a self-destructive and certainly self-defeating way in the family, the peer group, the job, or the community. I also want to determine what is fair and reasonable to ask of the patient and the family. If both parents are overwhelmed by the patient's behavior, or if it is a single parent who works nights when the child is not in school, it is not reasonable then to lay down a treatment plan that would require a significant degree of supervision by the parent as part of the intervention process.

Sometimes one-parent and two-parent families are just flat burned out and can't really function, and of course if the youngster has a significant underlying psychiatric disorder, this too is more likely to indicate the need for acute-care intervention. There are many substance abusers who are not at all suicidal; there are others who are consciously or unconsciously very self-destructive, and these inclinations need to be determined.

Second-level intervention is *residential treatment center (RTC)* care. This is the level of care at the clinic where I practice. We have a specialized substance-abuse program for youngsters who have been stabilized in the hospital and have been transferred to us for the substance-abuse program. We also care for youngsters who don't require the acute care of hospital-level intervention and are admitted directly to our clinic. The RTC substance-abuse program in our setting is for those kids for whom booze or other drugs have become a core part of their lives.

Partial hospitalization is a level of intervention for those kids who:

- need therapeutic intervention during the day, including educational intervention,
- can participate intensively in individual, group, and family therapies of the recovery program,
- be involved in an intensive Twelve-Step Program along with their families,
- can handle the responsibility of being home at night and on the weekends,
- and those whose families can handle that responsibility as well.

Sometimes kids are admitted directly to the "partial" level of care, and sometimes kids have graduated from acute care to partial, or from acute care to residential to partial.

Finally, the *outpatient level* of care is the level of care which most youngsters receive as their entire treatment process. It's the desired level of care when at all possible, because it means that the youngster continues to participate in the family, in the job or school setting and with the peer group. Also, he is able to do so with a reasonable degree of internal sense of well-being and functioning.

At all levels of intervention, I believe youngsters need to have the surface behavior problems of their substance abuse dealt with through a very aggressive Twelve-Step program which includes a didactic portion, the study of the Alcoholics Anonymous "Big Book," and so forth. In addition, if they're inpatients, the youngsters can start attending community-based Alcoholics Anonymous or Narcotics Anonymous programs. The AA/NA and Twelve-Step approaches are very important, in my opinion, for inpatients, for kids with partial substance-abuse problems, and for outpatients, because these programs have a heavy emphasis on the family aspects of this problem.

Recapping Joe's Advice

Joe's summary of treatment when you suspect your youth is getting into booze is basically simple: *Recognize, evaluate, and intervene.* Let's hope you never have to move through those steps. Let's hope your teenager has done his or her own evaluation and decided not to be a number on a substance-abuse statistical chart.

What Can a Teenager Do About Alcohol Abuse?

The list is pretty simple for a teenager who faces the drinking issue head-on. Here are some suggestions to pass on to teenagers you know:

• If you're under age, it's illegal for you to drink alcohol. Don't drink.

• If you're of drinking age in your area, decide for yourself what you'll do about booze—don't let advertisers or peers or problems twist your arm into drinking against your own better judgment. See the discussion called "Whatsitgonnabe?" in chapter 8 to get a grip on some basic principles that will help you form your own standards about drinking

• If you're under age and you're offered a drink, assert your independence to say no. There are probably enough rough stories of alcoholism in your community or your family; simply refer to the situation and say, "I'm not going to end up with a drinking problem, so I'd rather have a Pepsi or something." Practice role-playing your response; you *will* be offered an alcoholic drink sometime. Don't be intimidated by comments; practice some comebacks such as, "Oh yeah, booze is too tough for me to handle, all right. I wish I could be as mature as you. . . !"

• Don't get into a car whose driver has been drinking. Always have enough change to call home or call a cab in an emergency. And remember: Friends don't let friends drive drunk.

There are many creative ways teenagers can help cement their standards on alcohol use. They can join school or community programs to fight alcohol and other drug abuse. They can even get a realistic glimpse of the painful toll alcohol takes on their town by volunteering at the local hospital. Here's a letter from a kid who has decided to go straight because of what he's seen in his volunteer position at an emergency room:

> I am a teen. Not yet old enough to think things through as well as I ought to sometimes, but I'm old enough to look around me and just observe the things happening in my own community.
>
> So I volunteer in the emergency room of our town's hospital. And I am asking other teenagers like me if they have the guts to do this every week, because what I see in the emergency room will forever keep me from driving with someone who has been drinking.
>
> Watch who comes into the hospital on a stretcher. You may recognize a face or two. Watch what the doctors have to do to help them, and how their family feels. Then watch them try to recuperate.
>
> Sometimes it doesn't all stop the minute you crash a car. . . . If you're lucky enough to be alive, it will be with you for a long time.
>
> Volunteering gives me a chance to help other people. But it also helps me learn about life . . . and what I can do to save it.

Teenagers need to believe they, too, can do something about saving lives from the ravages of alcohol and other drugs.

I know they can; because as a teenager I began the changes in my own life that eventually would help my alcohol-cursed and addiction-driven family to wholeness. Our story of hope and victory just might be the incentive you need to work to rid your family or your neighborhood of the substance abuse that's killing our kids.

Read on.

11

My Own Story

I've been sharing bits and pieces of my own and my family's story of our battle with alcohol abuse. To round out what we've gone through, and to encourage you and your family toward wholeness, let me share, as Paul Harvey says, "the rest of the story."

How to Kidnap Your Own Mother

Mom's drinking got completely out of control. The entire family braced itself, knowing her deplorable condition could not go on indefinitely. When an alcoholic retreats from life to virtually nonstop drinking, the end is inevitably near. By the time Mom's drinking reached crisis proportions, she had a flower shop. But she was spending very little time there; it was mostly run by her employees. When Chris and I would drive past my parents' home during the day it would seem to us like an alcohol-haunted house. Every shade was pulled down, the curtains were closed, and the doors were shut and locked.

Mom's isolation was a cry for help—that was very clear to see. At this time, she was drinking nearly a quart of vodka a day! Later, after we had forcibly committed her to a recovery unit, Chris, and my brothers' wives went to clean Mom and Dad's house from top to bottom. By the time they had thrown the last bottle in a trash can, it was filled to the brim! Liquor bottles were found everywhere—in the closet, in the dresser, behind furniture, under the bed, etc.

Normal people don't live like a hermit or a recluse, existing in some dark cave. Three signs, among others, that signaled to me that Mom was on her last leg were isolation, binge drinking, and not stopping to eat. People who have dramatic differences in their eating and sleeping patterns, are obviously signaling that something is critically wrong. I think Mom was basically "out of it" most of the time in those days. Mr. Alcohol was manipulating her like a puppet on a string.

Everyone in the family always got together for all the major holidays—Thanksgiving, Christmas, and the small kids' birthdays—at Dad and Mom's house. I hate to admit it, but I dreaded those get-togethers, particularly when Mom was on the last lap of her spiral down. It was horrible. We all knew she was in trouble, but we weren't doing anything. Or so I thought.

After our conference with a medical center's alcohol-recovery director, we all felt our "enabling"—ignoring—response was over. One of my brothers had read Betty Ford's book tracking her own victory over alcoholism. Armed with more evidence that we had to do something, we held secret meetings to discuss the problem.

These conferences came to the agonizing conclusion that we should forcibly commit Mom to the recovery unit of Baptist Hospital. My mom is a strong lady, the mother of five, who had been drinking for years. We knew she was not going to pleasantly walk into the care unit and commit herself to a twenty-eight-day residential program. We knew we would have to abduct her! Planning to kidnap your own mother is a very interesting experience. When, where, how—and what if something went wrong?

Dad was very uneasy. His prayer-oriented approach to Mom's deliverance left little room for abduction and forced admission. However, the five of us boys immediately overruled and silenced him. Awakened to how long we had done nothing, there was no turning back now.

Because I owned a long, customized van, my vehicle was selected. We all felt equally that we had to move immediately. Our strategy was simple. We would go to Dad and Mom's home Friday night at 7 P.M. (By committing Mom on a Friday night with our signatures, the hospital could hold her over the weekend until she could be assessed by a doctor as to her alcoholism.)

We signed Mom in for a full twenty-eight-day stay. She still remembers every detail of that episode:

"I wouldn't speak to Jerry," she now recalls. "I wouldn't speak to any of the boys for about two weeks. Many times, I would walk to the elevator and just look at it, thinking it would be great to get out of there. Then one of the nurses would walk by and say, 'Don't even think about it; don't even look at the elevator.'"

Mom was humiliated by the abduction, and the pain and trauma for her and for all of us family members often seemed as if it would never end—that it *could* never end. But then, my mother had a husband who wouldn't give up.

He Wouldn't Quit Believing

My remembrances of Mom chained to alcoholism are limited, because I was just one of five sons. My dad lived with the problem every day and every night. And he never stopped believing God could change Mom's life and give her complete victory over her addiction.

John W. Johnston is a man of unusual personal disciplines. I suppose much of my personal security and confidence comes from the fact that Dad is everything I want to be. Even to this day, when I have a major problem or need direction on a decision, I go to Dad. We talk together and pray together.

Dad reads his Bible through every one hundred days—five chapters in the morning, ten at night, and twenty on Sunday! Every year, he has read the Bible three and a half times. Every morning Dad prays before he leaves the house.

And he feels he must pray on his knees. He does this every day. Or, to use his words, "A discipline is something you do every day without fail."

If I show up at my parents' house and his "reading" for the day is not completed, he doesn't come down until it is. And I understand!

Through the ups and downs of my mom's problem, Dad never stopped loving and believing. He was always there, encouraging Mom, gently reminding her of her relationship to God and her responsibility to her family.

Mom could be a tiger on the bottle! But Dad was always there. I used to think my dad was an enabler. I've changed my mind. Dad believed all along that God could change Mom's life. And through prayer, and prayer alone, Dad was committed to that goal. When we abducted Mom, he was reluctant. When Mom relapsed, he was quiet and looked Godward.

I used to chide Dad that we had to put "legs" to our prayers, and do something. I was upset and my hostility was evident. Dad quietly continued to look to the Lord. He believed, truly believed, God could work the impossible.

I have often thought, through our ordeal with Mom, how many more alcoholics, drug addicts, and traumatized people could be reached if they had in their lives a true believer and prayer person like Dad.

After our forced abduction of Mom and her subsequent relapse, she went downhill fast. From August to March of that year, things got very bleak. Mom became a prisoner in her own house. She stopped going to her flower shop almost entirely. Her drinking got out of control.

Brokenness and Healing

At that same time, I physically collapsed in Winston-Salem, North Carolina, during a week of speaking in all the high schools, with a culminating rally at Memorial Coliseum with seven thousand people. I had gone too hard for too long that year, speaking 410 times all over the nation. It took me months to get my strength back. And this experience was sovereignly used by God to draw me close to Himself. The Lord used this time to break me and make me dependent upon Him in a new and fresh way. Reminded of my own spiritual responsibilities, I started fervently interceding for Mom in my basement study each morning—while Dad was doing the same.

I sensed I had undergone a spiritual cleansing and overhaul. Renewed and invigorated, I had a mountain-like faith to wrestle with God in prayer. That's when I distinctly remember praying that dangerous prayer, "God, do whatever You have to do to get Mom's attention, to show her You love her, and can free her."

Chris knew the ramifications of what I was praying, and reminded me of the seriousness of it. My basement study is a glorious place. Books on every wall insulate it so it is almost noiseless. I enjoy having my devotions there, because no one can hear me. I feel totally uninhibited. God is there with me in that study. He helped me see that my physical collapse at my greatest point of need was all in His plan.

Our prayers for Mom intensified.

Unknown to us, Mom started bleeding internally. By March, she was almost bedridden. She didn't say a word, but she had to be scared. Of course, we didn't even know she was losing blood, until my dad called a registered nurse to the house. She was so taken aback by Mom's yellowish coloring she called a doctor and begged him to come to the house. The doctor, at Mom's bedside on that Friday, told her she needed to be rushed to the hospital. Mom resisted and said she would go Monday. He answered that she would be dead by Monday if she waited.

The paramedic unit carted Mom down the stairs of the house to an awaiting ambulance. Watching that scene, my awful prayer—*Do whatever You need to, God, to get Mom's attention*—was echoing in my mind.

Diagnosed at the hospital, she was placed in the intensive care unit. Unmoved, Dad quietly continued to look to God.

It was in this crisis atmosphere I had to leave and go to Atlanta, Georgia to speak in every high school in Cobb County—to more than twenty thousand students in five days. Each night I was to speak at the large Roswell Street Baptist Church in Marietta, which seats four thousand. Dr. Nelson Price is the pastor of this highly respected Atlanta congregation. Weekly, he speaks to not only Cobb County's movers and shakers, but to the entire city via channel 11, which carries his message live each Sunday morning.

I don't know what it was about Nelson Price that drew me to be so confidential and honest with him. I truly believed he was a man of faith and knew how to pray. During our grueling week together, we spent time talking and getting to know one another.

Wednesday night at dinner with Nelson, his wife Trudy, and Chris, I broke down crying, and blurted out, "Nelson, my mom's an alcoholic. She's in the hospital dying. Somehow I haven't reached her."

Instead of seeming shocked, Nelson calmly said, "Jerry, God loves your mom and God wants to heal her. Let's pray right now that God will touch her and change her."

Well, I certainly wanted to believe it could all happen that matter-of-factly, but my logical mind and years of enduring this sad saga said, *impossible*. I passed off Nelson's simplistic antidote, blaming his lack of knowledge as to the intensity of the problem.

My faith was so small that night. I was run down from going day and night that week. My schedule was so tight we even had to take one of the TV station's helicopters from school to school. Yet it was more than fatigue that had worn me down. I was unbelieving.

I answered Nelson's suggestion quite mechanically that night. "Okay, will you pray?" I said. Nelson took my hand and asked God to deliver Mom. There is no doubt his faith was in perfect unison with Dad's. Nelson's prayer was specific; he asked God to completely deliver Mom.

My mom has never had a drop of alcohol since, even though several years have passed. I still can't get over it. So many times Mom has said to me, "Jerry, in the hospital God took the desire away!" Mom has said she is not even tempted to drink now. In that hospital, our miracle came. And it was real. The difference in my mother now is inexpressible. She has said that the thoughts of her old self are like watching old black-and-white movies.

Dad stood true, and I have watched God bless his obedience. He and Mom are like new lovers. Their relationship is brand new.

If God can change my mom, He can change your loved one. Believe!

With Alcohol, It Ain't Over 'Til It's Over

Mom, set free from the bondage of alcohol, was quickly growing in her faith and freedom. Each month I could see the transforming, maturing difference in her life. I waited two years before I started talking to her about writing a book on the alcohol dilemma confronting youth and parents, and my desire to integrate her story into the book. Little did I know the intricacies that her story would entail.

Quite honestly, I was apprehensive about how to broach the subject to her. My hesitancy was in the newness of talking about the complete victory and freedom God had given Mom over the bottle. However, I knew that the Johnston family had gone through this taxing, long trial for a reason. I firmly believe that all—*all*—things work together for good (Romans 8:28). But I was aware that to Mom it was a very new thing to openly admit that she was and is a recovering alcoholic. Obviously, the "what-will-people-think" fear initially set in. However, when I finally summoned the courage to suggest it, Mom was more than willing to endure any embarrassment to reach out to others victimized by addictions.

I flew into Kansas City after speaking at the Fellowship of Christian Athletes national convention in Indianapolis, and Mom picked me up at the airport. It was a brilliantly sunny morning. We went to eat lunch at our favorite restaurant. "If it will help people who are like I was," was her reply. We laughed and talked that day more like best friends than mother and son. With alcohol removed from Mom's life, she is such a radiating, sweet person. I cautioned her that a book would have wide circulation. "Everyone will know. . . . Are you sure?" I asked.

Her reply came again without hesitation: "If it will help someone, yes! But why would anyone care what I have been through? Who would be interested?"

I thought again, off alcohol, just how humble and selfless she was.

Toronto Trauma

Planning for the release of this book, I decided to accept an invitation for not only myself, but also for Mom to appear on a TV show taped in Toronto, Canada. This would be Mom's first TV show to share her deliverance from alcohol. Originally, the guest coordinator of the show had scheduled us to appear Monday, January 25. Later, however, the date of the interview was postponed to Wednesday, May 30, which coincidentally was Mom's fifty-sixth birthday. I now know why the date was changed!

During her three-year comeback from alcohol, Mom would have intermittent spells of bleeding internally, losing significant amounts of blood. Each time, we hospitalized her and, like a car out of gas, they would fill her back up with blood by several transfusions. Because of liver degeneration brought on by the years of excessive amounts of alcohol, Mom's viscerous veins would drastically hemorrhage. Blood would escape to her stomach and it was not uncommon that she would vomit extensive amounts of blood. This problem is very common in alcoholics. Her doctor wanted to perform surgery to reroute blood circuitry to and from the liver, thus releasing the pressure on the viscerous veins.

For a long time, Mom had forbidden such surgery. But she finally conceded and allowed her Kansas City doctor to scope her veins in the esophagus and perform sclerosis, a process in which the viscerous veins are injected with a sealant in an attempt to prevent further hemorrhaging. The procedure went very well. But although we thought all was safe, we were actually headed for a harrowing showdown.

On Tuesday, May 29, we flew from Kansas City to Toronto. That night I spoke downtown. Mom and I enjoyed a meal before the meeting. We left the auditorium and got to the hotel late. I got Mom settled in her room. The next morning, the TV show's guest coordinator came early to the hotel to eat breakfast with us. Mom called my room and I encouraged her to go on down to the restaurant and begin eating with him.

By the time I got to the table, Mom and the coordinator had gotten acquainted and gone over some of the procedures for the taping.

I was nervous that the TV show might be too much strain for Mom; but when we started the interview, she surprised me! Calmly and sincerely she answered every question with poise and clarity. Mom shared her resentment at the time of our abduction and forced admission into the hospital's recovery program. She made clear the agony of life dependent on a bottle and the release when God "took the desire away."

Her genuineness not only captured the audience on the set, but also those who watched the show. I was amazed at the rapport she established so quickly with the audience, and the simplicity with which she credited her comeback and abstinence to the Creator. She became a positive inspiration to all those still struggling for freedom. Her message was not one of condemnation, but caring, prayerful patience for all people to believe in God's plan for the traumatized one in their families. It occurred to me that this is what true faith is: believing God for the impossible case we know. Never in all those long years of Mom's alcoholism would I have believed that she would be on a TV show, sober, giving God all the glory! God didn't honor my faith—He honored my dad's faith and tenacity to not quit believing in the miracle of transformation for Mom.

The driver dropped us off at the Toronto airport about sixty minutes before our departing flight, so Mom and I had plenty of time to clear customs and board the plane. I suggested we go to the airport restaurant for a quick lunch. The restaurant was rather full and Mom seemed distant. I inhaled my lunch and had just begun my pecan pie when Mom said she felt queasy. She stood up to leave for the restroom—but her dizziness was so visible I encouraged her sit back down.

Suddenly, she started furiously vomiting something red. It was blood—and it was everywhere. It covered the table. Immediately I stood at her side, scared to death, thinking that this couldn't be happening! I kept wiping Mom's bloody chin, holding her hand and talking to her. Amazingly, everyone just stared and did nothing!

I ran to the cashier and begged her to call a paramedic unit. Racing back to Mom, I noticed that her eyes didn't seem to be focusing. Blood was all over her light tan coat and green dress. I continued rubbing her hand, telling her to hold on. A Royal Canadian Mounted Police officer strolled by. I screamed at him to get on the walkie-talkie in his hand and do something. By now, the whole restaurant was observing our every move.

When the paramedic arrived, he quickly got Mom to the floor. I knew she was bleeding to death, and when her eyes fixed wide open, almost the size of quarters, I remember praying, *Oh, God, don't let her die!* Mom's blood pressure had plummeted.

On oxygen, and with two IV's immediately inserted in the backs of her hands, she started to recover. Then she said, "We can still catch the plane, Jerry." She whispered she was afraid she would ruin my schedule for the week.

Here again I saw just how beautiful and lovely my mom is. At death's door, after vomiting so much blood that we learned later her hemoglobin count was a mere 4.5 (14 is normal for women)—she was afraid she would ruin my schedule for the week.

With me riding in the front, the ambulance raced to Etibicoko General Hospital in nearby Rexdale, Ontario. After checking Mom in, the emergency-room doctor said she needed to stay and be treated and carefully observed for several days.

Emergency

I left the hospital at 4 P.M. with Jeff Bergen, my associate, intending on returning at seven to spend the evening at Mom's bedside. They told me by the time I returned, Mom would be in room 1046.

Three hours later, I hurried into room 1046—and found a dead man in the bed! A nurse quickly sent me back to the emergency area. Mom had started bleeding again, and the doctor told me that her condition was life-threatening. If they could not get the bleeding stopped, she would die. Then I was ushered completely out of the emergency room into the waiting area. My mind raced back to the comment Mom had made to me shortly before I left her at four that afternoon. "If anything happens, I want to be cremated, Jerry," she'd said.

I rebuked her for even suggesting the thought of death.

"You never know, Jerry," she said.

Within minutes, Mom was being rushed out of the emergency area to a waiting ambulance to be transferred to the Toronto General Hospital downtown.

I followed her stretcher, almost jogging to keep up, and was taken aback at how bad she looked. She was shivering as though she were in a blizzard; her body had started swelling. "Mom, I'm right here with you. I'm not going anywhere; I'll be here for you," I said, attempting to console her, but knowing I was staring into the face of death.

A team of nurses and a doctor scrunched into the ambulance with Mom—tubes, wires, and blood and IV bags swung from racks over their heads as the vehicle's doors closed and it raced away.

As I stood there alone, under the roof of the emergency receiving area, I shoved my hands in my pockets—and felt the business card of a man who had been in the restaurant when Mom had collapsed earlier that day. He had knelt beside me as I hovered over Mom and asked, "Are you Jerry Johnston?"

"Yes," I replied tersely.

"I am John, the pastor of a church nearby. If I can help in any way, please call."

In the chaos of the moment, I had crammed the card deep into my pocket and responded with a weak "thank you" as I hurried away, assisting the paramedics in getting Mom out of the airport and to the hospital.

It was later that night, after I had called John and asked, "Will you come?" that I learned the strength that could come from a Christian brother. John held me up, encouraged me, and most importantly, prayed with me. God had planted John in that airport restaurant at that exact time. *All* things do work together for good.

At 1:30 A.M., John and I were headed toward downtown Toronto General Hospital. The doctor there informed me in the waiting room that they could not stop the bleeding. As though he were wrestling with a tiger, he had had to force a tube down Mom's mouth, throat, and esophagus, without any sedation, to blow up a balloon in her stomach to put pressure on the bleeding veins in hopes they would stop hemorrhaging. As a result, she had somewhat stabilized; but she was still hanging on to life by a thread. John prayed with me and spoke words of faith.

All things *do* work together for good. Mom was forced to have the surgery her Kansas City doctor had recommended—but she had it at Toronto General Hospital, an eminent teaching hospital that was, the Kansas City doctor told me later, the best place for all of this to have happened. Toronto, he said, was the Mecca of the medical world in handling this kind of serious surgery.

I remembered the original date Mom and I were to have appeared on this talk show, and how it had been postponed from January to May. Although it was an unpleasant birthday experience, Mom, now at home in Kansas City, beams with pure delight that her roller-coaster days with internal bleeding are over. Her hemoglobin count is stable now, at its highest count ever, and doctors say her viscerous veins look excellent. There's even evidence that her liver is regenerating. So our family is overwhelmingly convinced: All things do work together for good to those who love God.

In some ways, the whole Toronto incident was just another scene in the life-long saga of my family and alcohol. And as usual in the hangovers of alcoholism, the situation continued to have its ups and downs. One occurred as I returned to Kansas City, and my dad arrived in Toronto. I'll let him describe those days of crisis. The rest of this chapter is his story; parts of it are reprinted from his journal.

If Only I Could Help Her

It was a matter of daily trusting God to provide for Joyce's health. She had hemorrhaged so many times, and I had had to rush her to the hospital for emergency treatments because of her internal bleeding.

She would become nauseated, then vomit old and new blood. Her hemoglobin count sometimes was as low as 3.9. I'd feel so bad, so weak, unable to help her, except to pray to God for His healing hand to touch her body and stop the bleeding. I would look at her and see her skin color and fingernails turning so white, and then I'd know she was still bleeding internally. If only I could help her. But I could do nothing except encourage her. And I could pray.

It's been great to be with her, especially these last few years, because there has been no alcohol. But her health has been so bad. Amazingly, though, she is strong, even with the constant threat of bleeding to death; she has still been so strong, so courageous. How could anyone be this strong, with the threat of death hanging over her head? How? Joyce believed that God would heal her from all the lingering effects of alcoholism.

She believed that God could do anything, and so did I. Why? Because man, nature, professionals in medicine can do anything described by the laws of physics, chemistry, botany, medicine, etc. But God can do anything even beyond the laws of nature. God performs miracles, inexplicable miracles. I believed that the medical professionals would do all they could to heal Joyce; but beyond that, God would have to take over.

You just take one day at a time. Forget yesterday; don't worry about tomorrow. Just get through today!

Joyce's strength, courage, and faith radiated to other members of the family. I could see it. The daughters-in-law marveled at her strength. With her hemoglobin so low, she would still go to her flower shop and work, plus she still "kept house" for the two of us. Unselfishly, she would always rather buy a gift for her children or grandchildren than for herself.

All of these wonderful attitudes came after she stopped drinking. Prior to that, while drinking, Joyce was just the opposite. The only thing that mattered, really, was alcohol. All through her drinking, I would leave her love notes. I would sign them: "John 3:17, I love you."

The Bible verse reminded her—and me—that if Christ did not come to earth to condemn us, but only to save, why should I condemn? So I didn't.

Toronto. I have never seen so many tubes attached to one body. Looking at Joyce's sad, swollen form, I felt so helpless. I told her she looked beautiful, that I loved her, and everything was going to be all right. I held her hand and told her I was going to pray with her. She couldn't speak. But she tried to write something on my hand. I couldn't understand how she could have the presence of mind to try to communicate with me, because she was so ill. But that was Joyce's strength coming out.

I learned from Joyce later that she was writing, "Take the tubes out, please; they hurt." Joyce believed that if she could only make me understand, I would persuade the doctors to do it. She believed in my love for her, my willingness to do anything for her—even "to take the tubes out."

But I couldn't figure out what she was writing; so I couldn't look into her eyes. When I started feeling faint, the nurses noticed it, offered me a chair, brought me sweetened orange juice, then suggested I wait out in the ICU lobby . . . where the loved ones of Leon, Tom, Pircha, and many other patients were also waiting. I prayed for them. I still do.

What is it like to go through another crisis caused by alcoholism? Let me share my diary entries from those days at the hospital:

- It's raining; when are we going home?

- Joyce appearing on TV.

- Joyce and Jerry's trauma in the airport.

- My fear; time to go to Canada.

- Notice of Joyce taking twenty units of blood. I forget my fear.

- Apparent recovery; Jerry and Chris return to Kansas City.

- Setback: more bleeding.

- Shunt operation performed.

- Other trauma cases include Mr. C., grandfather of a young man named Pat.

- Doctor assures us that shunt will prevent more bleeding.

- Another trauma case: Tom, a good Samaritan who stopped to render assistance to someone and was hit by a drunken driver. Skull fracture, broken bones. Critical.

- Another trauma case: ethnic Russian family.

- The nurses are so wonderful.

- Apparent recovery.

- More bleeding.

- Rush for tests—angiogram.

- Surgery? Shunt closed? Won't work.

- No! No! Thought to be old blood.

- Bleeding. Waiting for doctor to explain.

- Trauma case: two women killed by locomotive. They were homeless alcoholics; one was a former beauty queen.

- Lonely, and scared—but everyone is so nice.

- Sons visit. Thank God for a few hours of pleasure. Visit Skydome.

- Apparent recovery; sons return home. I love my five sons so much. Wish I was a better dad.

- Bleeding—old blood, I hope.

- Today's news: Major league baseball players unhappy, want Skydome closed for the game—too windy. Why do they complain so much? Joyce doesn't. Crime in the streets. N.Y. Yankees fired Bucky Dent. Steinbrenner still upsetting the team. Construction strike. Big cranes idle. Why can't men negotiate in earnest, good faith?

- Canadians of all ethnic groups touch you when they greet you—seem to love you.

- Where is God in all of this? Answer: Right smack in the center. He knows all, is in total control. He knows Joyce and all the patients.

- The people look down to the floor as they pass, but if you speak to them, they will talk your leg off. That's Canada.

- Joyce snores, her hair is messed up. But she is beautiful.

- She just looks, stares, looks away. She wants to go home.

- Eighth day. It's raining, foggy, can't see the construction cranes. Joyce is so pitiful, losing blood, getting more IV blood.

- God is in control, even though it doesn't appear so sometimes. God is in control.

- Read the Bible, believe, trust, pray, meditate.

- One nurse calls her patients "Love"; she's nice.

- Lots of delusions of reference (*Why are they looking at me? Because I'm a foreigner? Because I carry my Bible everywhere? Why?*). My mind must be playing tricks. *Get strong, JWJ; your wife is sick.*

- Joyce is stable this morning—no bleeding last night. Only knows her name, can't remember much else.

- Pray for Joyce: God please heal her; help her not to bleed. Make her conscious, alert—in accordance with Your will.

- Nurses and doctors say they will come and get me to go in and see Joyce, but they forget; they are so busy.

- *Toronto Sun* article June 9, 1990 about man who got his sleeve caught in the subway and was dragged, pummeled, thrown over the gate into the tracks and killed. Whose fault? He was drunk and on drugs. What terrible deaths and illness due to drugs and alcohol. What a terrible condition in life.

- I look out the window a lot from tenth floor of the hospital.

- Joyce took liquids, sat up seven minutes. Pray she doesn't bleed and continues to recuperate. Praise God.

- Joyce looks better today, Sunday. Wants me to stay with her and not go to church. OK—I'll minister to her.

- Life takes on new meaning when there is trauma in the family. Why couldn't we be kind and caring in life without trauma?

- I said to Joyce, "You look simply marvelous." She smiled.

- In retrospect, points of conflict in life seem very unimportant during times of trauma.

- I hear more news about the two women killed by train. One was thirty-two, the mother of two sons, ages twelve and fifteen, an alcoholic who drank to escape tragic memories—a former beauty queen and a beautiful person who ended up on the streets. She ran toward the engine of the train and was followed by another street person, who apparently was trying to prevent her from running into the train. Both were killed (*Toronto Star,* June 9, 1990).

- The hospital gardener planted rows of little flowers about four inches apart in thirty-foot rows five days ago. Each day he sprinkles water on them (when it doesn't rain). Now you can see the hearty ones and the apparent weak ones. Some will live; others will die. I wish all of them would live. The water and rain and sunshine will help them. Loosening the soil will help. Some fertilizer will help. But some will probably die. Why? Which ones?

Ten days after Joyce and I got home, a young man I'd met at the hospital—Pat—let me know that his grandfather had died.

The whys are endless.

——Epilogue——

A Word of Encouragement

by Joyce Johnston

In the previous chapter, I stated that recalling my life of drinking was like remembering an old black-and-white movie. After reading through the completed book, I realized I should have said it was like seeing a bad, bad movie. After I finished reading, I cried for two days, thinking I did this to myself and to my family. Then I got mad at myself for falling into the clutches of alcohol.

If anyone reading this has anyone in his or her family, or knows of a friend who might have a situation like this, don't give up. There is light at the end of the tunnel.

"Commit thy way unto the LORD; trust also in him; and he shall bring it to pass" (Psalm 37:5, KJV).

—Appendix A—

Articles of War

by Zig Ziglar

Drugs: Impossible Problem or Incredible Opportunity

I. A Formal Declaration of War

To win the War on Drugs, I want to begin by encouraging President Bush to call a joint session of the Congress and ask them to issue a formal declaration of war. Historically, America has never lost a war we have declared. We lost the war in Vietnam; we're coming painfully close to losing the war on poverty and the war on crime, and many say we have already lost the war on drugs. A formal declaration of war will clearly establish the fact that we are serious about this war and will unite our people against a formidable opponent.

In the spirit of President Bush's call for one thousand points of light, I present these plans as a starting point for action. Obviously, experts on the firing line will contribute other ideas and handle the important details and procedures. We win wars we plan and expect to win.

II.   Special War-Time Powers Enacted

The President can ask the Congress for special wartime powers to cut the red tape and mobilize our citizenry in this all-out effort. Citizen support and involvement, much like we had in World War II, is the only way we can win this war. Every citizen must become involved in the solution because every citizen is suffering due to the problem. To quote Richard W. Fisher, Chairman of the Institute of the Americas, *"Drugs are the enemy. To be sure, our newfound enemy does not possess the capacity for nuclear attack. It does not have troops massed along our frontier. Yet, it is nonetheless threatening—indeed, it already has accomplished what the Soviets and the Nazis before them never accomplished. It has invaded our territory, placed armed agents on our soil, taken hundreds of thousands of Americans prisoner, and set in motion a frightful challenge to the American way of life."*

III.   A System to Reward Informants

We must devise a plan so that drug addicts, drug dealers, illegal users, average citizens, automobile dealers, bankers, and people from all walks of life will be interested in turning in drug dealers for prosecution.

From September 27 until October 6, 1989, 77,000 pounds of cocaine were seized in five operations, with a street value ranging anywhere from $4 billion to as much as $35 billion, depending on what your source of information might be. This is equal to 7.5–9.8 percent of the estimated cocaine produced in 1988 in Peru, Bolivia, Colombia, and Ecuador; yet this apparently had a minimal effect—if any—on availability and price of the drug on the streets. That's serious!

Suggestion: Establish a national hotline with an 800 number. When anyone observes drug activity, he or she calls this number. Under the same protection afforded CrimeStopper reporters, the informant is given a reward and remains anonymous. Officials seized 20 tons of cocaine in Los Angeles because a local citizen was suspicious of the truck traffic in his neighborhood and called to report. Over $12 million in cash was recovered. A reward system would encourage everybody to be on the lookout. Nine percent of adults and 17 percent of our youth have friends who are selling drugs (*USA Today,* August 15, 1989). Reward the informant with the first $10,000 in recoverable funds from cash recovered, automobiles, houses, airplanes, buildings, jewelry, furs, etc., which are sold on the marketplace. Reward the informant with 50 percent of everything recovered from $10,000 to $50,000 and 25 percent of all monies or valuables recovered over $50,000. With this plan, the $12 million cash recovery would have netted the informant over $3 million! Incentives like this would encourage citizens from all walks of life to turn in drug dealers via the national hotline. Our national drug enforcement people would contact, via their computers, the local law enforcement people.

Dealers will turn in other dealers. Addicts in debt to their dealer will turn in dealers. Citizens of all kinds will observe more drug-related activities and turn in dealers. Automobile dealers, jewelers, furriers, etc., will report luxury cash purchases from questionable purchasers. Bank employees will keep their eyes open for money-laundering schemes. Boats, houses, cash, and businesses will be impounded because thousands of citizens will get involved as they see there *is* something they can do. This program will take dealers and hardened criminals off the streets in wholesale quantities.

IV. Special Judges Empowered

We might appoint special judges to handle only drug-related cases so that these cases could be dealt with expediently. While visiting Australia, I read that two men climbed into a zoo and cut the throats of some kangaroos. Three days later they started their jail sentences. They had been tried, found guilty, sentenced, and began serving their time. Fast action on drug arrests will serve as a tremendous deterrent to drug dealers.

V. Discourage the User

A major thrust of the War on Drugs should be the recognition of the fact that the profits are simply too great to completely stop the flow of drugs into this country, or for that matter, into our heavily guarded jails and prisons. Nor can we totally stop the production of speed, ice, ecstasy, etc., or the growing of marijuana. We must continue our interdiction efforts, but we must deal with the user. <u>This program is primarily designed to get all of America involved in discouraging the user</u> while at the same time looking for workable means of stopping the dealer from peddling his deadly product.

VI. Children Helped

We might establish a national hotline. Youngsters see their friends on drugs but do nothing because they don't want to be a *"narc"* or *"snitch."* Yet they know their friends are either killing themselves or jeopardizing their futures. The hotline could work this way: A young person sees a friend using drugs, calls the hotline, gives the drug user's address and parents' names to the hotline. A cover letter addressed to the parents should include some drug information. These parents will then know how to spot drug users. The letter is non-accusatory and simply states that since their child is in the *"at risk"* age bracket, this approach is part of the preventive aspect of our War on Drugs effort. The drug user too often becomes addicted before the parents discover he is even a user. This packet of information will simply alert the parents to the fact that a potential problem exists and give suggestions on how to spot the problem and what they can do about it.

VII. Vocabulary Changes

It is ridiculous to talk about *"casual"* users and *"recreational"* users. There is only one kind of illegal-drug user, and that is an *"illegal"*—or criminal—user. When anyone buys marijuana, crack, ice, speed, cocaine or heroine, he is breaking the law and probably financing the Mafia and the Colombian Drug Cartel. The buyer is contributing directly to murder, crime, cocaine babies, and countless other unspeakable crimes. No one starts out to become an addict, but every illegal user is putting himself at risk to do exactly that.

VIII. Close the Pipeline

U.S. News & World Report, September 11, 1989, reports that it is a rare case, indeed, when an illegal drug user does not start with tobacco, alcohol, or marijuana, and well over 95 percent of marijuana users learned to inhale by starting with tobacco. The entrance drugs for illegal drugs are *"legal"* drugs. *Over one hundred times* as many lives are lost each year because of tobacco and alcohol as are lost because of illegal drugs (*Dallas Morning News,* October 9, 1989).

> **NOTE:** We lost 406,000 men and women in World War II. We lose 390,000 each **year** to tobacco and 150,000 to alcohol.

Our major premise is that if we can shut down the pipeline, we will have largely solved the illegal drug problem. If we wanted to stop the flow of the Mississippi River, we would not go to the Gulf Coast. Instead, we would go to the source in Minnesota. That would effectively close the pipeline and the river.

We slow the pipeline by utilizing one of the special wartime powers of our President. Here's the way the proposal works: Establish a *"War-On-Drugs Stamp"* which would be attached to every pack of cigarettes and every can of smokeless tobacco. The stamp would cost $1.00 and would be labeled *"The War-on-Drugs Stamp Fund."* Up to $500 for each smoker would be tax-deductible by turning in the stamps when they file their tax return. This would raise an estimated $20–25 billion. We would use the same basic approach on beer and wine, so that an additional $20.6 billion would be raised. We would use the same stamps on hard liquor and liquor by the drink to raise yet another $20 billion. Simultaneously, we would cease all subsidies to tobacco farmers. (Article IX explains how funds would be used to offset losses from these subsidies.)

The next question is, "How do we overcome the hypocrisy of adults lecturing the kids on drugs while at the same time the adults sip beer, drink cocktails, and smoke cigarettes?" How do we explain to our young people that it makes sense to spend billions to keep illegal drugs out of our country (which we should do) while spending billions advertising legal drugs which kill over a half-million Americans every year (which we cannot continue to do)?

The answer lies in a mammoth public relations and advertising campaign to inform everyone about the problem. We must call for leaders at every level in our country to pass the necessary legislation to deal with the problem and begin to set the proper example for the youth of America.

Let us eliminate all beer and wine advertising from television. When this was done in Sweden, alcohol consumption immediately dropped 20 percent. With the combination of the stamp and the discontinuing of television advertising, we would have an immediate reduction in alcohol consumption of about 30 percent, which means we would still raise approximately $28 billion to fund some important activities.

The tobacco, beer, wine and hard liquor stamps, combined, would bring in between $40 and $50 billion.

IX.   Investing War Stamp Funds

Investing money for the restoration of American youth, America's elderly, and the underprivileged, as well as the chronically ill, would help in the revitalization of our society. The following figures are simply ideas. Obviously, experts would be relied upon to give more specific direction.

First phase: Take $9.4 billion of this money and give them to the effort President Bush is making in the War on Drugs. This is a bipartisan idea and would eliminate the need to curtail defense spending and cut back on some of the essential programs which are now being considered for reduction.

Second phase: A major financial investment to make with the *"War-on-Drugs Stamp"* funds would be for the tobacco farmers. We would reward farmers who elected to stop growing tobacco, which many will do since a reduction in demand will be inevitable. Compensation would be on the basis of the last seven years they raised a tobacco crop. We would look at their income tax, factor in inflation, and reward the farmers with the same amount of money, on average, for the next seven years that they earned the past seven years on the tobacco crop, provided (a) they quit raising tobacco, and (b) they start raising other crops (fruits, vegetables, herbs, flowers, shrubbery, trees, or fish crops like catfish, shrimp, etc.). Those foodstuffs could well be used to help alleviate not only hunger in our nation, but in the world. Certainly the nutritional level would be an improvement over the tobacco crop, and it could well be that the financial rewards would also be greater.

We would take a significant sum of money and use it to retrain tobacco field workers and workers in tobacco plants. Many tobacco farmers and factory workers are people who recognize the damage tobacco does, but economic necessity forces them to continue to raise the crops and work in tobacco or cigarette factories. This would give them a realistic substitute while enabling them to maintain their dignity and standard of living. The education or training could be in community colleges, mechanic schools, computer courses, etc.

Part of the stamp money would be used to re-tool tobacco factories, liquor distilleries, and breweries. Stockholders own these businesses. By structuring them to produce beneficial products, we would give these people an ongoing income, protect the stockholders, possibly raise the standard of living of the workers, and substantially reduce the toll in lives and human misery directly caused by alcohol and tobacco.

Next, we would establish a common-sense program so that drug users from their first arrest would be dealt with in a manner that would not only discourage further use but would improve the quality of life in America. It is unrealistic and impractical to think of putting all drug users in jail or prison, although the need for more incarceration space is obvious. Realistically, less than 2 percent of drug arrests result in trial, conviction, and imprisonment. Consequently, most users and dealers literally laugh at the law.

Solution: Persons arrested for the *first time* for illegal substance use, and underage users of tobacco and alcohol should be placed in a thirty-day rehabilitation program of two to three hours of drug education per day, combined with two to three hours of mental or manual labor, depending on educational capabilities. If they are functionally illiterate, they should be placed in a class and taught to read and write. If they are educated, they should be pressed into service to help teach the functionally illiterate to read and write. Details could be worked out by retired educators and handled through the public school systems where the buildings are largely unused in the evening hours.

Third phase: Use $2 billion or more to establish scholarship funds, telling youngsters from fifth through twelfth grade that scholarship money awaits when they graduate from high school if they neither smoke, drink, nor do drugs.

Fourth phase: Set aside $4 billion for 1 percent financing of low-priced housing. Maximum mortgage would be $50,000; the average would probably be less than $40,000. This money would be available to those who meet minimal financial requirements and neither smoke, drink, nor do drugs. This would enable many people to upgrade their housing and create numerous jobs. **Thought:** Since former President Carter is so active in the Habitat for Humanity, Inc., he could spearhead this program and establish a partnership arrangement so that retired carpenters, plumbers, electricians, masons, etc., could have apprentices do the work, and train these people at the same time. The benefits are obvious.

X.   Incentive Contests

We could establish an essay contest to involve every schoolchild in America (as well as their parents and teachers) from the fifth grade up. Each child might write a 300-word essay entitled, **"Why I Will NEVER Smoke, Drink or Do Drugs."** A $1,000 award could be given to each school which produces a winner in district competition. The student, parents, and teacher could be given local publicity via radio, television, and newspapers. The winners from each school (student, parents, and teacher) could have dinner with the principal, and the winners at the district level could have dinner with the superintendent. The school which produces the winner for the state could receive $10,000 and the student, parents, and teacher could have dinner with the governor. The national winners might be given a trip to Washington, where they could have an opportunity to meet the President. The schools which produced national winners could receive $25,000.

In addition, each teacher with a student who won an essay could be given a 10 percent raise at the individual school level, a 15 percent raise if his/her student wins at the district level, a 20 percent raise at the state level, and the teachers of the national champions could be given a 25 percent raise in salary. Think of all the publicity that would be gained by this! Young people all across America would be talking about why they don't smoke, drink, or do drugs. Good kids who avoided drugs would be recognized and rewarded.

XI. Song-Writing Incentives

We could enlist the aid and cooperation of our song-writing public. Let's establish an anti-drug song-writing contest, awarding the best song opposing drugs at the county level $5,000; the winner of the state contest $50,000; and the national winner, $1 million. The concept is simple: A prize that large would attract the most creative musicians in America who are already in the business of writing songs, as well as the millions who would be challenged to make the effort. Music speaks to the young people today. There would be literally thousands of songs created which would be played on our airwaves. We would be saturated with anti-drug messages via music. It would be the subject of the day for literally millions of our young people. The impact could be dramatic.

XII. Advertising

We should appropriate money for a massive advertising campaign depicting the real results of smoking and drinking. Publicize the statistics showing that over a thousand people every day die as a direct result of smoking cigarettes. Show public service announcements of old men or old women with a cigarette dangling from their mouths, as ashes drop on their tie or dress and let the viewers see how smoking has caused nicotine-stained fingers and teeth and wrinkled complexions. Show a young father walking away from an accident where he has killed his own daughter and her friend because he was too drunk to drive. Show a jail door clanging shut on an innocent-looking sixteen-year-old who dealt in drugs and is paying the price. Graphically show somebody who is so sick from drinking that he's vomiting. Caption these pictures with such things as, *"Drinking is fun?"* *"Smoking is glamorous?"* *"Drugs are the 'in' thing?"* I believe negative publicity, in this case, could have a sobering impact on people who are considering the use of drugs.

    Note: In California, the state added twenty-five cents to the tax on cigarettes, and used the money to show the real side of smoking. Now Californians are quitting smoking twice as fast as the national average.

XIII.   Help for the Abusers

We should establish a rehabilitation fund for smokers, drinkers, and drug addicts, giving them encouragement and help in breaking their addictions. At this time, they are looked down on if they admit their problem. Structure the presentations and advertising so that it is obvious that the only ones who are looked down on are those who have the problem but who are unwilling to seek a solution (less than 10 percent of those with drugs and drinking problems acknowledge their problems). Make it clear that no punitive action will be taken if they enter treatment; but if they refuse to volunteer for the treatment, they will be subject to disciplinary action, including the loss of their job if their addiction affects their performance. (General Motors says that during the twelve months preceding treatment, addicts are absent 50 percent of the time.—*New York Times* News Service)

XIV.   Education in Our Schools

Start a character-building, motivational program in our school system, beginning with kindergarten. According to Dr. Bill Kirby, Commissioner of Education for the State of Texas, Japan has a course starting in kindergarten and continuing through high school for one hour each day. During this time students are taught the importance of honesty, hard work, enthusiasm, positive mental attitude, thrift, free enterprise, respect for authority, responsibility, and patriotism. Japan's drug problem is only a minute fraction of what America's is. Statistics prove this approach works.

XV.   Recreational Funds

We can establish a fund for building motivational, athletic, and recreational facilities in the inner-city areas where many of our youngsters are at risk. These facilities would be staffed by teachers, coaches, educators, business people, and specialists who are genuinely concerned about America and her future. Evidence is solid that motivational input and athletic or recreational activities literally put young people on a motivational high, giving them both an emotional lift and a physiological boost. This would enable the kids to get high on life while reducing the desire to get high on drugs. Evidence is solid that kids do not primarily start on drugs because of peer pressure; many get on drugs because they're lonely, bored, and are seeking a *"high."* This approach provides our young people with an exciting alternative.

XVI. Catastrophic Insurance

We should set aside a significant amount of money for catastrophic illnesses. Newscaster Paul Harvey says that 49 percent of all medical bills and hospitalization are the direct result of smoking and drinking. This money would take care of the major catastrophic illnesses, and it would mean that the people with these illnesses will have financed their own health care, since many of those illnesses can be traced to drugs and alcohol.

XVII. Subsidize Positive Crops

We might set aside a significant amount of money to subsidize the coffee crops in Colombia, Peru, and Bolivia. This will provide the economy of these nations a boost so they do not have to grow coca, from which cocaine is derived. At the same time, we could prohibit overseas exports of tobacco (our own deadly drug). It is just as immoral for us to export our deadly drugs or alcohol to other countries as it is for Colombia to export illegal drugs to America. Additionally, in cooperation with these countries, we should train their military and law-enforcement people in counter-terrorist activities to combat the drug cartel people.

XVIII. Positive Celebrations

We should encourage soft drink companies to approach all athletic teams with the idea of celebrating with fizzing soft drinks after they win their pennant or national championship. The picture presented all too often is that if a person is going to be socially, sexually, and financially successful, he must drink alcohol. How marvelous it would be to see World Series and Super Bowl winners drinking soft drinks instead of pouring champagne all over each other! Economically, this makes sense. At the moment, the athletes receive nothing for pouring booze on one another. A $10,000 fee to each winner would be eagerly accepted and the soft drink company would have an incredibly effective *"commercial."*

XIX.   Involve Our Law-Enforcement Officials

We could adopt a law-enforcement recognition program whereby we would encourage schools, churches, and service clubs to regularly invite law-enforcement people for special recognition, free meals, and a general thank-you for the work they do. We would encourage parents to talk about their friends in law enforcement. When the occasion permits, have Mom and Dad introduce their children to law-enforcement officers and thank them for the part they play in making America drug-free.

XX.   Some Added Thoughts

Let us encourage parents, again through a media blitz, to prohibit—or certainly to discourage—their sons and daughters from dating anyone who smokes, drinks, or does drugs.

Let us encourage businesses all over America to post signs at the entranceway to their businesses saying, *"Welcome to our smoke-free, drug-free environment."*

Let us promote bumper stickers which say, *"Smoke-free airways, alcohol-free highways."*

Let us educate employers on the costs of smoking, drinking, and drugs. It costs $4,611 more each year to employ a smoker than it does to hire a non-smoker—and those are 1981 figures.

Let us eliminate all cigarette machines in the country. Ninety-three percent of people under eighteen, according to the Tobacco-Free Youth Project, buy their cigarettes from machines. We could impose a $100 fine on any merchant who sells cigarettes to a youngster under eighteen on the first offense; a $1,000 fine for the second offense; and remove the tobacco license for the third offense.

Let us encourage leadership at every level of our country to set the example by not smoking and drinking. It would be marvelous if our president, along with every senator, congressman, governor, and the mayors of every major city would personally declare a one-year moratorium on smoking, drinking, and the serving of alcoholic beverages at any official function!

Let us encourage corporate leadership in America to run ads in major newspapers identifying themselves as being committed to no-smoking, no-drinking, and no-drugs. On other occasions publish the names of all the sports heroes from high school, college, and professional teams who have sworn to abstain from the use of tobacco, liquor, and drugs as role models. This would have a dramatic impact on young people everywhere.

Return to the Basics

Let us not overlook our most important resource. During World War II, President Roosevelt regularly called on the religious leaders of America to involve themselves in prayer for the war effort. I would encourage the president to urge Congress to set aside a specific day of prayer for victory in the War on Drugs. I would also encourage him to schedule a seminar at the White House for all major religious leaders in our society on the role they can play in the War on Drugs, encouraging them to preach on the evils and dangers of tobacco, drug, and alcohol use. It's ironic that in virtually every successful drug and alcohol rehab program in the country the mention of God saturates the literature, but the same God is left out of all prevention literature.

Let me summarize with a very important thought. The following words are taken from a book which shares something all of us need to know. "In 1787 at the Constitutional Convention, America's elder statesman, Benjamin Franklin, stood up and made a speech. 'In the beginning of the contest with Britain, when we were sensible of danger, we had daily prayers in this room for Divine protection. Our prayers, Sir, were heard, and they were graciously answered. All of us who were engaged in the struggle must have observed the frequent instances of a superintending Providence. In our failure have we now forgotten this powerful Friend? Or do we imagine we no longer need

His assistance? I have lived, Sir, a long time, and the longer I live, the more convincing proofs I see of this, that God governs in the affairs of men, and if a sparrow cannot fall to the ground without His notice, is it probable that an empire can rise without His aid?' Immediately thereafter, things began to happen in a very real way."

In World War II the president regularly called on every preacher in America to get all of his people involved in prayer for our country. The last speech that President John F. Kennedy would have made would have been one of his very best. This is what he was to say: "We ask, therefore, that we may be worthy of the power and the responsibility; that we may exercise our strength with wisdom and restraint; that we may achieve in our time and for all times, the ancient vision of peace on earth, good will toward men. That must always be our goal, and the righteousness of our call must always underlie our strength, for as it was written long ago, 'Except the Lord keep the city, the watchman waketh but in vain.'"

Powerful words. Powerful thoughts. In 2 Chronicles 7:14 we read: "If my people, which are called by my name, shall humble themselves, and pray, and seek my face, and turn from their wicked ways; then will I hear from heaven, and will forgive their sin, and will heal their land" (KJV).

Putting all of that together, we come to the inescapable conclusion that America is a world leader with an enormous responsibility. Our very fabric has been weakened. These methods will help us regain our strength and occupy our position as the central force in the world today. Every citizen needs to get involved; every citizen needs to ask Almighty God to intervene and help us win the most important war we've ever fought. With His help, I am totally confident we'll do exactly that.

Let us challenge every American to join the "Army" and actively fight to win this war with the double question—If not me, who? If not now, when?

NOTE: For additional information write:

The Zig Ziglar Corporation
3330 Earhart, Suite 204
Carrollton, TX 75006
(214) 233-9191

—Appendix B—

Resources

It's astounding how much information there is on alcohol abuse. Take advantage of this information, and also the services in your local area such as those offered through organizations listed below.

If you have a son or daughter, or an adolescent in your guardianship who is victimized by an addiction to alcohol or drugs and needs recovery care, let me introduce you to the number-one program in America specializing in turning kids around: Century HealthCare Corporation. Century's uniqueness lies in the variety of programs it offers to help young people grow strong against any addiction that threatens happiness in life.

Century cares, and its fifty-two different programs in more than seventeen cities are ready to help by simply making a toll-free phone call: 1-800-SV-A-TEEN (800-782-8336). Century does not limit its health care only to inpatient hospital beds; it also provides preventative education services, evaluation, outpatient services, crisis intervention, residential treatment, partial hospitalization, in-home therapy, and sub-acute care.

Century's philosophy of treatment dictates the use of the least expensive, most appropriate, and least restrictive of these alternatives. Most major insurance carriers underwrite the cost of Century's specialized program.

Give Century a call and tell the receptionist I recommended that you call. Distance from a Century program need not be a concern with its specialized travel-assistance program.

Century has my total endorsement and that is why I am affiliated with them.

For more information about Century HealthCare, contact:

Century HealthCare Corporation
7615 East 63 Place South, Suite 200
Tulsa, OK 74133
918-250-9651
918-250-5624 (fax)

Regional Century HealthCare programs

Albuquerque area:
Desert Hills of Albuquerque
5310 Sequoia NW
Albuquerque, NM 87120
505-836-7330

Denver/Colorado Springs area:
Cheyenne Mesa
1353 South Eighth Street
Colorado Springs, CO 80906
719-520-1400

Houston area:
Champions
14320 Walters Road
P. 0. Box 73327
Houston, TX 77273-3327
713-537-5050

Iowa:
Gerard of Iowa
3801 Fourth Street, SE
P. 0. Box 1353
Mason City, IA 50401
515-423-3222

Greater Los Angeles area:
Newport Harbor
1501 East 16th Street
Newport Beach, CA 92663
714-642-9310

Minneapolis-St. Paul area:
Gerard of Minnesota
28th Street, NE
P. 0. Box 715
Austin, MN 55912-0715

Gerald Treatment Programs
11900 Wayzata Boulevard, Suite 104
Minnetonka, MN 55343
612-546-6996

Oklahoma City area:
High Pointe
6501 NE 50th Street
Oklahoma City, OK 73141
405-424-3383

Phoenix area:
Arizona Youth for Change
1500 South Mill
Tempe, AZ 85281
602-784-5592

LifeGate
367 North 21st Avenue
Phoenix, AZ 85009
602-256-0310

Westbridge
1830 East Roosevelt
Phoenix, AZ 85006
602-254-0884

Westbridge's Western Behavioral Center for Children
720 East Montebello
Phoenix, AZ 85014
602-277-5437

Saint Louis area:
West Rivers
15623 Manchester Road
Ellisville, MO 63011
314-227-2600

San Francisco/Oakland Bay area:
Oak Grove
1034 Oak Grove Road
Concord, CA 94518
415-680-1234

Tucson area:
Desert Hills
5245 North Camino de Oeste
Tucson, AZ 85745
602-743-7400

Tulsa area:
Shadow Mountain Institute
6262 South Sheridan Road
Tulsa, OK 74133
918-492-8200

Shadow Mountain Institute
Children's Services
1825 East 15th Street
Tulsa, OK 74104
918-749-9043

Other Sources of Help and Information

Al-Anon World Service Headquarters, Inc.
1372 Broadway
New York, NY 10018
212-302-7240

Alateen
P.O. Box 182
Madison Square Garden
New York, NY 10159-0182
212-254-7230

Alcohol and Drug Problems Association of North America (ADPA)
444 North Capitol Street NW, Suite 706
Washington, DC 20001
202-737-4340

Alcoholics Anonymous (AA)
P. 0. Box 459
Grand Central Station
New York, NY 10163

American Council on Alcoholism (ACA)
Health Education Center
5024 Campbell Boulevard, Suite H
Baltimore, MD 21236
301-529-9200

American Medical Association (AMA)
535 North Dearborn Street
Chicago, IL 60610
312-645-5000

Center for Science in the Public Interest
1501 16th Street NW
Washington, DC 20036

Center to Stop Drunk Driving (CSDD)
333 Pennsylvania Avenue SE
Washington, DC 20003

Highway Users Federation
1776 Massachusetts Avenue NW
Washington, DC 20036

The Insurance Institute for Highway Safety
600 New Hampshire NW, Suite 300
Washington, DC 20037

MADD National Office
P.O. Box 541688
Dallas, TX 75354-1688

National Clearinghouse for Alcohol and Drug Abuse Information
(NCADAI)
P. 0. Box 2345
Rockville, MD 20852
301-468-2600

National Council on Alcoholism (NCA)
12 West 21st Street, Eighth Floor
New York, NY 10010

National Federation of Parents for a Drug-Free Youth (NFP)
8730 Georgia Avenue, Suite 200
Silver Spring, MD 20910

The National Highway Traffic Safety Administration
400 Seventh Street SW
Washington, DC 20037

National Institute on Alcohol Abuse and Alcoholism (NIAAA)
5600 Fishers Lane
Rockville, MD 20857
301-443-4733

National Institute of Drug Abuse (NIDA)
5600 Fishers Lane
Rockville, MD 20857

Remove Intoxicated Drivers (RID-USA) National Headquarters
P.O. Box 520
Schenectady, NY 12301

Rutgers Center of Alcohol Studies
Rutgers-The State University of New Jersey
New Brunswick, NJ 08903
201-932-2190

Students Against Driving Drunk (SADD)
P.O. Box 800
Marlboro, MA 01752

Canadian Resources

Alberta
Alberta Alcohol and Drug Abuse Commission Library
10909 Jasper Avenue, Seventh Floor
Edmonton, Alberta T5J 3M9
403-427-7303

British Columbia
Alcohol and Drug Programs Library
300-307 West Broadway
Vancouver, British Columbia V5Y 1P9

Manitoba
William Potoroka Memorial Library
1031 Portage Avenue
Winnipeg, Manitoba R3G 0R8
204-786-3831

New Brunswick
Chemical Dependency Library
65 Brunswick Street
Fredericton, New Brunswick E3B 2H4
506-453-8507

Newfoundland
Alcohol and Drug Dependency Commission of Newfoundland and
  Labrador Library
Prince Charles Building, Suite 105
120 Torbay Road
St. John's, Newfoundland A1A 2G8
709-937-3600

Nova Scotia
Nova Scotia Commission on Drug Dependency
Lord Nelson Building, Suite 314
5675 Spring Garden Road
Halifax, Nova Scotia B3J 1H1

Ontario
Health Services and Promotion Library
Jeanne Mance Building, Fifth Floor
Ottawa, Ontario K1A 1B4
613-954-8590

Quebec
LaMaison Jean La Pointe
Centre de Documentation
Le Cours Saint-Pierre
111 Rue Normand
Montreal, Quebec H2Y 2K6
514-288-2611

Saskatchewan
Saskatchewan Alcohol and Drug Abuse Commission
3475 Albert Street
Regina, Saskatchewan S4S 6X6
306-787-4656

Bibliography

In addition to articles from periodicals that are cited in the text, the following sources were consulted during the writing of *It's Killing Our Kids*. Many are cited in the text by title, author's name, and the page number, to indicate a direct reference. You may find many of these sources helpful in your own study of problems related to alcohol.

Arterburn, David. *Drug-Proofing Your Kids.* Pomona, Calif.: Focus On the Family Publishing, 1989.

Beattie, Melody. *Codependent No More: How to Stop Controlling Others and Start Caring for Yourself.* Center City, Minn.: Hazelden, 1987.

"Between Molecule [alcohol] and Mayhem [road crashes]: The Case for Humane Intervention and the Role of Social and Behavioral Sciences," in the *Proceedings of a General Motors Symposium on Human Behaviour and Traffic Safety.* Warren, Mich., September 1984.

Black, Claudia. *It Will Never Happen to Me!* Denver: M.A.C. Communications, 1981.

Dobson, James. *Preparing for Adolescence.* New York: Bantam, 1984.

Dollar, Truman E., and Grace H. Ketterman. *Teenage Rebellion: How to Recognize It, Deal with It, Prevent It.* Old Tappan, N.J.: Fleming H. Revell Company, 1979.

Donelson, A.C. "Preventative Measures in Alcohol, Other Drugs and Traffic Safety," *Proceedings of the Tenth International Conference on Alcohol, Drugs and Traffic Safety.* Amsterdam, September, 1986.

Facciolo, D. J. "Unfinished Business: Confronting Juvenile Substance Abuse," in *Children's Legal Rights Journal,* Vol. 8, No. 1, Winter 1987.

Fine, Louis. *After All We've Done for Them.* New York: Penquin Books, 1981.

Insurance Institute. *IIHS Facts 1989.* Arlington, Va., 1989.

Klaus, Tom. *Healing Hidden Wounds.* Loveland, Colo., Group Publishing, 1989.

Leerhsen, Charles with Shawn D. Lewis and others. "Unite and Conquer: America's Crazy for Support Groups." *Newsweek,* February 5, 1990. Pages 50–55.

Lewis, C. S. *Christian Behaviour.* New York: Macmillan Company, 1946.

Mann, Peggy. *Arrive Alive.* New York: McGraw-Hill, 1985.

Maxwell, Ruth. *Beyond the Booze Battle.* New York: Ballantine Books, 1986.

———. *The Booze Battle.* New York: Ballantine Books, 1976.

Miller, Alice. *The Drama of the Gifted Child: The Search for the True Self.* London: Virego, 1987.

Milam, James R. and Katherine Ketcham. *Under the Influence.* New York: Bantam Books, 1983.

Polson, Beth and Miller Newton. *Not My Kid: A Parent's Guide to Kids and Drugs.* New York: Avon Books, 1984.

Simpson, H. M. "Community-Based Approaches to Highway Safety," *Drug and Alcohol Dependence,* Vol. 20, 1987.

Subby, Robert. "Inside the Chemically Dependent Marriage," in *CoDependency: An Emerging Issue.* Hollywood, Fla.: Health Communications, 1984.

Tuchfield, B. S., R. R. Clayton, and J. A. Logan. "Alcohol, Drug Use and Delinquent and Criminal Behaviors Among Male Adolescents and Young Adults," in the *Journal of Drug Issues,* Vol. 12, No. 2, Spring 1982.

U.S. Department of Justice. *Juvenile Justice Bulletin.* Washington, D.C., July/August 1989.

Van Impe, Jack with Roger F. Campbell. *Alcohol, The Beloved Enemy.* Nashville: Thomas Nelson Publishers, 1980.

Wilkerson, David. *Sipping Saints.* Old Tappan, N.J.: Fleming H. Revell Company, 1978.

Woititz, Janet G. *Adult Children of Alcoholics.* Deerfield Beach, Fla.: Health Communications, 1983.

Youngs, Bettie B., Ph.D. *Helping Your Teenager Deal with Stress.* Los Angeles: Jeremy Tarcher, 1986.